Turbulence

Turbulence

Boeing and the State

of American Workers

and Managers

Edward S. Greenberg
Leon Grunberg
Sarah Moore
Patricia B. Sikora

Yale UNIVERSITY PRESS

NEW HAVEN AND LONDON

Published with assistance from the Mary Cady Tew Memorial Fund.

Yale University Press books may be purchased in quantity for educational, business, or promotional use. For information, please e-mail sales.press@yale.edu (U.S. office) or sales@yaleup.co.uk (U.K. office).

Set in Garamond type by The Composing Room of Michigan, Inc., Grand Rapids, Michigan.
Printed in the United States of America by Sheridan Books, Inc.

Library of Congress Cataloging-in-Publication Data

Turbulence : Boeing and the state of American workers and managers / Edward S. Greenberg . . . [et al.].
         p. cm.
   Includes bibliographical references and index.
   ISBN 978-0-300-15461-0 (hbk. : alk. paper)   1. Boeing Aircraft Company—Employees—Longitudinal studies.   2. Boeing Aircraft Company—Management—Longitudinal studies.   3. Organizational change.   4. Industrial relations.
I. Greenberg, Edward S., 1942–
   HD9711.U63B6388 2010
   331.7′629130973—dc22

                                                                    2010009957

A catalogue record for this book is available from the British Library.

This paper meets the requirements of ANSI/NISO Z39.48-1992 (Permanence of Paper).

10 9 8 7 6 5 4 3 2 1

To our spouses and families for the loving and patient support
that made this book possible

Contents

Illustrations

Tables

Acknowledgments

This book represents over forty years of collective effort as the four authors surveyed, interviewed, analyzed, and wrote about the employee experience at Boeing. However, this effort did not happen in a vacuum, and our ability to do this research and write this book hinged on the help and support of many individuals and organizations.

We are particularly grateful to five people who generously volunteered their time to review the entire manuscript prior to submission to Yale University Press: E. David Beaty, Ph.D., consultant, Beaty & Associates, Inc., Denver, CO; Jim Collins, author of *Good to Great* among other influential best sellers and articles; Mike A. Moore, Ph.D., Associate Professor of History (emeritus), Bowling Green State University; Ben Page, Gordon Fulcher Professor of Decision Making at Northwestern University; and Stan Sorscher, senior official of SPEEA, the union representing engineers and technical workers at Boeing. Their thoughtful comments and detailed suggestions greatly improved the final version of the manuscript.

We also appreciate the time invested by others who read all or part of the manuscript as it was being developed: Charles Boefferding,

Philip Gordon, Anna Greenberg, Josh Greenberg, Stan Greenberg, Sunil Kukreja, Susan Stewart, and Mike Veseth as well as two anonymous reviewers for Yale University Press who read and commented on our initial prospectus and chapter drafts. We offer a special thank-you to Emma Grunberg for suggesting *Turbulence* as the title of the book.

Our thanks also go to Lindy Schultz for compiling and managing our reference list, Deb Stumpf for her careful proofing and formatting of the final manuscript, and Nancy Thorwardson for her patient help in creating graphs and figures. Sugandha Brooks, Reggie Tison, and Shreya Vinjamuri provided efficient office support during the course of the study and production of this book.

Dozens of individuals provided valuable assistance in the collection of data and in the analyses that form the foundation of this book. We want to thank the many undergraduate and graduate students at the universities of Colorado-Boulder and Puget Sound for their enthusiastic work as research assistants. In particular, we thank Lauren Manheim, who oversaw the operational details for our first Attrition Survey.

We want to thank as well the colleagues who helped conduct qualitative portions of field research, especially Nancy Maki, who conducted and summarized numerous in-depth interviews for this project. We are grateful to Hannah Knudsen for managing the complicated logistics to get the study off the ground and to Richard Anderson-Connolly for his astute statistical advice. Each also co-authored papers with us.

Our thanks also go to Paul Roman, Distinguished Research Professor of Sociology at the University of Georgia, for encouraging us to seek funding from the NIAAA to support our research and to David Olson, Harry Bridges Endowed Chair Emeritus in Labor Studies at the University of Washington, for introducing us to IAM officials and shop stewards, and clearing several roadblocks in the early phases of this project.

We are grateful to several institutions that supported our efforts. The National Institute of Alcohol Abuse and Alcoholism (NIAAA) of the National Institutes of Health twice provided the funding that enabled us to conduct this challenging ten-year longitudinal study. The University of Puget Sound and University of Colorado at Boulder provided time, space, and financial support for our research and the writing of this book. A specific thank-you goes to Jane Menken and the Institute of Behavioral Sciences at CU-Boulder for their long-term support of Ed Greenberg and his research activities. In addition, we thank the Rockefeller Foundation for enabling Ed Greenberg and Leon Grunberg to spend a focused month at the Bellagio Center in Italy working on key sections of the manuscript.

A special debt of gratitude goes to the hundreds of former and current Boeing employees, managers, and executives, as well as the union officials of the IAM and SPEEA, who so generously gave of their time and shared their first-hand experiences of Boeing Commercial Airplanes. Their insights are the essential ingredient in the story we tell in the book.

Finally, we are very grateful to the staff at Yale University Press, with extra thanks to our editor Mike O'Malley, who was an early and enthusiastic believer in this book and the story of Boeing employees.

Turbulence

Chapter 1 Studying a Company and Workforce in Transition

Boeing Commercial Airplanes*—a key unit of the Boeing Corporation—is in many ways a remarkable American success story. For much of the twentieth century its name was synonymous with pioneering advances in commercial flight. Toward the end of the century, as it faced a more uncertain and fast-changing environment, Boeing had to fight hard to maintain its reputation as one of the world's great companies. In the midst of a period of great economic, social, and technological change, and in response to intense global economic pressure, Boeing dramatically transformed itself. It revolutionized the ways it designed and produced aircraft, cut costs, and retained its position as America's leading exporter.

Yet the Boeing story is also a cautionary tale. The very innovations and changes Boeing introduced to remain a leading producer of air-

---

* Unless otherwise noted in the text, we use Boeing to refer to the Boeing Commercial Airplane division throughout the book because that is the way employees referred to the division. The book is based on our research of the Boeing Commercial Airplane division.

planes—altered management strategies, pervasive technological changes, extensive outsourcing, broad global partnerships, massive layoffs, and drastically altered ways of working—produced stress and turbulence in the lives of workers and managers alike. Some of this stress was unavoidable, but some of it brought unnecessary pain to many employees and raised serious questions about Boeing's continued success in the marketplace.

A close study of the Boeing case can tell us a great deal about the state of large American companies and their employees, because Boeing and its employees have faced nearly every one of the challenges confronting globally competitive firms today. Moreover, they have faced these challenges from a particularly advantageous position yet still have experienced enormous difficulties. In many respects, the position of Boeing and its employees is as good as it gets in the American context. As one of only two manufacturers of large passenger jets in the world, Boeing occupies an extraordinary economic niche and has had generally enlightened policies, along with strong unions, to protect its employees. Many American companies and their employees, in virtually every economic sector, face similarly strong competitive pressures but without Boeing's advantages. If Boeing and its employees are struggling in today's economy, so are many other firms and their employees. We hope, therefore, that the positive and negative lessons to be learned from Boeing's story can help top executives, managers, and workers more wisely navigate through these turbulent economic times.

THE NEW WORKPLACE REALITY

American workers have been put through the wringer in recent years. Not only have their wages and benefits taken hits, but they have also been downsized, reorganized, merged, and digitalized, and have seen their work outsourced. For many workers and managers it's been a little like being on a roller-coaster ride without a seatbelt. Some have enjoyed the thrill and excitement of the ride. Many more have been shaken and bruised by the experience. This book seeks to describe and understand the effects on employees, including middle and frontline managers, of living through this unsettling period of economic and workplace change and what it might mean more generally for working Americans. What, for example, have been Boeing employees' responses to this avalanche of change? Have their attitudes to their work and to their company changed? Are they still as loyal as they used to be to the organizations many have toiled in for years? Do they find their new work arrangements to be exciting and challenging, or are they merely new ways for their company to squeeze more work out of them? And what did living through these tumultuous changes do to their mental and physical health and to their sense of wellbeing? These are some of the questions we address in this book, relying heavily on the voices of a broad cross-section of employees who had to navigate these difficult times at one of America's most important manufacturing firms. And, because we believe the Boeing story is pertinent to what is happening in many sectors of the American economy, we also consider the lessons it holds for the various corporate stakeholders and for public policymakers.

Change is often unsettling and disruptive, but it is sometimes necessary and may even be welcomed by those who experience it. The massive entry of women into the labor force and, increasingly, into management ranks, for example, has lessened women's economic dependence on men and has helped to change workplace norms and behaviors for the better. And although important aspects of human connectivity may have been lost with the digital revolution, as virtual relationships replaced face-to-face ones, and hands-on and tacit skills and knowledge gave way to computer programs, workers on the whole seemed to enjoy the challenges and flexibility created by these new ways of working. Many workplace changes, however, have shaken the foundations of the postwar employment relationship and set loose a deep sense of anxiety in large segments of the American workforce. The "organization man" model, characteristic of many large companies in the past, and which promised employees lifelong security in return for loyalty and devotion to the company, is giving way to more transient and market-based relationships within firms.[1]

Recurring episodes of mass layoffs caused by swings in demand and by more permanent changes in business strategy, such as outsourcing and lean production, have left many surviving employees increasingly unsure and worried about the long-term security of their jobs and the benefits that are attached to them, even in relatively successful companies. The shift by top executives to a more single-minded and short-term focus on the financial bottom line, sometimes referred to as the shareholder value orientation,[2] has created a sense among many blue and white collar workers alike that they are expendable resources to be used and discarded according to the calculations of distant investors and financial gurus. As in other reciprocal games of tit for tat, it seems that workers have responded with lower commitment and greater cynicism toward those who make many of the decisions that shape their lives, including, most especially, the people who run the companies where they work.[3]

These trends are widespread across the economy and there is no shortage of books by social scientists, journalists, and consultants describing their broad outlines or examining the strategic rationale of top executives as they transformed their companies. But there are few that tell the story of these changes from the point of view of those who work in the trenches of corporate America,[4] and fewer still that have followed a group of employees for several years as they lived through these changes or that have given voice to their reactions and concerns. We do so in this book, describing in some depth what the employees of Boeing said and felt about a decade-long process of change at one of America's most notable companies. We believe this is important not only because employees' reactions can affect the performance of their company, but because, in the pursuit of efficiency and profits, the well-being of individuals, as well as that of their families and communities, is also at stake. Strategic and tactical decisions made by leaders of companies have human as well as economic costs and benefits, and thus inevitably raise urgent questions for workers, union officials, company leaders, and public officials about the pace, extent, and nature of workplace change in the United States.

BRIEF STORIES FROM THE FRONT LINES AT BOEING

Here we present a handful of brief personal stories that describe how a cross-section of employees responded to a decade of change at Boeing. They prefigure some of the key themes that are woven throughout the book, such as the disquiet over outsourcing, the anxiety produced by mass layoffs and the need to cope with new technologies and to remain "marketable," and they give a flavor of some of the main findings we present in the following chapters.

Tom, a Tool and Die Maker

Tom is a proud tool and die maker who was recently downgraded to a production job after twenty-five years at Boeing. He had come to Boeing in 1979 as a young man to join what his recruiter boasted was the "best, most skilled workforce in the country—the elite." For two decades he used his extensive training, experience, and skills to build parts and machine tools for the various airplanes Boeing produced. As computers began to change his job, he decided he needed to "learn computers" and took evening classes at the local junior college in software programming and computer assisted design (CAD), an education Boeing paid for. Tom is a quiet, modest man, and there was no hint of arrogance as he asserted, "I can program any NC (numerically controlled) machine. I'm as expert in these areas as anyone in the country, and because of my math and science background, I enjoy the work."

But in the late nineties, things changed for Tom. Asset Utilization Teams determined there would be less need for tool and die makers, as tooling work was going to be outsourced. They would no longer build new tools but act as support staff for tools built elsewhere. Many tool and die makers were not laid off, however, but were offered work in production. Tom "was the last one to be downgraded." Tom said he understood the rationale behind Boeing's new business strategy of "getting away from manufacturing, outsourcing much of parts production, and then shipping the components to the line for assembly." Such a strategy made sense "in theory," but in practice it was flawed. Producing airplane parts required "incredible precision," but when Boeing outsourced the production of so many vital parts, it "lost control" of the process, with damage to the quality of the parts. The resulting increases in scrap rates and defective parts going to the assembly line required expensive rework and delayed deliveries. Tom ruefully noted: "What gets me is that I and my co-workers have done nothing for the 787 [the new commercial airplane] and this is the first airplane that will roll out late. In the past, we did all the tooling and we were never late; we were proud of that record."

Reflecting on his thirty years at Boeing, Tom gave a mixed assessment of his career with the company: "Boeing has been good to me and I look forward to a decent pension when I retire." But the most important lesson he had learned was: "Keep myself marketable; keep learning" because "you never knew if you might be laid off even if you're highly skilled." Working at Boeing meant you were always "on edge."

Sandra, a Manager in Information Technology

Sandra joined Boeing in 1989 with a degree in accounting and with strong math and computer skills. But after five years working in IT support services, she quit the company. Boeing was going through layoffs, and, as she told us, "I started seeing my friends going out the door. My best friend was laid off and it was all real emotional for me. We were young, of the same age and went out together, almost like a family. One of the reasons for me going to work was to hang out with people I knew and liked. I thought Boeing didn't care about its employees and I'd had enough of such a big bureaucracy."

Sandra spent the next two years away from Boeing, mostly working at a small, family run business—"the best job I've ever had"—but decided to join

Starbucks when the small firm was bought out by a large company. She recalls with humor the HR interviewer at Starbucks trying to persuade her that although the benefits offered were not as good as Boeing's, "you get 1 lb. of free coffee every week."

Returning to Boeing in 1996, she noted that "now I had learned about the world, Boeing didn't seem so bad. I came to appreciate the company and what it provides." She worked on the massive company effort to "standardize processes and systems" across the whole company with a program called DCAC/MRM. Although she acknowledged that many within the company thought the program was a waste of dollars and had been "too expensive and taken too long," she believed it was "enormously successful" because the standardization helped "change the culture by facilitating communication and movement of people across the company." Changing Boeing was difficult because it was "so big, like its own country," and because changes would swing too far in one direction or another, as for example happened when the company moved from a situation where managers had clear authority to make decisions to one where no one seemed accountable or in control. "Doing everything by committee means nothing gets done."

Sandra's hard work and competence resulted in rapid career advancement. Promoted to a first-line management position, she worked on the new 787 program from its inception and remembers how that job had "consumed her life" as she commuted to Everett, Washington, worked long hours, came home, made dinner, and then turned on the computer for another two hours of work. Being a first-line manager is the "worst job in the company because you're responsible for so much—customers, work statement, employee development —you get overwhelmed." But when she became a senior manager and had more experience, she learned to be a "lot calmer when things don't get done because Boeing will still be there. That's the advantage of Boeing being so big. When I'm done, I want to go home to my family. I visited the 787 group three months after I moved to another work group and a former co-worker told me I looked ten years younger."

Michael, a Manager on the 767 Program

After twenty-three years at Boeing, Michael, a level 2 senior manager, was passionate about his work despite the fact that his work life had been anything but trouble free when we interviewed him in 2003. Working sixty-five to seventy hours per week during the day shift while still maintaining daily communication with his night supervisors, Michael told us that the post-9/11 layoffs reduced the size of his immediate working group by nearly 50 percent, and he himself was laid off from Boeing for a time. In the past six years, he has had to adjust to five different supervisors and has overseen the work of eighty-six employees, some of whom he has personally laid off. Although this had not been an easy period for him, he nevertheless concluded: "Boeing has made dramatic improvements in communicating with employees since I began with the company, and they recognize that they need to put effort and money into management and people. I work for a great team. I feel a strong sense of satisfaction when people are recognized for the work they have done and can improve the efficiency of the operation."

Perhaps Michael stands as a successful example of the modern day organization man, one who has abandoned his belief in the ethos of mutual dedication between employee and employer and of hanging in there through thick and thin for thirty to forty years. Speaking of the company when he first hired on, he reflected dispassionately and almost disdainfully about the large Christmas parties at the cavernous Kingdome and the recognition "trinkets." He likes the company's new focus on working like a team and requiring performance accountability from everyone. "The change allows people to recognize that the company doesn't owe you anything," he remarked. "Some people believe they deserve certain things, but I think you have to earn your rewards and respect. Just because you hired into the company, the company has no obligation to you. You have an obligation to yourself."

Janice, in Customer Service

Janice appeared at our interview visibly shaken and upset. She had just met with her manager and learned she had been "downgraded" to a Retention Level B, meaning she was now at increased risk for layoff. Even more distressing, she was shocked and demoralized by her performance rating. She had not received any negative feedback over the last year and was frustrated that the poor rating came in "out of the blue." She wanted to continue the interview, however, because she felt the study was important and had looked forward to participating.

Her department, one that provided service support directly to Boeing customers, had "endured" many consultants over the last year, and numerous changes had been implemented without input from employees working on the front line. Work was "equalized" across employees so that the most complicated customer inquiries, which Janice used to handle because of her level of experience and expertise, were now shared across the group. She was spending a significant amount of time on the phone handling "101 level" customer problems and felt very undervalued. She noted also that she saw a "huge" increase in absences and "nervous breakdowns" among her colleagues after the reorganization. Several were now on medication, and the practice of staying late to help customers had become a thing of the past. The changes and downgrading had taken a toll on her health and she now had "horrible" sleep patterns, felt constantly tired, had used antidepressants briefly, and was on medication for stomach problems.

Customers were starting to complain about levels of service and she believed the department was shifting back to the "old ways." However, her self-worth was "in the toilet," as she believed she was downgraded as punishment for "not buying into the reorg." Her manager told her that her integrity, ethics, and product knowledge were "exceptional" and she was "one of his best people," but she was not skilled at a new job function (she received training the week prior to her meeting with her manager). These mixed messages left her confused—she could go to the EEO office but felt uncomfortable having to "do battle to prove her value." She always took pride in her work ethic and had a positive attitude toward Boeing, but after the experiences of the last year she will probably be more likely to ask, "What are you doing for me?"

Paul, an Engineer

As of 2003, Paul had worked as a Boeing engineer for over twenty-five years, coming to the company directly after earning a bachelor of science degree in aeronautical engineering and a master of science degree in nuclear engineering. He agreed to speak to us as it offered him a "great place to vent" about an earlier strike, an event that still held much emotion for him despite the fact that it had occurred some three years earlier.

From his perspective, morale among the engineers was still a serious problem. "Engineering 'rank and file' and upper management do not share a partnership," he told us, a feeling that boiled over during the strike. He compared the scenario to professionals such as accountants and lawyers who work hard and eventually rise to the rank of partner, where they and the management "are one." Paul said engineers have that same kind of professional ambition and desire when they come out of college, but with the dynamics of labor-management relations, engineering "feels more like a blue collar position." Management consistently reinforces this mindset by the phrasing they select for describing company initiatives or positions. For example, he said, "Management might say that they want to pay engineers 'fair market wages' rather than 'share in the profit.' It's a subtle difference, but one that carries a lot of significance for professional workers."

We asked Paul, then, if the strike of engineers and technicians was about more than just money. It was a difficult question for him to answer. Paul told us that when he was on the picket line, he met people from other parts of the company and said he "got a spectrum of reasons" as to why people were out there, so he could not really see a major theme with the engineers. "The e-mails that were flying around were about respect and all these very abstract kinds of things that I couldn't understand. To me, it was more of an underlying morale problem or malaise among engineers."

When prompted to consider what caused this rift between top management and engineers, Paul noted his father was a career engineer with Boeing and drew a stark comparison between his dad's experience and his own. "In the 1950s, my father worked on the missile and space programs. Management and engineering were shoulder-to-shoulder, forging a new frontier, and feeling like they were going to change the world. By contrast, the messages in the company's 'Vision 2016' mission statement frequently refer to 'increasing shareholder value.' Most employees don't really care about the shareholders."

WHY BOEING?

Boeing is in many ways emblematic of what is happening at many other large enterprises. There are few large companies that have not, for example, downsized, conducted mass layoffs, outsourced, seen an influx of women into their workforce and management ranks, introduced lean production techniques, and computerized operations across the board. And, as one finds at many other large, complex companies, the Boeing workforce includes a broad gamut of skill levels and occupations affected by change, ranging from managers and engineers to clerical and hourly production workers. Boeing is, therefore, typical of large manufacturing companies that have transformed the way they do business, and the stories we presented above could be replicated at many other American companies.

In that sense, then, we could have selected any large manufacturing or technology company to study. But what makes Boeing particularly compelling as a case study of what is going on in American workplaces today is not only how similar it is to other companies, but also what distinguishes it. For years the Boeing Corporation (and its Boeing Commercial Airplanes division) has been among the most successful enterprises in the United States, enjoying political nurturing and assistance as America's leading exporter by dollar value, and lauded by management experts Jim Collins and Jerry Porras as a "visionary" company that is the "best of the best" in its industry.[5] Moreover, Boeing employees have enjoyed some of the most generous wages and benefits in the United States, in some measure because of the efforts of a muscular machinists' union local that represented production workers, and, somewhat unusually, a "professional" union representing most of its engineers and technicians. In other words, during the years preceding and during our study, Boeing was not an organization with a poor reputation as an employer. It was a pretty decent employer; perhaps as good as any in the United States. Nor at the time of our study was Boeing's very survival at risk given its market position as one half of a duopoly and its important role as a defense contractor. As such, the trends and patterns we found there cannot simply be ascribed to some particularly idiosyncratic management practices, or to desperate actions to prevent imminent collapse, but are likely the product of deeper, more structural factors and are therefore likely to exist to varying degrees at many other large companies. That is why we believe employees at other firms will recognize their own experiences in the voices of the many Boeing managers and workers who fill these pages.

RESEARCHING WORKPLACE CHANGE
AND ITS EFFECTS AT BOEING

We began our study in the mid-1990s with a sense of excitement and also some trepidation at the enormity of the task of trying to understand employee reactions at a division of 80,000 to 100,000 employees—the number varied according to where Boeing was in the business cycle—with vastly different occupational identities and skill sets, located at multiple sites across the Puget Sound region in Washington State. The task appeared more daunting when some of our initial approaches to a few employees to set up interviews were met with suspicion about our independence and concern over whether what they told us would get back to Boeing managers.[6] As we began to lay the groundwork for the study by meeting with dozens of managers and a handful of top executives to learn about Boeing's plans to implement various new programs, touring several work sites, addressing hundreds of shop stewards of the machinists' union, and talking with the leaders of the professional union representing Boeing's engineers and technicians about the purposes of our study, the organization began to appear even more complicated and the task more complex than we had anticipated. Would engineers and scientists who designed highly sophisticated machines and who possessed college degrees view the workplace changes in the same way as semiskilled production line workers with high school diplomas? Would gender, site location, union membership, or age produce complicated patterns of employee responses to the changes? In fact, our data analyses did uncover some group differences. But as our study progressed over its ten-year duration, certain common patterns and trends began to emerge and overshadow these differences. For example, although there were differences among occupational or age groups as to the timing of changes in certain work-related attitudes, all employees, regardless of occupation or age, registered the same U-shaped pattern on many—though not all—of these attitudes, first with declines in positive attitudes toward their jobs and the company in the middle of our study, followed by rebounds to where they had been in 1997, at the start of our study. And on important indicators of positive job attitudes and well-being that did not rebound, the pattern was similar across demographic and job categories. When we examined employee concerns over the threat posed to job security by outsourcing, we found that, in 1997, engineers were far less worried about this risk than hourly production workers were, but by 2003 the level of concern was similar. So, the passage of time revealed common patterns and trends that more or less applied to the whole Boeing workforce as it went through a series of both episodic and continuous changes. That is why we believe the story we tell of employee responses and reactions to workplace change has coherence, even as it acknowledges the nuances and complexity embedded within the main story line.

The transformation of American workplaces is ongoing and encompasses multiple changes. It has already spanned several years, and the effects of the changes introduced during this transition likely will also play themselves out over many more years. To fully understand how these changes have affected the lives of workers and managers, therefore, studies should not only examine the multifaceted nature of the changes, but also track their effects over long periods of time. It also helps if studies can follow the same group of workers and managers through the transition so that researchers have a baseline (measures at the beginning of the study) against which to compare the impact of various organizational changes, such as layoffs or mergers, on worker attitudes and well-being and to have confidence that it is the organizational changes and not variations in the samples at different points in time that produced the observed effects. Such longitudinal panel studies are not easy to conduct. Companies may lose interest in the study or dislike the kind of results that are emerging and cease cooperating, research funding can dry up, and dropouts from the original sample may jeopardize the representativeness of the panel sample. It is hardly surprising to learn, then, that few studies exist that provide a longitudinal picture of the effects of workplace change on a broad group of American workers and managers. Our study does so by tracking the responses and reactions to workplace change of a cohort of Boeing employees over a ten-year period (1996–2006). By examining the same group of employees over such a long span of time, we are able to detect general patterns in the data and to identify which trends seem to have staying power and which are ephemeral or short-lived. Most of the figures and the statistics reported in the following pages, therefore, are based on the responses of the 525 Boeing employees who remained in the study for the entire ten years of its duration and participated in each of the surveys.[7]

We also believe that uncovering the deep and sometimes hidden mood or zeitgeist of a large organization is best served by employing qualitative as well as quantitative methods. In our early forays into the Boeing labyrinth, as we conducted a handful of focus groups and interviews in preparation for the first employee survey, we were surprised at the emotional intensity of the responses we heard. Boeing employees expressed powerful and deeply felt reactions to what *their* company was doing. These responses convinced us that we needed to supplement the surveys with extensive interviews of a wide cross-section of Boeing employees if we were to understand fully the impact of the changes on the workforce.

Over the next several years we conducted over one hundred interviews with workers, managers, and union officials of Boeing in their offices and homes, in coffee shops, and by phone. As the study was nearing its end, we wanted to give many more employees the chance to express their views about the changes they had lived through. We therefore added two open-ended questions to the 2006 survey asking respondents first to tell us what they thought were the most important changes they had seen at Boeing, and then to describe how these changes had affected them. To our amazement, considering how often employees are surveyed by Boeing and the length of our questionnaire (117 questions, with many having several sub-questions), 900 of the 1,100 respondents gave voice to their feelings and opinions. It is from these comments, interviews, and focus groups, as well as from the survey findings, that we construct the story we tell in the remainder of this book (see the appendix for a fuller description of the study's methodology).[8]

CHANGES AT BOEING DURING THE RESEARCH STUDY PERIOD

We launched our study in 1996 at a point when Boeing, which had been the dominant player for many years in the passenger airplane industry, was well into a process to cut costs and improve the quality of its products to meet market threats to its supremacy. Some have called this the "total quality" period, aimed as it was at incorporating many Japanese ideas for continuous improvement, lean production, and teaming. Our study also began when employment at the division was at its lowest level in many years and just after a bitter ninety-six day strike by the machinists' union in 1995 over wages, benefits, and job security—issues that would continue to be front and center in future labor management negotiations. Our first survey in 1997, then, was conducted at a time when Boeing was already in the throes of unsettling change—not the ideal baseline by which to assess the impact of the changes at Boeing. We were, as it were, jumping into the process of change after it had already begun rather than before, as would be required in a controlled experiment.

Nevertheless, the period during which we conducted the first three of the four employee surveys (1997 to 2003) saw not only an acceleration and intensification of the changes begun before the start of our study, but also the powerful effects of the merger with McDonnell Douglas. In what we could call the short-term "shareholder value" period, nearly everything about Boeing seemed to change—corporate culture and identity, business strategy, governing ethos and ethics, and more. Our interviews and surveys in this period capture the intense, almost shell-shocked reactions of the workforce to an avalanche of organizational change. Our last survey in 2006 came soon after the decision to launch a revolutionary new airplane, the 787. As orders flooded in to Boeing for this new plane, the mood of the workforce improved, though the new global partnering model with its heavy reliance on multiple outside suppliers became a growing source of concern for many Boeing employees. This synoptic view of the interrelationship between phases of our study and developments at Boeing is summarized in table 1.1, and a fuller description can be found in the appendix.

Of course, change didn't end at the conclusion of our study. For example, at the end of 2009, the 787 finally took to the air to undergo a year of flight testing, roughly two years behind schedule. Boeing executives, partly in response to problems with suppliers that helped delay the 787 program, took over a key subcontractor, Vought Industries in South Carolina. In a powerful signal to the unionized workforce in the Puget Sound region, executives announced that a second assembly line for the 787 would be built in Charlotte, South Carolina, after the workforce there voted to decertify the machinists' union. And as we write in early 2010, Boeing is whittling away at the very generous educational benefits its workforce previously enjoyed. Even though our study captures an organization in the midst of profound change, there are no signs that the pace or extent of change will slow significantly at Boeing or at other companies. Faced with the uncertainty and insecurity produced by such disruptive

Table 1.1 Chronology of major Boeing developments during the four employee surveys

Survey year	Developments at Boeing
1997 (Time 1)	• End of period of layoffs (20,000 over previous three years)
	• Major merger and subsequent culture change from an engineering and "family" culture to a "team" and shareholder value culture
	• Start of period of increased hiring (40,000 hired over next three years)
	• Start of massive shift to computerization of design and parts ordering and to lean manufacturing
2000 (Time 2)	• Start of extended period of mass layoffs; layoffs accelerate after 9/11
	• Computerization and lean spread across company; cycle times cut significantly
2003 (Time 3)	• Layoffs begin to slow down after 50,000 laid off since 1999
	• Ethics problems among top executives come to light in 2004 and 2005
2006 (Time 4)	• Increased use of outsourcing and global partnering
	• Modest rehiring
	• Company working on new or redesigned products
	• New CEO appointed; stock price now double or triple the value that it was during previous survey periods

Note: Table A.1 (see appendix) contains a fuller description of Boeing events and our various research activities.

change, employees are likely to find that their coping and adaptive capacities will continue to be severely taxed, with significant consequences for their attachment to their companies and for their health and well-being.

WHERE WE ARE GOING IN THE BOOK

We set the context for the book in chapter 2, describing why Boeing leaders believed they had to transform their company. We focus primarily on the cost revolution brought by airline deregulation, the competitive threat posed by the rise of Airbus, and the pressures to produce short-term returns in a capital market dominated by institutional investors. We show how the choices that Boeing leaders eventually made were shaped by best practices among other globally competitive firms; legal, cultural, and technical developments associated with globalization; and the growing commitment among many publicly traded companies to short-term shareholder value as a primary objective. We also show how Boeing revamped its entire system of planning, engineering, and production to maximize efficiencies.

Chapters 3–8 describe how many Boeing employees who lived through these changes were bruised and battered by the experience. For the most part, those who survived that period—those, that is to say, who were not laid off or forced into early retirement, or who left of their own volition to pursue other opportunities—adapted to the changes, with some doing better than others, and some carrying the scars of their experiences. Their attitudes about Boeing and their jobs, as well as their physical and mental well-being—already somewhat negatively affected at the time of our first survey in 1997 following a bitter machinists' strike in 1995 and the turn toward a hard-line shareholder value orientation immediately afterward—tracked dramatically downward in our 2000 and 2003 surveys, as workplace changes multiplied, outsourcing intensified, and Boeing fortunes dipped. Employee job attitudes and well-being had improved in a number of respects by the time of our last survey in 2006—though not to the degree that one might have expected—as engineering and process changes took effect and proved workable, company fortunes improved, and a new airplane program that excited employees was launched. At the end of our study, Boeing's long-term employees were more disenchanted than at the beginning; less involved in their jobs; more attuned to outside activities, families, and friends; less committed to their company; and deeply worried for themselves and their country about outsourcing. The end result might best be characterized as a tendency among Boeing employees working through the change process to feel more detached and resentful, as if they had fallen out of love with a longtime partner who had become indifferent to them.

To be sure, Boeing employees reported they were impressed and satisfied by many of the changes they had experienced. Many reported they liked and appreciated the new energy of the company and its transformation from the "Lazy B" of the past. Many said they liked the more open and collaborative supervisory styles of their managers, the greater flexibility in scheduling their tasks and hours, better access to information that helped them perform their jobs more effectively, and more opportunities to collaborate on projects with people from other departments and with other skill sets. And our respondents credited the company with dramatically improving the situation for women, with serious and mostly successful efforts by company leaders to move Boeing away from its "good ol' boy" environment to one where gender equality became a serious objective and benchmark for assessing the performance of Boeing managers. Women respondents generally reported that overt gender discrimination was a thing of the past, though many told us that more subtle forms of discrimination continued to exist. Women, however, were increasingly promoted to managerial and executive positions during the period of our study, and closing pay disparities became a company priority.

Having said this, the problematic side of multiple, rapid, and continuous changes were much more pronounced. Layoff episodes and long-term downsizing tied to productivity improvements, outsourcing, and global partnering took their toll as people began to feel expendable, worried about being laid off in the future, and were forced to deal with a work environment where they were required to do more with less and where many of their close friends and collaborators were gone. More than a few employees said they were afraid that outsourcing and global partnering at Boeing and other companies would prove harmful to the country over the long haul as intellectual capital drifted to foreign firms, limiting opportunities for their own children and future generations of Americans as the nation's industrial and engineering capacities were hollowed out.

Many employees also complained that while they had absorbed and adapted to strategic, process, and supervisory changes, and had helped turn the company around after 2003, their contributions and sacrifices were not properly appreciated and rewarded by Boeing. Indeed, what most saw, especially after the shareholder value became the mantra of company leaders, was a disproportionate share of financial rewards going into the pockets of shareholders and executives. And, the cultural change at Boeing that accompanied the focus on shareholder value also took a toll on employees. Many pointed out, perhaps more in sorrow than in anger, that the notion of Boeing as a *family*, where employees' contributions were respected as a source of competitive advantage, was a thing of the past, replaced by Boeing as a *team* where people and positions were expendable or interchangeable with other workers around the world.

Boeing employees also were battered by multiple and continuous changes with respect to their work and how their workplaces were organized and operated. Many complained about, and used the term "flavor of the month" to describe, the flood of new initiatives, some of which were incorporated into operations, but many of which enjoyed brief flurries of executive support and demands for employee buy-in, then were all but forgotten. Though often benefiting from technological breakthroughs, Boeing employees were more than a little overwhelmed by the number and scale of IT changes that affected nearly every aspect of their jobs, and they were often irritated and frustrated by the inundation of e-mails and the need to take on many of the tasks done in the past for them by the human resources and employee benefits departments. And employees had to learn to adapt to this cascade of initiatives even as pressures to "get the planes out the door" proved unrelenting.

Front-line and middle manager employees were at the epicenter of the turbulent changes at Boeing and found their new roles increasingly stressful during the years of our study. They were, after all, the intermediaries standing between the top executives, who were determining the overall direction of the company and deciding what kinds of changes were to be introduced and in what sequence, and other Boeing employees whose jobs were being changed or eliminated. Managerial employees were the ones who determined, once the top executives ordered layoffs, which employees—with the exception of those covered by the machinists' contract—needed to be let go; and they were responsible for delivering the bad news in person to people in their work groups. To make matters worse, managers often faced layoffs themselves and had to contend with fewer opportunities for advancement as Boeing reduced conventional career ladders in favor of projects and lateral movement between projects.

After detailing the effects of these multiple changes on employees in chapters 3–8, we turn in chapter 9 to the possible lessons the Boeing experience has for American companies, and for American workers and managers more generally, as many of them face similar pressures, stresses, and upheaval from global competition and technological and social change. We conclude that individual employees can do some things to adapt to change and protect their interests. We also conclude that companies can do better for their employees, workers and managers alike, using strategies for enhancing revenues and cutting costs that engage employees as full partners and co-beneficiaries. But, in the end, we suggest that employees and companies cannot do it alone given the deep structural forces that are at work in the American and global economies. Companies and their employees can best thrive in an intensely competitive environment marked by rapid change and uncertainty, we conclude, if government provides a broad and sturdy safety net to help protect, sustain, and enhance American workers and managers.

Chapter 2 How and Why Boeing Changed Everything About the Way It Makes Airplanes

TURBULENCE: WORKING THROUGH CHANGE AT BOEING

In order to appreciate how Boeing Commercial Airplanes employees coped, adjusted, and adapted—some successfully, others not so successfully—to the many changes Boeing leaders instituted between the mid-1990s and 2006 when we conducted our fourth and last survey, we must first look at the causes, nature, and extent of the many changes the company introduced. That is the purpose of this chapter. We want to know why so many big changes were introduced, what they looked like in practice, and how they reshaped the working lives of so many Boeing employees.

Boeing was on the upswing during the years between our third and fourth employee surveys in 2003 and 2006, suggesting perhaps that the company's top executives knew exactly what they were doing as they redesigned the way Boeing made airplanes and refashioned the company's long-term strategy for succeeding in the global passenger jet market. The new, revitalized Boeing ran into trouble, however,

soon after our last employee survey, as its promising new 787 airplane, the foundation of the company's revival, became mired in production delays and can-
celled orders as the economic crisis took hold in 2008 and 2009, even as orders
for the updated 747-8 fell dramatically short of expectations. Though it is no
doubt too early to know whether Boeing leaders took the right path in terms of
the health and vitality of the company over the long term,[1] it will become apparent that many employees and ex-employees probably had a harder time of it
than was necessary. And, while many employees eventually bought into the
changed company and benefited from new opportunities and ways of doing
their jobs, many others were confused, demoralized, and made anxious by them,
with many choosing to leave Boeing and others marking time until retirement.

THE CASE FOR MAKING BIG CHANGES
AT BOEING

Companies generally do not make big changes unless they have to do so.[2]
Large-scale modifications are simply too expensive, time-consuming, disruptive, and risky to tackle when things are going well. When companies are growing and profitable, those who urge patience and prudence control the agenda.
Change in growing and profitable companies tends to be incremental rather
than on a grand scale, and investors, executives, employees, unions, suppliers,
and customers have time to adjust and adapt. In such companies, short-term
(or what seem to be short-term) reverses do not necessarily trigger big changes
because most tend to assume from past experience with the "ups and downs"
of the economy and/or the fortunes of their own industry that another uptick
in the business cycle is likely to occur sooner or later to set things straight. No
use moving away from what has worked in the past. Why rock the boat when
the current is in your favor and the shore is in sight?

Here, a former senior executive at Boeing reflects on the difficulties in un-
dertaking large-scale changes when the organization has no sense of urgency:
"I joined the Boeing Company in 1978 as the organization was embarking on
what was then called quality improvement. It was my task to help lead the
journey. The company faced the usual obstacles, but it also faced a more unusual one: business was great! We were the No. 1 commercial airplane manufacturer in the world, and orders were pouring in. Companies we visited to educate ourselves told us we simply weren't desperate enough to make it work."[3]

Big changes started to happen at Boeing in the early 1990s and continued to
unfold to the end of our study in 2006.[4] During these years, various Boeing

leaders, including Carl Schronz, Phil Condit, Ron Woodard, Allan Mullally, and Harry Stonecipher, came to believe that Boeing had to change or face imminent decline. By the late 1980s, Boeing leaders, industry insiders, and investors were growing increasingly anxious, not only about Boeing losing its dominant position in the global commercial airplane market, but about its very viability as a profitable firm over the long haul. In their view, the traditional ways of doing things in the company no longer worked. A new kind of company had to be created, and, given the nature of the economic environment and the rise of an important rival, creation of this new kind of company needed to happen with some dispatch. In this chapter we ask why Boeing leaders felt that company transformation was needed and what specific steps they took over the course of no more than a decade and a half to achieve this goal.

The unions at Boeing played a very small role in decisions about the types and pace of change. The key decisions about the transformation of the Boeing Corporation and its passenger airplane division, Boeing Commercial Airplanes, were made by the company's top executives and board of directors. While a majority of Boeing employees were represented by labor organizations—the International Association of Machinists (hereafter, the IAM) for production workers and the Society of Professional Engineering Employees in Aerospace (hereafter, SPEEA) for engineers and technical workers—company leaders retained (and still retain) the power to make decisions about the most important aspects of the design, manufacture, and sale of airplanes. This included, for example, decisions about the organization of work processes, the deployment of new technologies, which models of aircraft to produce and which ones to discontinue, when layoffs needed to occur, when the head count needed to increase, and what business model to use in response to changing market conditions.

Though making periodic stabs over the years at playing a role in decisions about new technology, outsourcing, and the use of outside contractors in Boeing plants and offices, the IAM and SPEEA were most successful in negotiating agreements with Boeing on issues related to wages and salaries, benefits, and grievance procedures, but fell short on matters having to do with job security and control of the workplace, the introduction of new technologies, or the lineup of airplane models, a state of affairs typical of American labor unions.[5] Like other large manufacturing companies whose workers are represented by labor unions, Boeing has been willing, usually after tough negotiations and even a few strikes, to yield on wage, salary, benefits, and grievance matters, but has vigorously defended management's traditional prerogatives.[6] As Boeing CEO and chairman James McNerney put the issue in an e-mail to employees in 2008 during an IAM strike: "It would be gravely unwise for Boeing to agree to terms in any contract that would fundamentally restrict our ability to manage our business. Markets and business conditions can change quickly and dramatically. And we need to be able to react just as fast."[7]

In making decisions about the way ahead for the company, Boeing leaders were well aware that the formula for long-term success in large publicly traded companies is fairly straightforward: earnings must be large enough to reward investors and fuel additional growth in the value of the company. A company whose costs exceed revenues for some number of years will likely disappoint investors as share prices stagnate or fall, face difficulties in the credit markets, have trouble holding on to talented employees, and cease investing in its own research and development for long-term growth. Though Boeing did not slip completely into such a negative hole in the late 1980s and 1990s, the overall health of the company was not good in the first half of the 1990s. So, for example, Boeing suffered serious declines in earnings and saw its stock price decline.[8] During this period, Boeing executives, board members, and investors came to believe that disappointing earnings were the product of bad performance on both the revenue and cost sides of the ledger and that something needed to be done regarding each. The fastest road to increasing shareholder value, a term used over and over in conversations with Boeing executives about what they were trying to achieve in the mid- to late 1990s and the reigning mantra in the business management literature in those years,[9] was to get the costs of manufacturing airplanes under control. Boeing strategies for enhancing revenues included forays into new markets (mainly space and military contracting) and some attention, though very belatedly and with mixed results, to designing and launching new and improved airplanes.[10]

Cost Pressures

The airline industry was heavily regulated between 1938, when President Franklin D. Roosevelt and Congress created the Civil Aeronautics Board (CAB), and 1978, when the old regime ended with passage of the Airline Deregulation Act. For four decades, nearly everyone associated with the airline industry made money—the large airline companies; American airplane manufacturers such as Boeing, Douglas, and McDonnell; and members of the various labor unions associated with airlines and manufacturers. Under the federal regulatory regime, the CAB had the final word on the routes particular airlines could fly, the rates they could charge passengers and shippers, and their schedules. The system was designed to stabilize the airline industry and protect the major players from unsettling competition, from either the other established airlines or upstarts. Cost was hardly an issue for any of the players in the system because any increases in fares, airplane prices, or new amenities could be passed on to the paying public, both leisure and business travelers. The public had no choice but to pay the higher tariff because the CAB rarely allowed competition on the most profitable routes.[11]

During this forty-year period, then, it is hardly surprising that not a single major airline among this group went bankrupt nor saw a new airline appear to challenge the majors on any of their most vital interstate or international routes. This was a cozy world indeed for the major airlines; commercial aircraft producers such as Boeing; labor unions representing pilots, maintenance, and cabin personnel; engineers and technicians; and machinists.

Former Boeing Commercial president Ron Woodard went on, almost wistfully, about the good old days in a 2007 interview with us: "Everyone made money; the airlines [were] regulated. You'd come up with some great idea and you would sell that to Pan Am or United or somebody, and they'd go off to the government and they would get their prices enough to pay for the whole thing, and you know, everybody made money with it. There was no nasty discounting, no low cost carriers."

In a regulated world, where costs were almost an afterthought for airlines and airplane manufacturers, Boeing and other producers could concentrate on engineering and building the products they wanted to create. Until the late 1980s, Boeing was known in the industry as an engineers' company, where costs played second fiddle to design and quality. One close observer of Boeing described the company in the following terms: "Boeing was willing to spend money—lots of money—to make long-term investments in new ideas. If those ideas took a while to make money, well, that's how it was because, at Boeing, the engineers, not the accountants, called the shots. . . . Boeing's philosophy could be summed up as go-for-it-and-damn-the expenses—but not damn the quality."[12]

It was surely a wonderful environment in which to be an engineer at Boeing, as Woodard pointed out: "We had our ten [engineering] design standards that you're supposed to make every decision with and there wasn't a single thing about cost, relevance to the customer or anything else. It all had to do with doing it faster and being safer . . . intentionally, no one knew what anything cost because they didn't want engineers to know what anything cost."

In the midst of the economic troubles in the United States during the 1970s —stagnation joined to high rates of inflation ("stagflation") and a perceived decline in global competitiveness to Japan, Europe, and the so-called Asian tigers—an intellectual shift occurred among a broad swath of economists, business leaders, elected officials, and the public regarding the necessity and efficacy of government regulation of economic activities. Among a strange group of bedfellows, including the conservative Chicago School of economics and the center-left Brookings Institution, a consensus began to emerge that many aspects of the regulatory state were becoming increasingly irrational and burdensome, stifling innovation and competition, and contributing to inflated prices in many sectors.[13]

Though virtually every major airline resisted its passage, the Airline Deregulation Act was passed in 1978. The Act gradually phased out the CAB's control over fares, routes, and schedules, and made it difficult for the CAB to deny market entry to new airline companies. The CAB itself was to be abolished after a four-year period.

Rather than stable profitability, which was the norm during the regulated period in the life history of airlines, the post-1978 world for them became highly cyclical, with revenues tied mainly to the rise and fall of the business cycle. Because airlines, whether legacy or newcomers such as Southwest, Frontier, and JetBlue, cannot change the course of the overall business cycle, their only hope over the long term was and remains to control their costs, with the biggest costs on their balance sheets going to labor, fuel, and airplanes (whether bought outright or leased). This post-deregulation focus on costs transformed Boeing's world, accustomed as it was to designing and building the planes it wanted to produce, knowing that the airlines would pay whatever price was required. Now Boeing had to worry about the sales prices of its airplanes and the cost of parts airlines needed to buy to maintain them. It was all a bit of a shock.

Though it took some time for the implications of this new, post-regulation world to sink in, Boeing executives and investors eventually came to believe the company had to get its costs under control. Overstretched legacy carriers and their low cost competitors were simply not going to play by the old rules.[14] As Woodard observed, "The damned airplanes were so expensive . . . we knew we had to change and we were trying to do it."

The Airbus Challenge

Another reason Boeing leaders and investors favored company transformation was the emergence by the middle of the 1980s of a formidable global competitor, European Airbus, which was willing and able to match Boeing not only on price but on the quality of its airplanes.

Boeing leaders didn't take Airbus seriously for a long time. When Airbus was created in 1967, Boeing was the dominant producer of passenger airplanes in the world. It had already zoomed far ahead of its postwar American domestic rivals, Douglas, McDonnell, and Lockheed, with the first commercially successful passenger jetliner, the 707. By the time Airbus was reorganized as Airbus Industries in 1970—having not yet produced a single plane—Boeing had launched the world's first jumbo jet, the twin-aisle, four-engine 747, the aircraft that would dominate this particularly lucrative market, particularly after Lockheed and the merged McDonnell-Douglas company failed to meet sales expectations with their Tri-star and DC-10 jumbos. A year later, in 1971, while Airbus was still in the throes of its birthing difficulties, Boeing rolled out its first 737–200, the beginning of a family of airplanes designed for the short-to-medium-haul market (130–190 passengers) that would prove to be the best-selling airplane model in aviation history. In the early 1980s, when Airbus was beginning to make its presence felt in an important way with the 200-plus passenger A300, Boeing rolled out two planes that would be fairly successful over the long run in this market—the 200-plus passenger 757 (single aisle) and the 250 passenger 767 (double aisle). Lockheed and McDonnell Douglas had no answer for either of these planes, nor for the Airbus A300, wasting most of its engineering and financial resources on the race for the jumbo market.

By the early 1980s, then, Boeing was the clear leader in terms of market share, at around 60 percent; Lockheed and McDonnell Douglas were in terminal decline in the commercial airplane part of their operations, while Airbus was beginning to make its mark. It was clear to all that Airbus was introducing some terrific airplanes into the marketplace[15] and taking sales away from Boeing because, according to industry observers, it was listening to airline customers about their needs, incorporating important technical innovations in its planes,[16] and making cost-saving breakthroughs in the manufacturing process.

The rise of Airbus started with the introduction in 1974 of the twin-engine, two-aisle, wide-bodied A300, aimed at the medium range, 250-passenger plane market (direct flights within Europe and one-stop flights across the United States) then not being served by any other manufacturer. It followed with the less commercially successful but innovative A310 in 1982 (two-person cockpit where three had been the norm, color-coded instrument panel, and carbon fiber tail fin) and the wildly successful A320 in 1988. Not only did the A320 compete very well against the venerable Boeing 737 in the medium range, single-aisle 150–180 passenger market—it was the fastest-selling airplane in aviation history until the appearance of Boeing's 787 almost two decades later— but it was the most technologically advanced passenger plane of the day, with a fully digital "fly-by-wire" flight control system,[17] the first LCD displays in a passenger jet filled with digitalized up-to-the-second information of each of the plane's operating systems, and a fully computerized guidance system.[18] In 1993 it began deliveries to the airlines of the A330, a medium range, twin-engine, 335-passenger plane, and its twin (common cockpit, avionics, and flying characteristics), the A340, a long-range, four-engine plane for 295 passengers, proving to the aviation world that Airbus was ready and able to provide a full family of technologically sophisticated aircraft for its airline customers. Boeing was without an answer for these twins for over two years—its own 757 carried only about 200 passengers in a two-class configuration, while its wide-bodied 767–300 carried 269—until it began deliveries of the 400-passenger 777–200 to airlines in 1996.

Both McDonnell Aircraft and Douglas Aircraft folded under these competitive pressures (they merged to become McDonnell-Douglas, which was then absorbed by Boeing in 1997), their places rapidly filled by Airbus. Though Boeing leaders, workers, and supporters tied the rise of Airbus to the generous subsidies the company received over the years from European governments to develop new aircraft, and to its consequent ability to sell planes below the costs of production because of this government backing, it cannot be denied that Airbus was producing attractive and technologically advanced airplanes aimed at markets where Boeing planes were beginning to feel old and tired (the A320 challenge to the 737 falls into this category), or where Boeing had no planes to offer at all (the A330 and A340, at roughly 300-plus passengers). As a result of these efforts, Airbus surpassed Boeing for the first time in orders for new airplanes in 1994;[19] Airbus also increased its market share—measured by number of planes delivered—from 16 percent in 1988 to 37 percent by 1996,[20] the year before our first employee survey. For Boeing leaders, who at first ignored Airbus and then disparaged the oddly organized and run company, Airbus's sales achievement in 1994 was the exclamation point to their slowly growing realization that their company had to change radically or face decline and a permanent secondary status to its vigorous European rival.

WHAT BOEING LEADERS DID TO TRANSFORM
THEIR COMPANY

Responding to these escalating cost and sales pressures, Boeing leaders Carl Shrontz, Phil Condit, Ron Woodard, Allan Mullally, and eventually Harry Stonecipher changed Boeing root and branch from the mid-1990s through the mid-2000s. During this relatively brief period of time, they introduced a broad range of changes in the way Boeing went about its business.

Changing How Boeing Designs and Manufactures Airplanes

While Boeing made scores of changes in the complex processes by which it made airplanes, the most important of them in terms of engineering and manufacturing, as well as the working lives of employees, were lean production, the digitalization of all important design and manufacturing processes, and outsourcing and partnering.

VIRTUAL DESIGN

The computer revolution has transformed much of the everyday lives of employees at every level of skill and position at Boeing. Word processing, desktop publishing, digital design tools, Web-based tools for doing personal and collaborative work, as well as doing one's own human resource planning (company-based medical and pension and 401k planning, for example), and, most especially, e-mail became ubiquitous.[21] In these respects, Boeing employees experienced computer-driven changes in their everyday work lives similar in type and scale to those of many other American wage and salaried workers. What has been going on at Boeing would feel familiar to many other people in workplaces across the country, indeed, across the entire rich industrialized world. But there is much more in the way of digitalization beyond these routine changes, if you will, that shaped the direction and fate of Boeing and the everyday work lives of its employees during the years of our study: the computer-based virtual design of airplanes and a program to plan and track the engineering and manufacturing processes. We talk about the first of these in this section, leaving the second for the section below on manufacturing.

The virtual design of new airplanes took off at Boeing with the 777 under project director Alan Mulally.[22] For Boeing, the 777 was the first plane completely designed on a computer, bypassing the traditional "mock-up" stage of the design process in which a full-scale plane model is built from the ground up to ensure that all the pieces fit together properly and that no more than one part occupied a single physical space. The 777 was designed on a single computer system with massive computing power from Dassault/IBM[23] that allowed for the three-dimensional design and representation of the entire plane. Boeing distributed over two thousand computer terminals linked to IBM mainframe computers to Boeing design team members. The computer-linked common design system enabled engineers from diverse parts of the company to collaborate, all the while consulting with airline customers, parts suppliers, and in-house manufacturing experts. The designs for parts and tooling were then released to subcontractors in the United States and abroad to fabricate parts and sections for planes, which were then brought together in Everett for final assembly.[24] This system eventually spread throughout the company and became standard for design and engineering on new versions of existing planes such as the 737 NG.

Computer-assisted design and engineering took a giant leap forward with the 787 project, which was announced in 2003. For this airplane, Boeing leaders pursued a strategy of global partnering (which we will describe in more detail in the section "outsourcing and partnering" later in this chapter) rather than subcontracting. In the 787's global partnering arrangement, engineers at Boeing and at partner firms around the world work in close collaboration to design the airplane and its component parts and sections. Partner companies then design and build the tooling to make parts and sections, and then manufacture them in multiple locations in the United States and abroad. Shipment and delivery scheduling for final assembly in Everett are done collaboratively by Boeing and its partner companies on a common computing platform.

All of this is possible because of dramatic increases in computing power and advances in designing and engineering software packages well beyond what was used for the 777.[25] As one Boeing engineer described it to us in 2006, "Information technology and communications technology have enabled Boeing people to be in touch at all times from anywhere. Design anywhere, build anywhere is now possible. True globalization is now possible."

Computer-based airplane design was clearly beneficial for Boeing on a number of levels, including dramatic cost savings and greater efficiencies in engineering. For Boeing employees, however, these powerful new computer design systems meant that proportionally fewer Boeing engineers and technicians were required on new projects, a product of both increases in productivity—each person could do more—and the company's easier access to global engineering talent.

MANUFACTURING

Lean Production. Companies going lean hope and expect to do much more for much less with fewer people. Indeed, the lean mantra from Richard Womack, who co-authored the book *The Machine That Changed the World*[26] about the Toyota production system and who is a consultant to many major public companies (including Boeing), is straightforward and unambiguous: "half the space, half the time, half the people, half of everything." By all accounts, Boeing leaders embraced lean principles with a vengeance once the company announced in 1996 that lean would be central to all Boeing operations. One industry observer noted that the company "has . . . an almost fanatical dedication to lean manufacturing," having sent over 1,500 executives, managers, and frontline employees to Japan to study Toyota's methods from 1993 through 1998.[27]

Central to lean is an effort to cut waste in every aspect of production and to get rid of anything that uses resources without creating value. Typically in manufacturing, "going lean" means diminishing inventory in favor of just-in-time delivery of parts and subassemblies (partially built sections rather than individual parts); replacing large-scale inflexible tools with mobile, flexible, multiuse tools; standardizing as many parts and processes as possible (meaning less customization); giving workers more information about the details and pace of production and the power to correct problems when and where they occur; and using workplace teams to identify and eliminate inefficiencies and waste. Boeing had adopted these mechanisms on the 737 NG production line by 2002 and on the 777 by 2005. These included: just-in-time; mobile tooling jigs to replace huge fixed-in-place tool scaffolding surrounding airplanes as they were being built; quality control teams; a moving assembly line; feeder lines delivering preassembled parts and tool kits to fixed spots on the moving line; prominent visual displays on the production line of manufacturing progress; workers empowered to stop the line to fix problems immediately; and accelerated improvement workshops for all production employees to identify waste and inefficiencies, all to very good effect. Before lean production was introduced, for example, much time was wasted as mechanics assigned to airplane assembly first went to pick up the tools they needed for the day, then went to a different part of the plant to assemble parts. After lean was introduced, mechanics found packets of tools and parts waiting for them at their workstations at the start of the day, with new packets arriving as needed throughout the day.

Where these reforms were fully in place, the results were impressive. In 1999, for example, Boeing workers took twenty-two days to assemble a 737 NG, using three shifts (one production shift and two shifts to remove tool scaffolding, move the planes forward to the next position, and configure the scaffolding on the next plane in line) backed by two years' worth (twenty planes) of parts in inventory. By 2005, they needed only eleven days to complete the task, using two shifts, with 60 percent fewer parts in inventory.[28] Ominously for jobs, even as orders increased for the 737 NG, by 2005 two assembly lines were able to produce all the planes Boeing needed rather than the three it had previously required.

Getting lean processes up and running, not surprisingly, was time-consuming, often disruptive, and not always fully realized, though production cycle times in Boeing plants decreased as expected. The 787, however, being a brand new airplane developed in collaboration with global partners for final assembly in the Everett facility, was planned to be lean from the beginning. There the 787 is assembled on a single line, with planes configured in nose-to-tail configurations, with entire subassemblies from global partners delivered just-in-time at the point of use, alongside kits containing tools and parts for the assembly task at hand. Of course, as is well known at this writing, problems with the quality and timeliness of delivery of airplane sections and subassemblies from global partners in 2007, 2008, and 2009—after our study of Boeing employees was completed—disrupted 787 production, putting deliveries more than two years behind schedule by 2010.

Airplane Definition and Parts Management. Introduced in 1993, the inelegantly named Define and Control Aircraft Configuration/Manufacturing Resource Management (DCAC/MRM) was a massive computer system for streamlining the process of putting planes into production in the factories, providing drawings for them, and tracking and ordering parts during the manufacturing process. It is an extremely complicated system whose purpose, paradoxically perhaps, is radical simplification. The first part (DCAC) divides airplanes within each model category into three types. The first is a standard product for which the customer can order only a handful of options (color of the interior, for example) and for which engineering drawings already exist ready for downloading from the computer system. Boeing leaders hoped and expected that this type of order would make up the bulk of orders, dramatically lowering engineering costs. The second type might be termed "standard-plus," a mostly standard product for which a much wider range of options is available, but limited still. This way of ordering is similar to how a consumer might order options for a car from an auto dealer. Again, all engineering drawings for the broader set of options are complete and available for downloading. The third is a heavily customized plane, built on the base model to be sure, but with many modifications to satisfy the needs of a particular customer. Such a plane requires very high-end engineering attention and time, resulting in the highest cost airplanes.

Boeing wants less of this third type in favor of a more commodity-type, semi-mass-produced plane like the first and second types, though the third is most similar to the traditional way of doing the engineering drawings for the manufacturing process. In the view of virtually all industry observers, the old Boeing engaged in way too much customized production over the years, something that added tremendously to rising costs. One story has it that over a thousand different engineering drawings existed for bulkheads for the 747. When a customer ordered a nonstandard bulkhead configuration, over 2,500 parts on the airplane were impacted in one way or another, something that had to be accounted for in engineering drawings.[29] Reducing the number of available options and cutting back on customization was the objective of DCAC and its successor system.

The MRM part of DCAC/MRM tracks and manages airplane parts during the manufacturing process. The 777 was once described as four million parts flying in formation.[30] Keeping track of these parts throughout the manufacturing process, ordering additional parts when supplies run low, and keeping a record of the parts going into each plane are done for the purposes of airplane maintenance after sale and to meet FAA requirements (mainly to aid in the investigation of crashes, should any occur). Prior to MRM, Boeing had to keep huge supplies of parts in inventory, and many mistakes were made in the tracking system (wrong numbering on drawings was said to be quite common).

Here is how Ron Woodard, former president of Boeing Commercial Airplanes, compared the old and new way of doing things under DCAC/MRM in an interview with us in 2006:

> We called it DCAC/MRM, but it was a new release system—basically, how do you release things to the factory floor in an efficient manner? We had this old release system that was so complex that [for] every airplane or every customer you basically had to re-release the whole airplane [every time there was a new order. For example,] if this cup were in the galley and you're going to order an airplane we'd have to go back to this cup drawing and tabulate that drawing so it would be on that particular airplane, so you're constantly opening every single drawing for every single part. One thing that we were trying to do is get it so you could say this is or isn't on this particular airplane. We tried to get it so when you're building this airplane you push a button and it lists everything that's on the airplane so you don't have to go [through] every single drawing in the whole Boeing drawing system to find out what makes up an airplane; you can go to the airplane top drawing and find out what's in it. It was a completely backwards way of doing it but it's what grew out of the military, which wasn't a problem because all military airplanes have almost the same stuff. If we started from a clean sheet of paper, we wouldn't have that problem.

The introduction and deployment of the parts tracking system were not without problems. Not only did many find that the system had many bugs to work out, it also came along at the same time as other changes were occurring in the factories, including a range of lean-related initiatives. For employees, as we report in later chapters, the pace of change and the need to learn how to use new processes on the fly contributed to rising stress levels. Further, deployment of this new and complex system, coupled with a dramatic uptick in airplane orders and problems with parts suppliers, led to a meltdown in the factories in 1997, with both the Renton and Everett facilities forced to shut down until the backlog could be cleared out. Anticipating the disaster, one consultant told a group of Boeing executives: "The prospect of doubling production rates in the face of such change is like attempting a four-and-a-half somersault off a 50-foot board into a pail of water."[31]

Eventually, the bugs in DCAC/MRM were worked out, manufacturing employees became proficient in its use, and it became for most of them the way parts management and tracking were done. In 2000 the DCAC/MRM system was upgraded to a Web-based, single interface system called Metaphase from the company Teamcenter, and within a short time it was being used throughout Boeing's manufacturing facilities. By 2006, at the time of our fourth and final employee survey, over thirty thousand machinists, technicians, and engineers were using the upgraded system.

Outsourcing and Partnering

Outsourcing is the practice of contracting aspects of design, production, and distribution, as well as a range of company infrastructural operations (such as accounting, human resources, and IT), to businesses outside of a company. Most major manufacturing companies in the United States and abroad source activities that were at one time done in-house as a way to decrease costs, gain entry to new markets, and tap into deeper talent pools.[32] Boeing has distributed portions of the design and manufacturing of airplane parts to other companies, some in the United States and some abroad, for a very long time, though the pace has increased dramatically in recent years. Engines for Boeing airplanes, for example, almost from the beginning of Boeing's life as a company, have been designed and manufactured by outside companies, usually because these companies have been at it for a long time and design and build engines better and less expensively than Boeing could do on its own. Starting with the 707 in 1958, General Electric and Pratt and Whitney in the United States, and Rolls-Royce in Great Britain, have been the sole suppliers of engines for Boeing commercial airplanes, up to and including the new 787.[33] Other major airplane component parts, such as landing gear and overhead storage compartment units, typically have been sourced to outside companies, again for reasons of perceived economic efficiency and quality.

Offsets—formal and informal arrangements to subcontract work to a country in return for favored access to its markets—are another reason for sourcing, though the rationale is less about engineering and production efficiencies and more about selling airplanes to foreign airline customers. Thus, for many years Boeing has awarded contracts to non-U.S. companies as a way to influence the purchasing decisions of government-owned or government-subsidized or otherwise government-privileged airlines in favor of Boeing products (Airbus, as well as McDonnell Douglas before its merger with Boeing, has long done this). Four Japanese companies manufactured the fuselage panels, floor beams, and cabin doors for the 777, for example, an airplane that was then ordered in substantial quantities by Japan Airlines and All Nippon Airways (ANA). To take another example, Chinese-based airline companies dramatically increased their purchases of Boeing planes after six Chinese companies were awarded contracts in the mid-1990s for production of parts of the aft section of the 737 NG as well as aluminum and titanium forgings for a range of Boeing models.

The "make-buy" program that was introduced at Boeing in 1993 made outsourcing more systematic, more strategically central to Boeing's fortunes, and much more widespread in practice. Though company publications and handouts to employees are often confused by new and ambiguous terminology, complex diagrams, and murky action plans, "make-buy" was really pretty straightforward: to identify and keep in-house core products and competencies and outsource everything else. In only eighteen months, Booz Allen consultants helped Boeing identify every major part in every one of its airplane models and examined how well and at what cost Boeing produced or might produce such parts in the future. With this information in hand, Boeing began subcontracting out noneconomically viable parts production to a range of companies in the United States and abroad. Over the long run, of course, moving substantial design and production activities from in-house to out-of-house status meant that Boeing required fewer employees in their several Puget Sound area factories and offices.

The pace of outsourcing was ratcheted up even higher for Boeing's newest airplane, the 787. According to industry sources, only about 30 percent of the fabrication work on this revolutionary plane, much of it made of lightweight composites rather than aluminum, is being done by Boeing in its U.S. plants. Though final assembly is being done in Everett, north of Seattle, many of the new plane's major subassemblies and completed sections are coming from companies in the United States and abroad. A consortium of three Japanese companies is supplying the wings and center wing box that connects the wings to the fuselage, for example, elements of an airplane once thought to be a core competency, even a crown jewel, of the Boeing company. A partnership of an American and an Italian firm is supplying part of the center and rear fuselage. Several Chinese firms are involved in producing important parts for the vertical fin. In fact, parts for the 787 are being produced in about 135 sites in two dozen countries, all to be brought together in Everett for final assembly. Boeing and industry people refer to the 787 as a "snap-fit" airplane, one that is snapped together, as it were, much like model planes. The process is more complicated than this, of course, something Boeing discovered to its considerable discomfort in 2008 and 2009 when many of the sections neither snapped nor fit properly, but it gives some sense of how different the production of this plane is from the way Boeing produced airplanes throughout most of its history.[34]

Outsourcing on the 787 project is even greater than for other projects because firms are involved with Boeing not as subcontractors but as full partners, as we suggested above. The partnering strategy for the 787 is, in part, a way to share the huge costs of the huge up-front financing required for this high risk project; to secure advance orders from airline customers here and abroad; and to tap into the broadest possible pool of engineering talent. To be a full partner means that American, Asian, and European firms are required to put money on the table to launch the project (Boeing president Harry Stonecipher's condition for giving the go-ahead on the project in 2003),[35] collaborate in the plane's design, take on responsibility for engineering the tools and manufacturing process for their area of responsibility, build new factory space to produce sections of the plane that Boeing would have had to do otherwise in its own plants, and ship them to Boeing for final assembly.

As partners, U.S. and foreign firms are responsible for every aspect of their portion of the airplane project (subcontractors generally do what the contracting company wants, following directions given to them): assume financial risks for their participation, hold intellectual property rights on the components and systems they design and produce, and share in the rewards, namely, a portion of the revenues from airplane sales. The upshot is that much of the design and engineering work that would have in the past been done by engineers and technicians in Everett, Seattle, and Renton is now being done elsewhere as part of global teams, so fewer of them are needed in the long run. Though this more elaborate outsource partnering was only relevant to the 787 during the final years of our study, and while production snafus and glitches in coordination of the complex partner supply chain led to painful and expensive delays in delivery of the 787 to airline customers,[36] many industry observers and Boeing employees believe this form of collaborative design, engineering, fabrication, and assembly of airplanes will eventually spread to other airplane models. More than a few engineers we interviewed in this study worried that this will result in the bleeding of engineering knowledge and jobs to global partner companies, hurting both Boeing and the United States in the long run.

Though both the IAM and SPEEA have raised the issue of outsourcing and job security during recent contract negotiations, neither union has been very successful in slowing the former or improving the latter. We look in more detail at these layoff-related issues in chapter 4.

THE EFFORT TO PUMP UP REVENUES

An important part of the story of change at Boeing that so affected the company's fortunes and the lives of its employees was the company's goal of getting costs under control by going lean; digitalizing design, engineering, and manufacturing on a broad front; and outsourcing and partnering. But reducing costs was only one part of the equation for increasing earnings and establishing a strategy for long-term success at Boeing. The other part of the strategy was to increase revenues, primarily by moving more heavily into space and defense contracting. Another possible route, according to most industry observers, was a greater effort to offer its airline customers newer and more innovative airplanes, something Boeing didn't get around to until 2003 when it announced plans for the 787 Dreamliner.[37]

Boeing bought and merged with longtime rival McDonnell Douglas in 1997, just a year after it had acquired Rockwell Aerospace and Defense. The deals to buy Rockwell and McDonnell Douglas were the brainchild of Boeing president and CEO Phil Condit who long had wanted Boeing to become a company that did much more than produce commercial airplanes. He had a number of strategies for doing this, ranging from providing computer services to providing in-flight entertainment systems and consulting on systems integration, but he was most interested in space and national defense. Though Boeing had some presence in these areas, it was still way behind McDonnell Douglas and Lockheed, especially as a defense contractor. Condit saw a more diversified company as being more profitable in the long run, especially one more directly tied to lucrative government contracts and less dependent on the vagaries of the commercial aviation market, with its periodic boom-and-bust cycles. The merger with McDonnell Douglas did not go smoothly and resentment about it was very strong among Boeing people, many believing that Boeing got "taken to the cleaners" and that McDonnell Douglas people, with their notorious, GE-inspired short-term shareholder value orientation, had taken control of the company, dramatically changing its culture and how people were treated.

Here is what Ron Woodard had to say about it in our interview with him in 2007: "I was dead-set against the merger. . . . We thought that we'd kill McDonnell Douglas and we had it on the ropes. . . . I still believe that Harry [Stonecipher, then head of McDonnell Douglas] outsmarted Phil [Condit] . . . and his gang bought Boeing with Boeing's money. We were all just disgusted. We had the commercial guys dead. The military guys had them totally out of business. Condit went off, and it was another one of his solo deals . . . and [we] paid way, way too much money, and we're still paying for it. We wrote off so many tens of billions of dollars for that whole mess."

We will have much more to say about the merger with McDonnell Douglas and its effects on employees in chapter 3 on Boeing's changed corporate and workplace culture. Our interviews, focus groups, and survey questionnaires suggest that the merger was and remains one of the most consequential changes affecting the sense of long-term well-being and commitment of Boeing employees. Whether the merger was a good or bad thing for Boeing and its employees is something we shall explore throughout this book. But the deal and the subsequent shift in emphasis at the Boeing Company—exemplified by the relocation of its headquarters from Seattle to Chicago in 2001—seem to have achieved an important goal of the Boeing leadership. Today, Boeing's Integrated Defense Systems company is the world's second largest aerospace and defense contractor and accounts for more than half of the parent company's revenues.[38]

Transforming design, engineering, and manufacturing processes to control costs and adapting to the merger with McDonnell Douglas dominated the agenda at Boeing during the 1990s. While in the process of fixing airplane designing and manufacturing, and dealing with the consequences of the merger, Boeing leaders failed to introduce any new airplanes, something the company needed to do if it was to hold off Airbus in the commercial market. Indeed, more than a decade elapsed between the first commercial flight of the then new 777 in 1994 by United Airlines and the announcement by All Nippon Airways in 2004 that it had ordered fifty of the new 787 planes, though first deliveries of the Dreamliner may not happen until 2010 or 2011. This "failure of innovation" by Boeing was, according to Lawrence and Thornton, mainly responsible for Boeing's loss of its leading position in the commercial market and the emergence of an Airbus-Boeing duopoly by the turn of the new century.[39]

Boeing mostly chose the "derivatives" path during the 1990s and early 2000s

—making improvements to existing models—apparently unwilling to spend the enormous amounts of money and thereby assuming the risks involved in designing, producing, and selling entirely new airplane models. The idea was to generate profits out of existing models by finding ever more cost-efficient manufacturing methods. To be sure, it improved almost every aspect of its 737 and 777 models during this period, making them bigger, faster, and more fuel efficient, allowing them to go longer distances as the need arose.[40] But even here, Boeing wasn't as nimble as it needed to be. It introduced the 737 NG derivative very late in the game (1997), for example, losing market leadership in single-aisle planes to the wider and more comfortable Airbus A320. It tried to answer the challenge of the super-jumbo Airbus A380 without incurring the burdensome up-front development costs of a new plane with the 747–8 series, a redesigned stretched version of its once dominant 747 model, but the new model had found few airline customers by late 2009. (This was a good thing, perhaps, because the transfer of engineers from the 747 project to the troubled 787 project put the former way behind schedule.) The last delivery of the 757 was made in 2005, while the 767 was on its last legs by 2007 and 2008, when there were no new orders for it at all.[41] Meanwhile, as suggested above, Airbus had a presence in virtually every global market niche (defined by number of passengers, range, and cost) with an innovative and popular airplane model. By 2006, the last year of our study, Boeing had only two products—the 777 and the 737 NG derivatives—with a reasonable product life cycle remaining that were still being manufactured, while the 787 Dreamliner was still in the development stage.

Boeing chose not to compete with Airbus on a super-jumbo, concluding that there was simply no market for an expensive, giant (525 passengers in a standard three-class configuration and 800 in an all economy class one), hub-to-hub airplane in an era when passengers and the airlines who flew them seemed eager, in Boeing's view, to avoid such overtaxed hubs in favor of more point-to-point journeys. Not only would a super-jumbo be enormously expensive to launch and produce, Boeing leaders concluded, but the size of the market it was likely to serve didn't amount to much in their view and would not be getting much larger. The debacle of the A380's start in life—breathtakingly high engineering and manufacturing costs, manufacturing glitches that delayed delivery of the new airplane for more than two years, far-below-expected initial orders for it—at first seemed to have proved Boeing right in not pursuing the super-jumbo direction. However, the A380 was flying commercially by late 2007 and proved popular with the flying public, airline customers, and aviation writers. It will no doubt dominate long, high-density routes between major hub cities in the world, replacing the 747, but whether or not it ever turns a profit for Airbus remains to be seen.

Rather than a super-jumbo, Boeing went in a different direction with the radically innovative 787 "Dreamliner," designed to carry about 300 passengers for very long distances, in greater comfort, and for point-to-point service (avoiding hubs), and to do so with a fuel savings of about 30 percent over similar size planes because of its mostly carbon-fiber construction (stronger and lighter than normally used aluminum). By 2007, the 787 had piled up orders faster than any aircraft in commercial airplane history. The new airplane excited industry watchers, Wall Street, and, most especially, Boeing's own workers, who began to regain some confidence about the financial future of the company in the period between our 2003 and 2006 surveys. As one engineer reported to us, "The most important change at Boeing in the past ten years is the commitment to build a new model of airplane, the 787. This shows that Boeing has the innovation and faith to invest in the company. . . . The new 787 is exciting and makes work more interesting hearing about [its] progress."

Another engineer could hardly contain his excitement: "We are meeting the subsidized Airbus competition and winning!!"

As we have discussed (and after our last survey of Boeing employees in 2006), the 787 eventually ran into production difficulties, mostly tied to Boeing's inadequate oversight of global partners and secondary suppliers (that is, parts suppliers to global partner companies), and to difficulties in the manufacture of carbon fiber sections, which led to repeated and embarrassing delays in the delivery date of the new airplane to airline customers. And the 2008 and 2009 recession, with its associated steep declines in passenger and air freight traffic, caused some airlines with orders on the books to delay deliveries further, and still others to put off purchasing decisions on any new planes, causing a drop in business and further layoffs at Boeing in 2009. How all this will play out remains to be seem.

CONCLUSION: ON WORKING
AT A CHANGING BOEING

Over the course of a decade and a half, beginning in the early 1990s, a generation of employees at Boeing experienced a flood of dramatic changes in the company that affected the core of their jobs and the operations and feel of their entire work environment, as well as their job security and future prospects in the firm. In this chapter we have tried to describe the main ways in which the company changed and why Boeing leaders felt that company transformation was essential for long-term economic viability. Boeing clearly could not have continued to operate in the ways it did during the 1980s and early 1990s and flourish in the new global commercial airplane market. We do not mean to imply, however, that they made the right decisions along the way or implemented them in the best ways for either the long-term health of the company or the well-being of their employees.

We conducted the first three of our four employee surveys during a period when Boeing leaders were focused on maximizing short-term shareholder value. From roughly early 1996 through 2003, Boeing's top executives were intensely focused on maximizing returns to investors. In practice, this meant relentless cost-cutting (including a heightened pace of downsizing and outsourcing, going lean in production, taking a tougher line during contract negotiations with the IAM and SPEEA), avoiding risky investments in developing new airplanes, offering generous stock repurchase programs to reward investors, and moving more boldly into space and defense contracting. You will see in the chapters that follow that these years were tough on Boeing employees, with most workplace attitudes and measures of well-being tracking downward.

Between 2003 and 2006, when we conducted our last survey, things improved at Boeing on a number of fronts, including record orders for the 787, a new leadership team untainted by ethical issues, and the apparent success and widespread acceptance of previously introduced technologies and processes for engineering and manufacturing. Not surprisingly, many measures of job attitudes and individual well-being improved during this period, though many important ones did not, suggesting lingering damage from the most turbulent years. And, worries about the effects of the global partnering model for the 787 on Boeing workers, the company, and the country, as you will see, became even more salient.

For the remainder of the book we turn our attention to the questions of how Boeing employees experienced and interpreted these multiple, complex, and cumulative company changes over a relatively brief period of time—in other words, how these changes affected them and shaped the way they came to feel about their jobs and the company for whom they worked. Using information from interviews, focus groups, and surveys we conducted between 1996 and 2006, we look at the organizational change process through the eyes of ordinary employees, workers and their immediate managers, who bore the consequences of change, whether for better or worse. Because many Americans are living through similar changes in large, globally competitive firms, or soon will be, we think the story we tell in these pages is broadly consequential.

Chapter 3 Boeing's Changing Culture

In the eyes of top executives, it was not enough to change Boeing's business strategy and operations in response to the new, more competitive, and uncertain business environment. Boeing's culture also had to be transformed; the values and behaviors of its employees needed to become more aligned with the company's new focus on efficiency and the bottom line. If there was to be a new ethos to guide Boeing's operations, Phil Condit and Harry Stonecipher made it clear it was to be a more explicit and aggressive pursuit of shareholder value —one, moreover, that would be more responsive to the needs of Wall Street than to those of all its stakeholders. This was not an easy or popular shift for Boeing workers or managers to make, but it was one that they, like millions of workers at other large companies, would have to navigate. Top executives wanted to hurry this transformation, but organizations and the people who inhabit them tend to change more slowly. Values, social relationships, and the emotional bonds that develop over decades, and shape the culture and identity of companies, establish institutional practices and beliefs that linger in memory and frame employee understanding and responses to change.

It would be wrong to say that employees disapproved of, or resisted, all the changes Boeing undertook during the decade of our study. Many saw the necessity, in this more competitive business environment, of adopting more efficient design and manufacturing processes and appreciated the attempt to increase worker involvement through teams and softer, more participative supervision. But few could swallow the realization that in the pursuit of what CEO Phil Condit called "enhanced shareholder value," they would become expendable units of production to be used or discarded according to the vagaries of strategic and financial calculations. At the height of the cultural changes from 1997 to 2003, as Boeing merged with McDonnell Douglas, moved its headquarters to Chicago, and slashed its workforce, employee attitudes toward the company deteriorated almost across the board. In a remarkable tribute to people's resilience, by our 2006 survey, as the company's fortunes turned around with the spectacular flood of orders for the new 787 Dreamliner airplane, and with stable employment levels, many (though not all) attitudes toward the company improved and returned to their 1997 levels. But there are signs in the 2006 survey results, and particularly in the comments made to us at that time, that a decade of tumultuous change had taken its toll. Employee comments revealed powerful feelings of loss and regret at the change in Boeing's identity mingled with anger at the more ruthless behavior of top executives. Like longtime partners who feel betrayed by their lovers, many employees became disenchanted with Boeing and began to distance themselves emotionally from the company they had once admired.

To understand why so many workers disapproved of what the company was becoming, we need to know something about what they were leaving behind. Feelings of discontent require some comparative frame by which to measure the present. As we will see, many Boeing employees, whether design engineers, office staff, or production line workers, evaluated the emerging identity and culture of Boeing by comparing them with what they had been in the past. The declaration of an executive to employees that Boeing "was no longer your father's company" rang true for many long-serving employees. Using the words of many of its employees and top executives, this chapter will explore what kind of company Boeing had been, what it became, and how that transformation took place.

THE CULTURE OF LEGACY BOEING

> Boeing had an engineering culture. Engineers were in control; we put
> Apollo on the moon, not the finance guys.
> —*Charles Bofferding, a former Boeing engineer and until 2007 executive
> director of the Society of Professional Engineering Employees in Aerospace*

There is a temptation to gild the past when the present is difficult. Certainly a
fair number of Boeing employees recalled the Boeing of the 1960s, 1970s, and
early 1980s with fondness, pride, and a degree of wistfulness for a disappearing
world. They referred to Boeing as having an engineering culture where engineers "ruled the day" and where the emphasis was on making "cool products"
that were technically sophisticated; making profits was secondary. Several employees conveyed intense pride at Boeing's international reputation for quality
products. An engineer nearing retirement after thirty-eight years at Boeing told
us that "when I was in engineering college in the U.K. we used to dream about
working for Boeing. Boeing had a good reputation." He added, "I had wanted
my children to work for Boeing." Sadly, he now felt that this was no longer the
case. The sense of pride in Boeing's achievements was often expressed in very
personal terms. An office worker in her mid-thirties recounted in 1996 how
everyone in her work group felt proud and excited when new airplane orders
came in as though they had contributed to the sale. She noted that some of her
friends didn't understand that feeling: "When I say to my friends, 'We sold
eight planes today,' my friends tell me, 'You didn't sell the planes, Boeing did.'
What they don't understand is that we are Boeing—I am Boeing. You don't just
work for them, the company is part of you. . . . Around here you tell people you
work for Boeing, and it's no big deal. Abroad though, people are really impressed and that makes you feel good."

Almost universally, long-serving employees referred to the old Boeing as a
family that cared about its employees, so much so that numerous employees
would encourage their relatives to come and work there. Indeed, hiring relatives
was so prevalent, according to an official of the local machinists' union, that 9
percent of the machinists in 1995 had a spouse who also worked at Boeing. She
recalled that some jokingly referred to this hiring practice as the "FBI system"
for "friends, brothers, and in-laws." Boeing was a place, many recalled, where
work was fun, and where Christmas and individual and collective achievements
were celebrated with parties. These sentiments were echoed by Ron Woodard,
the former president of Boeing Commercial who had worked his way up
through the ranks over thirty-two years of service. He described the family feel-

ing as one where "you were all in it together and you were all going to work together and support each other." He went on to note that Boeing's reputation was built on its "great products" and the fact that it was an "extremely honorable company."

There is no doubt that for senior managers Boeing was a secure and protected environment, where insiders rose through the ranks and where no senior manager ever got fired. As a consultant working with the leadership team told us in 1996, "The culture for over eighty years has been not to fire managers but to let them retire with dignity." Woodard, who was pushed out in 1998, described himself as "incredulous that my Boeing career . . . ended the way it ended,"[1] and in an interview several years later recalled with some poignancy that he did not remember "anybody ever being fired, or humiliated, or penalized for trying and not getting there" before Boeing changed in the late 1990s.

But if these recollections of the Boeing culture describe a rosy picture of what Boeing used to be like, it is also possible to draw a decidedly more nuanced and ambiguous portrait of the past. As we will see in chapter 4, Boeing's nonmanagerial workforce was not spared periodic layoffs. Hundreds and sometimes thousands of workers would be laid off and then recalled as orders fell and rose. Hourly employees especially had to anticipate and save for these recurring blows to their income. On the factory floor, moreover, some workers remembered old-style managers ruling in a rigid, "dictatorial," and crude manner. An employee in a 1996 focus group recalled how managers "used to be bull-headed, wanting to do things their way by pushing you around," and went on to note that most of those supervisors were now gone.

A woman administrative assistant in 1998 explained this old managerial style by noting, "Boeing is a typical, traditional, tall organization with a military-like chain of command. Men who hold these managerial positions are rigid, Theory X types who, at the core of their being, are incapable of relinquishing any power. They have deliberately created a culture of fear where the average worker is scared to voice any problem they may see with a proposed suggestion."

This view is given credence by comments from Boeing executives we interviewed who were working hard to create a "threat free" environment when they were implementing various change initiatives in the 1990s. Even as late as 2003, a study conducted by the Ethical Leadership Group at the behest of Boeing noted that "many employees expressed fear of being retaliated against" if they reported ethical problems to an Ethics Phone the company had set up.

Another legacy of Boeing's past as a builder of military equipment for government was its large, bureaucratic, and, some argued, wasteful structure. A lax work ethic and an inadequate knowledge about, or control over, the cost of doing things seemed to plague parts of the culture of legacy Boeing. A consultant who assessed Boeing's culture in 1987 noted that Boeing was a "company of paradoxes," being simultaneously "the most loosely structured and informal system you'd ever want to see," but also "very rigid, formalized and bureaucratic."[2] Ron Woodard acknowledged the problems associated with being "like a government entity [that was] unbelievably big and bureaucratic and cumbersome and slow to do things," and recalled a press conference in the late 1960s when former CEO T. Wilson responded to a question about how many people worked at Boeing by saying, "About half of them."

This view was echoed by several workers we interviewed at the start of our study. They alluded to Boeing's reputation as "Lazy B" to signify the easygoing attitude to work effort that pervaded the company.

> You could spend virtually eight hours doing absolutely nothing and nobody would know it. There are people that do that. I know a guy here ten years. I haven't seen him to do a piece of work in ten years. So it's a gravy train. You can be a socializer. You can walk around with a clipboard, pretend you're doing whatever, and nobody'd know it. [a focus group participant in 1996]

> Boeing had many employees (20 percent) who just wandered around or slept at their machines and didn't produce and because of the union it was hard to fire people. [a male hourly worker with sixteen years of service, interviewed in 1996]

> Sometimes it seemed they worked slow during the week so that they could work on the weekends. You hear people talking about the Lazy B, and in a lot of cases that's the truth. [a female salaried employee with nine years' service, interviewed in 1996]

> Boeing is very different from other organizations. I was shocked when I first came to see many people, employees and supervisors, wasting large amounts of time during the day socializing. [a female employee with seventeen years' service, interviewed in 2002]

This cozy, engineer-driven, somewhat paternalistic identity of legacy Boeing, while popular with many workers, was about to be refashioned by a crop of new leaders responding to powerful external forces.

GROPING TOWARD A CULTURE OF EFFICIENCY

We saw in chapter 2 how deregulation and competition from Airbus were forcing the company to change the way it did business so that it could cut costs and increase profit margins and shareholder value. To cut costs and increase efficiency, it adopted a series of programs like lean production, computerized operations, the make-buy system for choosing which planes to produce and what to outsource, and the DCAC/MRM for releasing planes for production and tracking parts for them. These operational changes were the first phase in the cultural transformation of Boeing and were designed to set in motion a relentless cost-cutting mindset that would significantly increase the efficiency of the company, something that was and is an ongoing process in large American companies. However, the rapid introduction of so many programs and initiatives, one seemingly on top of another, must have seemed like an unstoppable avalanche that threatened to bury the workforce. A cascade of confusing acronyms heralding the changes fell upon a reeling workforce. An alphabet soup of programs—first WCC, which was followed by DCAC/MRM, the five S's, JIT, DBT's, and AIW's—were just some of the changes that bombarded employees in the 1990s.[3] The interviews, focus groups, and factory visits we conducted in 1996 and 1997 suggested an organization where, from the point of view of the employees, change seemed to have run amok, a place where the pace and complexity of the changes had created a kind of chaos in the offices and on the factory floors. Widespread employee cynicism and skepticism about management competence accompanied many of these changes, as we show in figure 3.1.

The comments that follow were made to us as these changes were being implemented in the mid-1990s and reinforce the sentiments revealed in the survey.

> The company is notorious for making 8, 10, 12 internal changes a year. Take the DCAC/MRM, it is a good thing but it's bad timing. It's like the top doesn't know what the bottom is doing. Right now people are caught. They might want to do something (make a change) in their organization, but they are afraid to do anything because they know change is on the way but they don't know when it is going to get to them. People are frozen and it is not constructive chaos. It's a joke after a while. In Everett the whole building was completely changed. They were going to put all the engineers in one place. People were moved all over. The company just tries to make too many changes at one time. [a professional/administrative, technical writer, employed seven years]

> A year, maybe two has been the maximum any one particular program has been, you know, the fair-haired child of the moment . . . the latest jingle-bell program, if you will. You can't change a bureaucratic organization like Boeing overnight or by taking a bull in a china shop approach. Every week there is some kind of training program, but these two-hour slots could have been spent doing my job. [interview in 1996 with a male cost management analyst with eleven years at Boeing]

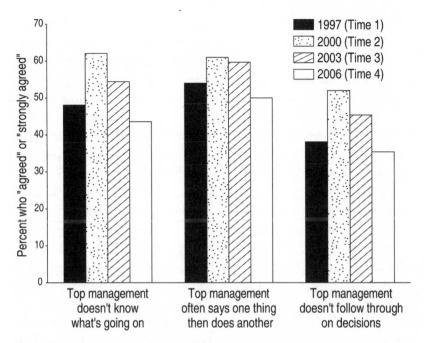

Figure 3.1 Employee level of mistrust of top management's competence

Buzzwords are used in meetings but no one really understands what it all means. For example, you go to all these meetings and they say DCAC/MRM, JIT, and so on and so forth. Pretty soon you're lost in buzzwords. [a focus group participant in 1996]

Some employees, even ones who had left Boeing, sometimes because of the seeming chaos at that time, pleaded with Boeing management to let things stabilize for a while and to follow through on the programs it introduced.

Stop the insanity of "flavor of the month" quality programs. Don't force them on people and then abandon them six months later. [a male employee with nine years of service who quit to take another job in 1998 or 1999]

[I] saw too many token attempts that were quickly abandoned. The attitude was, "Thank God we're through that, now let me go back to sleep." [I] never got to the point where it didn't matter—it always made me crazy. Therefore, I had to go. [a female employee with nine years of service who quit in 1998 or 1999]

Changing a large, complex organization like Boeing inevitably produces resistance and a certain defensive mindset, one that hopes that if one ignores what is going on then maybe the change agents will go away and things can continue in the old, familiar ways. Perhaps it was to overcome such resistance that the top management fostered such a sense of turbulence among the workforce. That was certainly the view of one executive level woman manager who recounted in 1998 that "about four or five years ago (1993 or 1994), we went through a period when Condit said our biggest problem was that we didn't have a crisis. So he did some things to create a crisis environment, because he strongly felt you don't change without a crisis that creates a constant sense of a lack of plan, a deer in the headlights fear. It's a philosophy. Some people do well in that type of environment. Some people don't."

Reinforcing the external pressure to change was the expensive advice of several management consultants the company hired during this period. Boeing's top executives, like many others across corporate America, had become enamored with management consultants in the late 1980s and 1990s. But, as Micklethwait and Wooldridge have pointed out,[4] consultants often offered advice that not only had very short shelf lives (the life span of new management ideas shrunk from a decade to a year or less), but also were frequently deeply contradictory, pulling these organizations and their top executives in conflicting policy directions. The push for quality conflicted with the need for speed; the goal of building trust conflicted with the need for flexibility or laying people off, and so on.

An example of this at Boeing concerns the successful 777 program and its aftermath. The development of this wide-body twin-engine plane under the leadership of Phil Condit (later to be CEO) and Alan Mulally (later to be president of Boeing Commercial and then CEO of Ford Motor Co.) pioneered a new way of designing and building planes.[5] Employees who worked on the project describe their excitement at working on the project and then their sense of betrayal as thousands of employees were laid off or jumped ship and took the generous voluntary buyout Boeing offered in 1995.

> I think at the start of the 777 program, those of us who were experienced at Boeing felt that there was a tremendous amount of support and a lot of promises made and we really bought into it . . . the 777 program was essentially a whole new company, a whole different way of doing things. . . . But at the start of the 777 program, our leader got up and said, "You build this plane in five years for me, you're part of the team, we will never let you go." They made all kinds of promises about "we're going to work together, we're going to do this and we've got lots on our plate." And I remember him talking, particularly about the concerns people had when this program ends . . . and he listed the programs we now are going into, but at the time, at the layoff time, they said, "Oh well, the business isn't right for it." In [avionics], we took

a 42 percent hit. With the retirements, we lost people with so much experience and skill. They didn't know they were taking that experience away from us. It was a process that they had learned over 25, 30, 35 years of doing business and it was just so incredible that this is just the way it's done, they didn't think about document-ing what they were doing. And in losing that we just had some terrible results from that in that we had to reinvent the way to do things. Then on the other side, we lost all of the really young. We lost such bright kids coming out of college. [focus group participant, 1996]

I worked tremendous hours as probably everyone on the 777 program did because we bought into the "working together, together we're going to take this company to the edge of technology, we're going to do the best we can and build the best air-plane" . . . and we did it. And then it was, "Okay, 42 percent, you're out the door. There's nothing we can do about it." . . . Morale is at an all time low, even now, a year later. [focus group participant, 1996]

Another example of the tensions among company goals and the gap between rhetoric and reality is illustrated in an interview in 1996 with an hourly em-ployee with sixteen years of service at Boeing who comments on the introduc-tion of Quality Improvement Teams in the late 1980s and the introduction of the World Class Competitiveness (WCC) program in 1991. At the beginning, he recalls, many teams were formed and workers met once or twice a week and made several suggestions for change. However, management ignored or blocked these ideas and often argued the proposed changes were "too drastic," and they would just kill the suggestions by calling for additional meetings. The whole experience, he said, "accomplished nothing" concrete. (See chapter 5 for more on teams at Boeing.) Similarly, the 1991 WCC initiative touted that "employ-ees are our most valuable asset." Although people wanted to believe that, the program stopped because it took too much time and trouble. The subsequent layoffs and the return to a more traditional management style with little recog-nition and appreciation of employees soured people and left a "bad taste in people's mouths." In his view, these programs petered out because in practice production pressures took priority. First- and second-line managers worried that if they stopped to introduce programs they would lose production, so "they'd create charts and graphs to show that things looked good but really it was just a dog and pony show" to appease top management. He also felt that change was very difficult because Boeing was "huge like a city with a huge bu-reaucratic morass."

Woodard, who was one of the principal architects of the effort to create a more efficient design and production system, accepted that all the changes in this period might have seemed chaotic to those on the ground floor. "I'm sure it looked that way. . . . I was senior manager through all that time and we were just unbelievably frustrated because nothing would really get done. We had eleven to thirteen levels of management and we used to start out retraining everybody, and two years later they [the changes] still hadn't hit the factory floor because we're so big, so encumbered with everything that we'd be saying one thing while two years later they were still going through the system. The real problem was, it was almost impossible to change what we were trying to change."

As managers and employees repeatedly told us, at bottom Boeing was a schedule-driven organization that responded to trends in airplane orders. When orders built up and schedules tightened, the imperative was to get planes out the door on time. As one worker put it, "You've got a deadline and you're expected to do more, faster, and faster and faster." When orders drop, layoffs were the order of the day. These imperatives also worked to stymie and slow attempts to change the Boeing culture. But, however halting and confusing the steps, the groundwork had been laid to change the way Boeing designed and produced airplanes. The drive to create a culture of efficiency had been set in motion. As described in chapters 2 and 5, lean manufacturing techniques and computer-aided design and parts ordering systems were transforming how work was done in the offices and on the factory floor. What was still unclear was whether the governing ethos of the company, its identity and sense of itself, would also change. Over the next decade, the answer was yes; Boeing became a very different company. What we see is a type of cultural transition that has been going on at most other large American companies as they shift the way they produce their products and services.

CHASING SHORT-TERM SHAREHOLDER VALUE

According to many employees, nothing changed Boeing and its culture more than the merger with McDonnell Douglas in August 1997. The merger was both a way to insulate revenues and profits from the recurring and periodic downturns in demand for commercial airplanes by expanding Boeing's military and space business, and a catalyst to accelerate the transformation of Boeing into a company focused on financial metrics and shareholder value. Although Boeing seemed like the dominant partner in the merger, keeping its name and continuing with its commercial airplane product line, there was a pervasive sense among the employees that it was McDonnell Douglas's top executives who had gotten the better end of the deal and who emerged as the power holders within the merged company. The two largest individual shareholders of the merged company were Harry Stonecipher, the CEO of McDonnell Douglas, and John McDonnell, chairman of McDonnell Douglas's board. Stonecipher's compensation package as chief operating officer was also considerably larger than that of Boeing's CEO, Phil Condit. One employee summed up the sense among many workers that McDonnell Douglas had been the real winner in the deal by saying that "McDonnell Douglas bought Boeing with Boeing's money," echoing a comment apparently made by former Boeing CEO T. Wilson[6] and repeated to us in many conversations.

Stonecipher certainly saw himself as the change agent who would shake up a complacent and lax Boeing culture. In a series of speeches and interviews he gave in 1997 and 1998, he sent a very clear message to workers and to Wall Street. Boeing would no longer "buy orders" in the pursuit of market share as it had in 1997, when it recorded its first ever loss in fifty years; its aim was never to sell planes with zero margins as it had in 1998 but to aim for double-digit profit margins.[7] The emphasis was to be on shareholder return and unit cost. Reflecting on this period in 2004, he told a reporter, "When people say I changed the culture of Boeing, that was the intent, so it's run like a business rather than a great engineering firm. It is a great engineering firm, but people invest in a company because they want to make money."[8]

To ram home the seriousness of this new guiding ethos, Condit and Stonecipher pushed Ron Woodard, president of the commercial division and architect of the single-minded drive for market share at the expense of Airbus, out the door.[9]

Stonecipher's words in those early years after the merger had a remarkably powerful impact on employees' perceptions of Boeing. In a speech to the Rotary Club of Seattle in 1998, Harry Stonecipher warned employees that they had to "quit behaving like a family and become more like a team. If you don't perform, you don't stay on the team."[10] Workers interpreted this as heralding a new managerial philosophy, one that diverged radically from what had existed in the past. A female manager with twenty-four years of service at Boeing noted that company leaders kept reminding employees that "this isn't your father's company" to impress on them that things had changed, and that there were no unshakable bonds tying workers to the company. As she put it, "The feeling that if you take care of the company, the company will take care of you" was now a value from a bygone era. The family-to-team metaphor must have spread rapidly across the workforce because it was repeatedly brought up by employees in numerous interviews and comments, even several years later.[11] Workers talked about the loss of "family feeling," of Boeing going from a "family that valued its employees" to one where team members could be "traded for cheaper labor overseas." And they were not reticent in assigning blame: "[Things changed] when Harry Stonecipher said we are a team not a family. Our merger with McDonnell Douglas was a nightmare. We lost our way, our moral compass, our business vision. . . . I hope and pray that [current CEO] McNerney can save this company and bring it back to where it can and should be. If he can't, history will write that the merger was the beginning of the end" (a female manager with twenty years' service).

Employees also spoke in very direct, emotional terms about how the sense of "fun" and pride they had felt as Boeing employees was lost after the merger.

> Merging with McDonnell Douglas brought in lots of new people and managers into legacy Boeing. This changed the culture from airplane builder to a focus on profits and stock price. [It also] brought in a new philosophy on employee to management relationships. Boeing used to be a family (picnics, lunches, friendly) which was turned into a team (competitive, everyone for themselves). Prior to the merger, I was proud of Boeing and proud to be a Boeing employee. I could take comments about "the Lazy B," knowing there were a lot of good folks dedicated to making good products. After the merger, as it became obvious where things were going, and particularly because of the "leadership," under Harry S., I quit wearing Boeing logo items and wasn't so proud of Boeing. I was angry at Phil Condit for "selling the company" and turning it over to Harry, who was ruining what was a national treasure. I had a bit of trouble getting over that bitterness. I believe Alan Mulally has done his best to save and rebuild Boeing Commercial (what's left of it). [male white collar worker with twenty-eight years' service at Boeing]

> In my early years at Boeing, we had fun and there was a feeling of family in the culture. Later, the family feeling went away and we had to please the stockholders, be more team oriented and worry about Airbus. The fun went away. Or I got older and jaded. . . . We had public problems, bad decisions; we were arrogant and lost our nerve. [female white collar worker with twenty-seven years at Boeing]

> The merger changed the whole complexion of the company. Whatever this corporation saw itself as, an image or ideal shattered at that moment. Then when the world headquarters moved to Chicago, I applauded the decision. But the company ties with the community and the workforce were severed and something broke that day. Call it loyalty, devotion, even love, that was very hard from true Boeing-bred-and-raised families. [female white collar worker, with eight years at Boeing]

As the sense of identification with and loyalty to Boeing eroded, several workers described an atmosphere where individuals began to think first of themselves and less about others or the good of the company.

How have the changes affected me? Seeing these changes has convinced me that no matter how loyal I am to Boeing, I cannot count on Boeing to be loyal to me. I need to have alternative career options in place. [male engineer with twenty-one years at Boeing]

The company has become less personable, more cold towards its employees. When I joined, it felt more like a family, now it's everyone for themselves. [a fifty-year-old female engineer with twenty-five years of tenure]

They have changed my attitude to be "why should I care" and to look out for myself as management won't. Also Boeing is no longer a premium company to work for. If I can find something (anything) somewhere else I'm gone. They got no loyalty to me, why should I have any to them? [male technical employee, twenty-three years at Boeing]

[The change] has made me more guarded; need to look out for myself since no one else will, both from a career development standpoint, very little mentoring being done today, and a welfare standpoint (i.e., ensure my saving will support me if I lose my employment). [male manager, fifteen years of service]

Several employees deeply resented what they perceived as Boeing's single-minded focus on the bottom line and how the company seemed to treat them as "numbers" or "chattel" and "commodities" to be used up and discarded as top management decided. A technical worker with eighteen years of service echoed a widely held view among Boeing employees when he observed that "the primary focus is shareholder value and short-term profits." He added, "If they could make profits without us, they wouldn't hesitate to dump us all." In response, many began to detach their emotions from the company. Some left the company, many told us they couldn't wait for the time they could retire, and others mechanically put in their time with little extra effort or care.

For me, the most important change was the merger with McDonnell Douglas. That was the beginning of my emotional detachment from the company. All company goals seemed to be focused on greed. I finally became fed up with it as a manager, and eighteen months ago, requested to leave management to be an engineer again. I am so much happier, and the pay is better! Now I just live for retirement. [a forty-nine-year-old woman engineer with twenty-six years of tenure]

I was fiercely loyal to Boeing. Now it is just a job. I do my job well, but I do it for my own personal satisfaction—I don't do it for "Boeing." I will retire early at fifty-five because of the way Boeing has changed. I have totally divorced myself from Boeing—at the end of the day I walk away and don't look back. [a fifty-two-year-old female professional with twenty-six years of tenure]

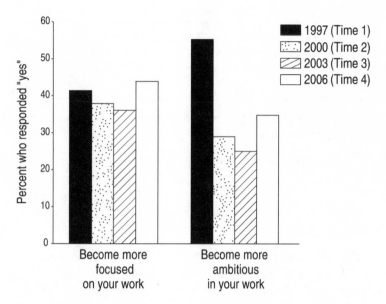

Figure 3.2 Responses to questions related to the degree of work emphasis: "In the Last Two Years, Have You . . ."

This emotional detachment sometimes resulted in a shift in priorities away from work and toward their nonwork lives. A fifty-one-year-old white collar worker with ten years of service noted that because of the changed ethos, she would do her eight hours but would now "think in terms of family and goals to be accomplished outside of work. . . . My loyalty," she continued, "is to my family, friends, and community, in that order."

Our surveys also picked up this shift in focus toward family, friends, and leisure activities and away from work (see figures 3.2 and 3.3). This shift in focus persisted throughout the ten years of our study, unlike many other attitudes that rebounded to 1997 levels in late 2006 as the company's fortunes improved. For many employees, and more so for older workers with longer years of service, a bond that connected them emotionally to the company snapped and could never be fully repaired. As in a long-lived marriage wherein one party was seen to have betrayed the other, the aggrieved party could no longer see the other in the same way. Anger or cynicism toward the company was often mixed with a wistfulness and sadness that the affection had gone out of the relationship.

The disenchantment toward Boeing manifested by these individual attitudes was highlighted when thousands of Boeing's engineers and technical workers went on strike in February 2000. With resentment building at their fading sta-

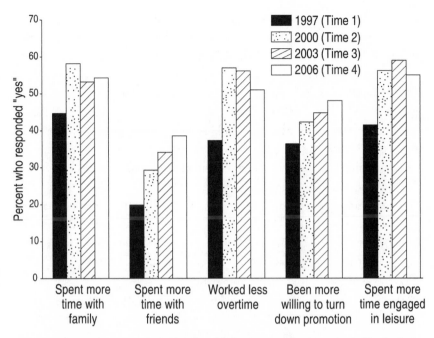

Figure 3.3 Responses to questions related to the degree of nonwork emphasis: "In the Last Two Years, Have You . . ."

tus in the company (the company's Vice President of People had remarked to the *Wall Street Journal* that "the engineers have to understand that they are no longer the center of the universe"), and with Boeing management trying to cut costs by offering SPEEA members less-generous compensation than the machinists had won in contract negotiations, engineers and technicians pushed back at the company and demanded "respect." It is rare to find professional employees going on strike and walking the picket lines. That those at Boeing did so for forty days is another powerful indication that Boeing had become a different kind of company.[12]

ETHICS TAKE A BEATING

Several ethics scandals hit Boeing after the merger, and, in the eyes of many in the workforce, they were powerful confirmation that Boeing had lost its way. The general feeling was that the values brought in by the McDonnell Douglas executives had led to a "winning at any cost mentality," which badly tarnished Boeing's reputation as one of the great American corporations. The year 2003 first saw several Boeing executives indicted for "swiping twenty-five thousand pages of proprietary documents" from Lockheed Martin as the two competed for air force contracts;[13] and then Mike Sears, the chief financial officer who came to Boeing from McDonnell Douglas with Stonecipher in 1997, was fired for shady dealings in winning the 767 refueling contract from the Pentagon. Sears was later tried, convicted, and sentenced to four months in jail for having offered a job to the second-ranking air force procurement officer while she was still at the Pentagon. And even though the ethical problems were primarily confined to the defense division and corporate headquarters, the whole Boeing workforce seemed to feel besmirched by the scandals. A white collar worker commented on how he had "totally lost respect for Boeing management's lack of personal and business ethics," while an hourly worker, noting how the "unethical actions" and "illegal behavior of higher ups" had eroded feelings of trust, added that "the fact that the board of directors ignored all of Condit's affairs and cover-ups is embarrassing."

Boeing's general counsel is reported to have asked a gathering of top executives at their annual retreat in 2006 whether Boeing "had a culture of win at any cost." Noting the many recent ethical scandals and the fact that fifteen vice presidents had been pushed out because of them, he ended the talk by asking whether the company had a "culture of silence," and if management bore the responsibility for the problems rather than the rank and file employees.[14]

In response to the ethical scandals, Boeing initiated a series of ethics training programs that much of the workforce had to go through, but some employees agreed with the implication of the general counsel's questions. It was not the rank and file that seemed to have the ethical problems.

> Each time upper management gets in ethics-related trouble they send me to training. [a male manager with twenty-seven years at Boeing]

> We are tired of signing and attending phony ethics papers and classes. It's the top management that seems to have the problems. I'm sure as hell not going to bribe anyone. I'm just a factory production rat! [male hourly worker, nineteen years at Boeing]

Nevertheless, with the departure of Condit at the end of 2003 and Stonecipher's resignation in 2005 after his affair with a senior female manager had come to light, there was a sense that the company was regaining its ethical balance. As one male manager with sixteen years of service remarked, "Getting rid of Stonecipher/Sears/Condit was a very positive change and excellent for morale." Our tracking of employee attitudes toward top management (see

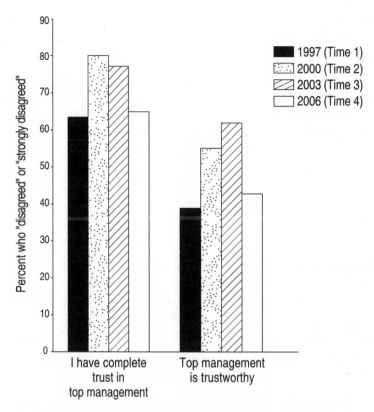

Figure 3.4 Employee level of mistrust of top management's credibility

figure 3.4) does indeed show that trust in the integrity of top management rebounded in 2006 after having dropped to a low in 2003, when over 60 percent told us they did not find top management trustworthy.

WORRIES ABOUT BOEING'S NEW BUSINESS STRATEGY

Making airplanes is a high-risk business. Billions are invested up front, and profitable returns on the investment are uncertain and typically accrue many years later. Boeing has increasingly tried to reduce the risk, as we saw in chapter 2, by spreading among many partners and suppliers the billions involved in the design and production of airplanes and by locking in buyers for these planes early in the process. Outsourcing, or off-loading, the design, engineering, and production of many of the components of the airplane is the most important strategic decision Boeing has made to reduce its risk. As Newhouse[15] asserts, "Under the leadership of Phil Condit and Harry Stonecipher . . . aversion to risk became embedded in Boeing's corporate culture." Boeing also sought to reduce risk by diversifying from its lopsided dependence on the highly cyclical commercial airplane division. The merger with McDonnell Douglas increased the defense side of its business and the move of the company's headquarters to Chicago signaled both its detachment from the Puget Sound region, home of much of the commercial airplane work, and its growing international focus. Employees, of course, were the ones who saw work they were once doing going to outsiders in the United States and overseas. Sometimes they were the ones who had to train the very workers who would replace them. Not surprisingly, they responded to the outsourcing with feelings of anxiety and worry about the security of their own jobs, as we will document in chapter 4. A female employee with twenty-two years of service with Boeing grimly joked that the paint job on new airplanes would "probably be done by Earl Schwab for $99.95."

Several employees also expressed deep concern in 2006 about what outsourcing and the new business strategy meant for the future of Boeing and for the availability of good jobs for Americans more widely.

> As the company sells plants, gives away its hard-learned and expensive know-how, it is opening the door for competition against itself and losing control of the prime components of its product. The long-term future is not being thought of. [a male hourly employee, twenty-six years at Boeing]

> Boeing's footprint is shrinking rapidly in the manufacturing sector. Very little of present and especially future aircraft is manufactured by Boeing. This cuts more of the middle class from our country as they send jobs we currently do overseas. This, in turn, cuts back further our national tax base. Not only Boeing is doing this, many huge companies are doing the same. [a fifty-four-year-old male hourly worker with thirteen years' seniority]

> I've seen the financials, so I know some outsourcing is required to offset rising union costs, but I worry about Boeing's longevity with regard to retaining intellectual property and the dilution of capability and skills and of America's incomes. My gut tells me there is significant risk in outsourcing so much work, which results in some anxiety. [a forty-two-year-old female manager with sixteen years of tenure]

> Outsourcing work, especially engineering work, should be outlawed. People are dying for our country, our way of life, while CEOs like Boeing's are outsourcing and effectively destroying our way of life for future generations. CEOs who out-

source work outside the U.S. should be hung for treason. [a male engineer, thirteen years at Boeing]

Outsourcing of skilled work will destroy the company. We will no longer have a skilled workforce, either professional or skilled labor. Ultimately, and not that far in the future, we will be unable to own the business or maintain our product development. Although we have better leaders, the business model is flawed and will fail. No one will know how to develop, build or support our products. [a male manager with seventeen years at Boeing]

Engineers in particular were concerned about the loss of specialized knowledge. Newhouse discusses a ten-page memorandum circulated by a group of Boeing engineers that complained about the "brain drain" and worried that Boeing would not be able to be a successful large-scale systems integrator if, as was happening, they were losing the technical knowledge needed to do the integrating. One engineer with twenty-seven years of experience at Boeing echoed these fears: "Outsourcing has increased business for Boeing but I fear this is temporary. Boeing will lose its engineering and design capabilities to other countries. We are giving away the farm."[16]

The growth of outsourcing around the turn of the century seemed to put the final nail in the coffin of the old legacy culture of Boeing. A smaller, leaner, and more globally networked company was emerging, one with fewer ties to any particular region, workforce, or country.

SOME POSITIVE RESPONSES TO THE CHANGES

These critical responses to the culture and business strategy of Boeing were widespread but not universal. A sizeable minority of employees told us they recognized that Boeing had to change and therefore welcomed the new direction and the new ways of doing things. A female manager with ten years of tenure at Boeing interviewed in 1998 noted,

There is a highly conservative, very, very, very, very conservative culture at Boeing. I'm very encouraged about our recent executive management changes. I am very excited because those people are more progressive and not so tied to the old boys network, to "this is the way we've always done things, we've done it this way for fifteen years, why do we have to change." It's an exciting time being at Boeing. We nearly hit rock bottom. It's been good for making change. It's difficult to make change in a company that's making money—why change? And so now, when you start to lose some of your airplane sales, there are more people willing to change the way they work. It's a good company, except for that conservative, arrogant past. It needs to change.

Among the changes welcomed by employees were the more open communication and sharing of information through the intranet and the greater freedom and flexibility given to employees to make decisions. A few endorsed the new business strategy because it enabled the company to focus on what it was good at—large-scale systems integration.

Several emphasized that, compared with other companies, Boeing was still one of the better employers around, even after accounting for all the turmoil caused by the changes. Not only were the pay, benefits, and educational and career opportunities generally more generous, but a female procurement agent, who had worked at several other manufacturing companies before coming to Boeing, observed that because few of her colleagues had worked elsewhere, they didn't realize just how "outstanding" the benefits were and how much security they had despite the layoffs. A similar point was made by a recently retired office worker in Human Resources. Noting the "phenomenal" education benefits, she recalled how Boeing had paid for her MA degree in leadership coursework and went on to observe that "when I was outside the company for three years, I realized how good the company was. When people complain about them, I say get real. Ten dollars per month for health insurance is not that big a deal in the big picture. Some don't realize how lucky they are." Along the same lines, a male manager pointed out that in comparing his experience to those of friends who worked elsewhere, Boeing's large size tended to result in "more evenhanded and fair" treatment of employees. He added that he couldn't believe how poorly people were treated at other companies. Other employees appreciated the greater work scheduling flexibility and the ability to telecommute, something that some 10 percent of the workforce was now taking advantage of, at least for part of the week. A technical worker also summed up a general feeling among the workforce that management's supervisory style had changed for the better when he noted that "it used to be a 'shut up and do your job' attitude but now employees have the ability to question and make suggestions."

There is no doubt that the recent success of Boeing in its competition with Airbus during the latter part of our study and the strong orders for Boeing's new plane, the 787, gave many Boeing employees a sense of optimism about the future. As one male manager put it in 2006, "I have become much more optimistic and proud to be a Boeing employee, especially in the past 12–18 months." Another manager believed that moving the headquarters to Chicago in 2001 had lib-

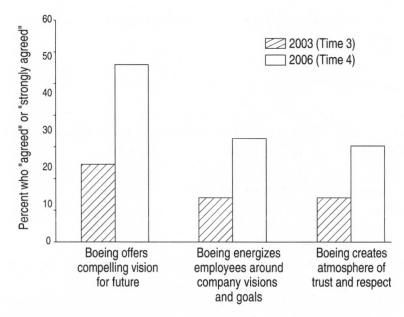

Figure 3.5 Positive attitudes toward Boeing's future and vision

erated the commercial division and allowed it to become "not just a company that makes derivative airplanes but one that can listen to customers, innovate and take risks, and build the best airplane for the world, the Dreamliner—the 787." There was a sense of gratitude among some workers that, in building this revolutionary new airplane, they could once again, as one forty-seven-year-old manager phrased it, "be part of history." Several employees talked of a change in the mood or atmosphere caused by the success of the 787 and the recent turnaround in the fortunes of the company: "The Boeing division in which I have worked most of my career is flourishing and this has made a tremendous change in the workplace for me personally and, I think, for many of my colleagues. All of my fellow workers want to believe we are working for a very technically capable, ethical, world leading company" (a male engineer with thirty-five years at Boeing).

These positive responses are symptomatic of the upturn we found in 2006 in several of their attitudes on such things as job satisfaction, level of trust in top management, and company support for employee needs. We also found that many of the strong negative assessments they had made about Boeing's goals, direction, and internal policies in 2003, when ethics scandals and mass layoffs were at their peak, had abated somewhat by 2006. However, as can be seen in figure 3.5, the increases in positive attitudes toward the company, though sizeable, were from a pretty low base and reveal how hard it is to restore goodwill once it has been damaged.[17]

CONCLUSION

Being part of something exciting and meaningful mattered for many employees at Boeing. They identified strongly with the old Boeing, the company that built the best airplanes in the world and which treated them as part of the "family."[18] Yes, these sentiments tended to idealize the past, but they also acted as necessary reassurance for workers that spending twenty or thirty years at one company was worthwhile and that their loyalty was reciprocated and valued. When the rules and norms changed toward the end of the century, a sense of disappointment, betrayal, even despair clouded the mood of many of these long-serving employees. Workers coming toward the end of their working lives after many years of service with one company are prone to ask some troubling questions. What did my thirty years of loyalty and commitment to this one organization add up to? Was it smart to put so much of my energy and emotional commitment into an organization run by leaders who increasingly focused on the financial bottom line and could, with little consultation, change direction and push thousands of my fellow workers out the door? Millions of other American workers probably have been asking themselves similar questions as their companies, responding to pressure from competitors and investors, change their business strategies and corporate cultures.

For many employees at Boeing, the answer seemed to be no, maybe it was wiser to rebalance their emotional investment, giving less to the company and more to their families and lives outside work. Workers, it seemed, would also begin to evaluate their employment relationship with the same marketlike rationality that Boeing executives had trumpeted after the merger. We will consider the implications of this more marketlike employment relationship for companies and individuals in the last chapter.

Chapter 4 Living

Through Layoffs

The misery of uncertainty is greater than the certainty of misery.
—*A male manager quoting the comic strip character Pogo*

Boeing Commercial Airplanes workers have lived with layoffs for a long time, though the reasons for layoffs have changed in important ways. For many years, layoffs were tied to fluctuations in the demand for Boeing airplanes from airlines and leasing companies, with people getting hired during good times and laid off during bad times. These were expected, broadly understood, and often planned for by Boeing workers. However, as Boeing transformed the way it planned, engineered, and produced airplanes, it has needed fewer in-house employees to produce aircraft. What this means is that the traditional business-cycle-related layoff patterns increasingly have been superimposed on a new pattern of a long-term decline in the number of employees Boeing leaders feel they must have on board to get the job done. This complex pattern, which involves cyclical layoffs happening within a general decline in the number of workers needed to produce the same number of commodities, is similar to what has been happening across a broad swath of industries in the United States.

Being laid off, of course, is an extremely painful experience, with broad-ranging impacts on laid-off workers and their families. There is ample evidence, for example, that being laid off can cause serious psychological and financial damage to many who suffer this fate. But it is also the case, however, as we have only recently come to understand, that the damage caused by mass lay-offs extends beyond those who are laid off. Survivors—that is, those who see their colleagues and work friends laid off but who themselves remain employed at the company—are also affected, sometimes very deeply. In the ten years of our study, we were struck by how few people at Boeing were spared the anxi-ety and pain that mass layoffs produce. There is no way to lay off thirty thou-sand people and not cause "collateral damage."[1] We discovered, for example, that hundreds and sometimes thousands of additional workers were made to feel vulnerable when they were identified as likely candidates for future layoffs. Other employees, primarily blue collar workers, were shifted to other jobs in the company, sometimes in a different plant many miles away. Still others were "bumped" from their jobs or were shifted to other jobs, thereby bumping those workers from their jobs in a cascade of musical chairs. A good number of those with particularly in-demand skills chose to jump ship and find work with other employers or become private consultants as they saw colleagues and friends lose their jobs and morale tumble. And, such tumultuous organizational change disrupted and often ruptured long-term social ties and sources of support among colleagues and work friends.[2]

Middle and frontline managers who had to do the actual work of imple-menting layoffs, moreover, were not insulated from the emotional turmoil; they were adversely affected in many ways as we describe in chapter 6. Even if they managed to escape the layoff axe themselves, they had to execute the par-ing down of the workforce mandated by higher executives. Some even came to see themselves, according to two psychologists, as "executioners."[3] The man-agers who supervised white collar workers, for example, had to select those in their work groups who were to be let go and personally deliver the bad news to those they were axing.

What we see here are the human costs of layoff actions that may seem at first glance perfectly justifiable in sheer market terms, as organizations, in this case Boeing, respond to external competition, customer demands, technolog-ical changes, or threatening cost pressures. But layoffs are also the mechanism that turns a company's financial crisis into a human and social one. Our purpose in this chapter is to convey the responses of workers as they lived through these layoff crises and to examine how the workforce and the organization were changed in the process. What threats to their job security did workers most fear? What kind of protection could the two unions that represented a large portion of the workforce offer these workers, keeping in mind that most private-sector employees in the United States are not covered by union contracts? What kind of psychological and emotional distress did mass layoffs cause to Boeing workers? Did a sense of pervasive insecurity affect workers' commitment to the organization? What did it do to their work effort and to the performance of the organization? And, finally, what happened to those who left the company during this turbulent period? Did they land on their feet or face very hard times? These are some of the questions we will explore in this chapter.

WORKERS' PERCEPTIONS OF THREATS
TO THEIR JOB SECURITY

Boeing workers perceived many threats to their job security during this period. They were concerned about the cyclical rounds of layoffs and rehiring that paralleled the fluctuations in demand for airplanes that came with regularity every ten years or so. They worried about the challenge from Airbus and how the loss of market share to their competitor could result in lost jobs at Boeing. Surprisingly, lean production and technological change were seen as low level threats by the great majority of employees. Only about 30 percent thought such changes would put their jobs at risk, and that proportion remained fairly constant throughout the period of the study. However, the outsourcing of work cast a growing shadow over their sense of job security. The proportion of workers who thought that outsourcing would put their jobs at risk grew from 31 percent in 1997 to 63 percent in 2003, before subsiding a little in 2006. Of particular interest is how the worry about outsourcing spread across the occupational groups in the workforce.

As figure 4.1 shows, hourly workers were the first, in large numbers, to express such concern. Close to 60 percent of these blue collar workers thought that overseas outsourcing could threaten their jobs "in the future" in 1997, and this percentage ballooned until the concern about outsourcing was almost universal. By 2003, the concern had spread to the rest of the workforce. And it spread not only to technical and nonprofessional workers whose jobs involved quite a bit of routine work, but also to the highly educated engineers and professional employees. By 2003 some two-thirds of engineers, for example,

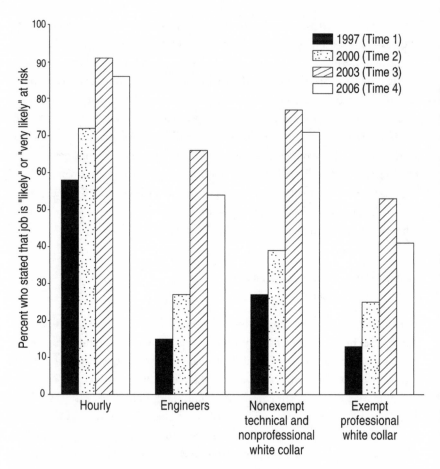

Figure 4.1 Percentage of workers who perceived their job to be at risk due to overseas outsourcing: by pay code in 1997, 2000, 2003, and 2006

thought outsourcing threatened their future job security, whereas less than 15 percent had felt that way in 1997. The pattern of responses was almost identical for their assessment of the risk to their jobs from subcontracting work to non-Boeing vendors, a form of outsourcing that could include domestic suppliers. As one official of the machinists' union told us in 2007, "We've been complaining about outsourcing for years, but now it is finally hitting everyone —the firefighters, security guards, engineers, human resource personnel, all are facing problems that the machinists faced decades ago."

So, on top of the familiar and expected cyclical and often transient threats to job security, Boeing employees also had to come to terms with structural changes that augured a more permanent termination of their employment with the company. Both the former president of Boeing Commercial and a former executive director of the Society of Professional Engineering Employees in Aerospace (SPEEA) agreed: Boeing was trying to have "more gentle fluctuations" or to "flatten the cycles" by doing more outsourcing and using more subcontractors. A more gentle fluctuation, of course, meant fewer workers laid off and hired by Boeing, but it also displaced the insecurity and uncertainty to contract workers and employees of other companies.

UNIONS STRUGGLE TO PROTECT JOBS

The local machinists' union, one of the strongest in the nation, fought a long and quixotic battle to protect its members' jobs. As long ago as 1992, surveyed union members of District 751 had signaled that job security was a central concern. By the 1995 contract negotiations, after the layoffs of several thousand employees, Lee Pearson, vice president for the International Association of Machinists' Western Territory, emphasized during the negotiations with Boeing that "job security overwhelmingly is the most important issue" for the District's members.[4] A few weeks later, the machinists went on strike for sixty-nine days to protect their benefits and to win "meaningful protections" against the threat to jobs from outsourcing. Their demands included being able to bid on work targeted for outsourcing and to limit the number of jobs that could be lost to this practice. The story of the 144 women making insulation blankets became emblematic of the competing goals between management and union. Boeing could slash costs by transferring the fairly routine work to a factory in Mexico, where women workers would earn seventy-six cents an hour to sew blankets that women in the Puget Sound region earned sixteen to eighteen dollars an hour to make. The Boeing workers, on the other hand, faced layoffs or reassignment to other positions even after they had "been so effective in reducing costs that top Boeing managers recognized their efforts with a commendation."[5]

In a pattern that was to be repeated several times in subsequent standoffs, Boeing yielded to the unions by sweetening its offer with more cash and improved benefits, but gave somewhat vague promises on job security and outsourcing. Boeing agreed to meet the union twice a year to discuss, as a press release put it, the "impact of subcontracting and offsets on planned layoffs with the intent of reducing, where possible, the impact on . . . jobs." It also accepted that the union could bid on work scheduled for outsourcing and promised that it would reassign or retrain workers whose work was to be subcontracted out. But crucially, management retained the right to outsource work at its discretion.

Boeing avoided another strike in 1999 when, at the last minute, Phil Condit, the new CEO, acquiesced to setting up "Work Transfer Committees." Union members would not only be on these committees but would also have access to company-supplied economic data so they could, in the words of Bill Johnson, then president of District 751, "assess whether there is a legitimate business case for sending work outside."[6] By 2002, in vastly changed economic circumstances, with airlines reeling from the 9/11 fallout and looking for ways to delay taking deliveries of ordered airplanes, Boeing took a much harder line in negotiations. In its weakened position, the union made little headway on job security even as Boeing was laying off thousands of its members. Indeed, Boeing chiseled away at existing workers' job security by winning the right to have outside nonunion suppliers deliver parts and tools directly to the assembly line, thereby threatening the jobs of hundreds of machinists.[7] Despite a twenty-eight-day strike in 2005, neither side gained much traction on the outsourcing or subcontracting issue.

It was not until 2008, with Boeing struggling to overcome an almost two-year delay in the 787 program, that the machinists had enough bargaining power to claw back some of the concessions they had made in 2002. After a strike of fifty-eight days, the union won the right to limit the delivery of parts to the assembly lines. Suppliers now had to deliver them to designated areas in the factory where they would then be tracked and distributed by Boeing machinists. However, this limitation would not apply to the 787 assembly lines or to military or new airplane programs. In what a reporter for the *Wall Street Journal* called "one of the country's last and most important battles over outsourcing,"[8] one of the most powerful union locals in the country had won a defensive, rearguard skirmish. It had limited and delayed the ability of Boeing to outsource work and, as it had done since the mid-1990s, managed to protect the jobs of a group of blue collar workers with some of the best pay and benefits in the United States. But the stark reality was that the number of machinists at Boeing had shrunk in that period by some 20 to 30 percent.

Job security was not a key bargaining issue for SPEEA, the union representing many of Boeing's engineers and technical workers, during the 1990s. Of greater concern to the union and its members were the distribution of merit-based pay increases and gaining respect for engineers and technical workers in the postmerger culture, a key subtext of the 2000 strike. It was not until well into the new century, with the heavier use of outside suppliers for the new 787 airplane, that SPEEA made outsourcing and the in-house use of non-Boeing contract workers important elements of its negotiations. In the 2008 negotiations, Boeing rejected SPEEA's request to limit the number of such workers or the length of their contracts. It did, however, agree to involve SPEEA in the outsourcing process. As Ray Goforth, SPEEA's executive director, put it, they had achieved "a voice, not a veto in the decision" to outsource. Boeing's negotiator, Doug Kight, saw it somewhat differently: the agreement maintained the company's flexibility and would help the union "understand the nature of Boeing's business strategies and plans regarding the use of non-Boeing labor and subcontracting."[9] A decade or so later than the machinists, Boeing's engineers and technical workers won the right to voice their concerns about a business strategy they increasingly feared would threaten their job security and the company's future.

LIVING WITH CONSTANT UNCERTAINTY

Despite the best efforts of their unions, employees of Boeing lived through two massive employment swings during the period spanning our study, as thousands of workers flowed into and out of Boeing's offices and factories. Boeing went from a high of about 87,000 employees in the early 1990s to a low of 64,000 in 1996, followed by a ramp-up to about 109,000 employees in 1998. Subsequently, policy changes, such as increased outsourcing and lean manufacturing, and the collapse of airplane orders after 9/11, triggered mass layoffs. By 2004, a year after the third survey, Boeing employed 48,000 people.

A modest recovery began in 2005 with the spectacular growth in orders for the 787 Dreamliner. The cyclical pattern began to repeat itself, but to a lesser extent than in the past. What was different, according to Boeing officials and observers in the business press, is that Boeing planned not to ramp up to employment levels anywhere near levels of previous peaks in airplane orders. And the changes Boeing made between the early 1990s and the mid-2000s to make itself a much more efficient producer meant that the company could produce more airplanes with fewer people in its Renton and Everett plants.

Taking the long view, one could argue that Boeing workers should have grown used to living through layoff and rehiring cycles. After all, it was no secret that Boeing had gone through several employment cycles since its founding. The most notorious, still referred to with amazement by old-timers who lived through it, was the precipitous downturn in the late 1960s and early 1970s when Boeing in the Puget Sound region went from a labor force of 100,000 in 1968 to just 37,000 employees in 1971. Boeing's employment booms and busts afflicted the region before this memorable event and continue to do so right up to the present. A female office worker in her mid-thirties gives us a sense of the frequency of layoffs as she recounted how her family's fate was repeatedly impacted by Boeing's layoff decisions: "I was affected by downsizing when I was ten years old and my father was laid off two days before we were supposed to go to Disneyland. I was so angry that I wanted to call 'Mr. Boeing' and yell at him. Later when I was in high school, I remember a day when my father, who was now an upper level supervisor, came home and began calling aerospace companies in an attempt to find his soon-to-be-laid-off subordinates other jobs. Most recently in these last rounds of layoffs (1995), my husband was laid off from Boeing while we were in the process of buying a house and I was responsible for determining which employees were going to be laid off and which were going to stay."

Despite the long history of employment booms and busts at Boeing, and the fact that many Boeing workers have lived through many of these swings, we found little evidence that the experience becomes less unsettling or troubling because workers had been through it before. The story is similar for the whole workforce, regardless of job classification or age. For example, the proportion of employees who told us they were worried about their job security more than tripled between 1997 and 2003, from around 20 percent to 65 percent. Workers invariably became acutely anxious living and working in a state of constant uncertainty and insecurity. A sixty-three-year-old female office worker who had survived the post-9/11 round of layoffs gave her graphic impression of the atmosphere during that time: "The layoffs were a terrible time for all of the employees regardless of their job description; for those being laid off and for those who wondered if they were going to get a WARN [Worker Adjustment and Retraining Notification Act] notice. The stress and pressure was tangible and you could cut it with a knife, so to speak. Everyone, management and otherwise, knew that absolutely no one was safe in keeping their job, and that everyone was vulnerable to being laid off. If one would scratch just below the surface, I believe that the employees had a general sense of terror, even if the word *terror* wasn't spoken."

Living with uncertainty is deeply unsettling. One hourly worker with a young family recalled how he and others would get notices giving them sixty days' advance notification that they might be laid off only to have the company extend their employment a week before the expiration of the sixty days. He described the actions of the company as "like putting someone on death row," and told us how his wife, toward the end of another sixty-day period, had said in exasperation, "just do it [lay him off] so we can get on with our lives."[10] In 1995, in the first wave of downsizing after Congress passed the WARN Act in 1988, requiring large companies to give employees sixty days notice before implementing mass layoffs, Boeing had handed out WARN notices to many more workers than were eventually laid off. Whether due to a certain cavalier carelessness or an inability to forecast correctly the needed size of the workforce by Boeing, these WARN notices caused needless anxiety and insecurity among thousands of workers. A participant in a focus group in 1996 observed: "I came within a month of being laid off. And they played this game that people got as many as five notices, and they'd go down within the last day or two and then pull it for whatever reason. So then you go on another thirty-day or sixty-day notice and then you do this all over again. Am I? Am I not? Should I try to get another job? No, I don't want to do that. You go right down to the end. And I've known people that had as many as five and that was very stressful."

Boeing learned a hard lesson from this experience, and in later downsizings was far more careful about calculating the number of WARN notices it doled out. Nonetheless, the fear and anxiety caused by large scale layoffs was palpable and pervasive throughout the decade. Even as late as 2006, two years after the end of one of the largest and longest-lasting episodes of mass layoffs, one woman professional told us that the memory of the "multiple layoffs" meant she "could never quite relax or make long range plans." A female clerical worker echoed that anxiety when she observed that although she "appreciated her job as I see more and more people losing theirs," she still felt "it is just a matter of time, the clock is always ticking."

Living in a state of heightened suspense and anticipation about a possible threat to one's job, described by a worker as trying to get on with one's life constantly aware that "a sword is hanging over you," is what prompted a manager with thirty-five years of service at Boeing and a survivor of seven rounds of layoffs to quote the comic strip character Pogo, who spoke about "the misery of uncertainty" being more painful than the "certainty of misery."

These anecdotal accounts by those who lived through this turbulent decade don't suggest that workers build up resilience by going through downsizing repeatedly. Going through it twice or three times did not make it less unsettling. In fact, the systematic data we collected show that both workers' sense of insecurity and their levels of depression increased with repeated exposure to layoff cycles.[11] Moreover, we found evidence that for some survivors the sense of insecurity produced by going through even just one downsizing event, especially if it involved getting a WARN notice, lingered for several years after the event. Nevertheless, by 2006, with the boom in orders for the 787 and some modest rehiring by Boeing, workers' sense of job security rebounded to levels close to those seen at the time of our first survey in 1997. But there was a twist to the pattern. Decomposing the job security scale into its three components measuring past, current, and future worry about job security, we find that surviving a decade of job uncertainty does damage employees' confidence in the *future* security of their jobs at Boeing. The proportion reporting that they were not confident about their future job security rises sharply from 15 percent in 1997 to 70 percent in 2003 before falling to 33 percent in 2006. There is a rebound, but now with twice as many skeptical and worried employees.

THE RHETORIC OF DOWNSIZING AND LAYOFFS

During the 1980s and 1990s, companies across the United States described downsizing and the mass layoffs that accompanied them in rather anodyne language. They talked of "rightsizing," or "restructuring," or "delayering" the organization in order to cut costs and compete more effectively in the global marketplace. Executives spoke of the need for companies to become lean and flexible so as to adapt more quickly to the changing economic environment. Boeing was no different. It, too, used the language of competition, cost, efficiency, and economic necessity to justify its mass layoffs. On the ground, in the offices, and on the factory floor, workers used a very different and more vivid language to describe what was happening. What we heard and read in the many comments made to us were descriptions of crisis and pain. One manager, for example, described the atmosphere during the post-9/11 layoffs as like "being in a war zone," with people developing short-term objectives centered on survival. He noted the irony when one executive in a speech reviewing the financial health of the company talked of how process improvements on the production line had allowed Boeing to make staff reductions. He did not think "making improvements to terminate people is terribly motivating." A female employee compared the layoff process to "a marriage falling apart where both sides know they should end things," but "most people stay . . . because it is their security blanket." A male manager compared being laid off to "being pushed out of the lifeboat and sacrificed for the good of the whole." An hourly worker said it felt like being "hit on the head with a hammer."

Several reached for metaphors of expendability to describe how they felt in these periods. One talked of Boeing using employees until they were a "burnt out cinder" and then "brushing them away" before replacing them with someone else. In the same vein, the wife of an hourly worker felt that Boeing "uses up people and tosses them away like used Kleenex." This feeling of being expendable was widespread and, in the view of many workers, flew in the face of the oft repeated claim Boeing made to its employees that "people are our most valuable resource." Cynicism about the sincerity of company rhetoric—"it's just propaganda" or "bullshit"—was a frequent worker response to the juxtaposition and resulting contradiction of soothing executive talk and harsh on-the-ground reality.

MASS LAYOFFS AND EMPLOYEE ATTITUDES TO WORK

Workers responded in a variety of ways to the uncertainty and insecurity of their situations. Several of those we spoke to told us they began to prepare for alternative careers. One of the benefits Boeing provides all its workers is the opportunity to pursue further education at Boeing's expense, even if unrelated to aerospace work. A male hourly worker who had received two WARN notices but had not been laid off started to take courses in nursing, "just in case." An engineer was training to be a massage therapist and claimed he knew many others who were preparing to work as consultants or contractors. Another engineer with seventeen years of service turned to preparing for a career as a math teacher. A female manager took courses with the University of Phoenix to complete her degree to increase her chances of continued employment whether within or outside Boeing. A female manager with twelve years of service, who admitted that not working for Boeing was "scary" and "used to be my biggest fear," made a conscious decision to "look outside . . . and got comfortable with the idea that I could go elsewhere and do a similar job." And a good number of Boeing employees actually left the company for other jobs during these times. A widely shared view was that often it was the most competent workers who left. One participant in a focus group in 1996 asserted: "It'll happen every time you go through a major cut in any company. The cream of the crop, the ones that are hotshots, the top 10 percent—they'll bail because they know they can get a better job." These individual stories are again supported by our survey results, which do indeed show that with each successive wave of mass layoffs, more workers reported they often thought about quitting their jobs and claimed it was more likely that they would look for a new job in the forthcoming year. By the 2003 survey, right at the peak of the post-9/11 layoff cycle, a third of respondents told us they often thought about quitting their jobs at Boeing, and one-quarter said they would probably look for another job in the forthcoming year.

In such a climate of anxiety and uncertainty, with many workers having half their minds on their precarious futures, it is not surprising that some believed that productivity suffered. This view was especially prevalent during the 1995 downsizing. A senior manager observed that "productivity is hurt because people spend so much time talking," wondering about who is likely next for the chopping block and perhaps through collective talk trying to assuage their anxiety. Productivity seems also to have been hurt by greater job search behavior by some of those who had been targeted for possible layoffs in 1995. A computer programmer noted that several colleagues in her department were "out of the office more because they were going out on interviews." Our analysis of company data on sick leave found that managers and professionals, who typically enjoy more work autonomy and flexibility, were absenting themselves far more often than other employees when they received WARN notices. However, the effect on other employees who received these notices, those with less authority and flexibility, was a lowering of their sickness absences, perhaps in an attempt to keep their heads down and minimize the risk of actually being laid off.[12] As one manager told us at the time, "Absenteeism is lower . . . because people fear the unknown."

In more recent downsizings, as layoffs were carried out in parallel with the introduction of lean processes, we heard more frequent complaints about increased workloads as surviving workers were asked to do more with fewer people. An office worker described how, after the most recent round of layoffs, work was "dispersed amongst the other office administrators who already had full workloads" and, with "no overtime allowed," how this had produced "incredible stress and pressure." An aversion to changes in work processes was also mentioned by some employees. A manager argued that the biggest impact of the constant threat of layoffs was the lack of willingness among employees to "make any improvements" in their work processes. For many workers, he said, "improved efficiency and cutting costs means cutting jobs." Under such circumstances, a woman professional worker wondered, "Why should I be happy to initiate ideas to lay me off?" even as she acknowledged that such ideas would help the company.

These divergent responses highlight the difficulty in accurately assessing the effects of layoffs on work performance. Although there is little doubt that layoffs and the resulting uncertainty and insecurity create widespread discontent, what they do to work effort and quality depends on a host of other factors, including the technical conditions of production and the balance of power between managers and employees. Technical changes in the design and manufacturing processes, for example, can massively improve productivity even in the face of worker discontent. And fear can be a powerful motivator, at least in the short run.

THE END OF THE PSYCHOLOGICAL CONTRACT?

There is much talk that the postwar social contract between workers and companies in many of America's large companies has ended.[13] This "contract," which implicitly promised workers lifelong job security and benefits in exchange for loyalty and commitment to the company, it is argued, has been replaced by a more instrumental and short-term arrangement. In this new accommodation, workers would now receive market rates of pay and benefits as long as merited by their performance and the financials of the company permitted. In return, workers would give the employer a "fair" or reasonable amount of work effort but would be under no obligation to go the extra mile in the provision of either effort or ideas. In the words of Jeffrey Pfeffer, a leading scholar of organizations, the relationship between the two would become more "market-like, distant, and transactional."[14]

Our study tried to assess whether such a change had taken place or whether there were signs of movement in that direction. As we saw in the previous chapter on the changing cultural identity of Boeing, many workers did indeed start to view the company in a very different way after the mid-1990s. The statement by one employee that "if I'm just a number to them, they're just a paycheck to me" is a blunt formulation of a central element of the new relationship. To uncover how widespread that view was and whether workers' expectations of Boeing's obligations had changed, we asked respondents to our 2006 survey to tell us what they believed Boeing had "owed" them when they were first hired and what they believed Boeing "owed" them now. Even if their memories may be less than fully accurate recollections of what they believed ten or twenty years ago, their responses do give us a sense of their current feelings about changes in their expectations.

As figure 4.2 shows, the items in which we see declines over time have to do with expectations that the company should provide employees with long careers at the company (career development), job training and advancement, and long-

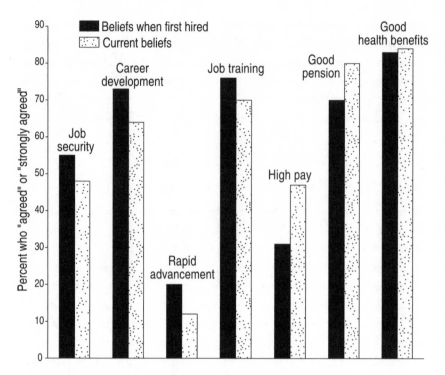

Figure 4.2 Employee beliefs about what Boeing should provide workers: comparison of current beliefs to those when first hired (from data collected in 2006)

term job security. Those that see an increase are expectations that the company should provide high pay and good pensions. These, along with the expectation of getting quality, affordable health care, which shows little change, indicate a shift in expectations away from intangible and toward tangible benefits. One might expect such a shift among older cohorts of workers as they approach retirement and begin to care more about their financial and health security than about careers and job security. However, this trend was not confined to older workers. Workers under the age of forty-six reported similar changes in expectations, suggesting that the trend might portend a more permanent shift in employees' expectations.

Part of the explanation for the change in expectations can be attributed to workers' responses to Boeing's actions. As Boeing repeatedly implemented mass layoffs and increased the outsourcing of work, workers' attitudes and expectations adjusted. Human relationships are built on reciprocity, and workers repeatedly told us that as Boeing started to treat them as expendable commodities or numbers, they no longer felt the same sense of loyalty to the company. For many it meant a weakening of their emotional commitment to Boeing. Some, as we have seen, went further and positioned themselves to pursue alternative job opportunities. Others accepted the inevitability of living with constant insecurity, even in periods when the company was expanding, because they believed that the growth of outsourcing or lean processes and other technical work improvements would continue to threaten their jobs. An official of the machinists' union noted that, in the 1980s and 1990s, job security was the primary issue for their members in negotiations, but more recently it had been displaced by concern about health care and pension benefits. She attributed the change not only to the aging of the machinist workforce but also to the acceptance among them that globalization and outsourcing are here to stay. She went on to say that, despite widespread worry about long-term job security, many workers "don't think job security is possible. They don't have a sense of what it would even look like, or how it could be framed, in this new world."

How did frontline and middle managers respond to this changing employment relationship? While we find that the difficult changes Boeing implemented eroded their sense of loyalty to the company, they still remained far more committed to the organization than other workers and were also more likely than others to accept the necessity of layoffs, either because they had access to financial data or because they had more fully internalized the ideology justifying company downsizing and outsourcing. Managers we spoke to tended to agree with the redefinition of the employment relationship away from lifetime employment and toward "lifetime employability."[15] One observed that the change "allows people to recognize that the company doesn't owe you anything." He went on to complain that some workers thought of the company as if it were similar to a "parent-child relationship." Whereas some believed they "deserved" certain things, he thought it was important that employees earned their rewards. These sentiments were echoed by another manager with twenty-six years of service at Boeing, who expressed the basis of the new relationship in this way: "Anyone in business has to provide their share of value in order to maintain their job. If a person stops doing that, then why would anyone think they have a right to a job? Some people at Boeing have the attitude that there is this big benevolent employer that should take care of them. As long as I'm providing value, the company owes me a competitive wage and benefits."

LAYOFFS AND WELL-BEING

> Leaving Boeing was like walking out of a cave into the light. I hadn't realized what a negative place it was to work until I wasn't there anymore.

Everyone at Boeing went through the layoff cycles, but not everyone was directly threatened with job loss or personally witnessed the layoffs of friends or co-workers. Stories and rumors did circulate across the whole workforce and it was impossible for employees to be unaware of what was happening when 25 or 30 percent of their colleagues were disappearing. But we found evidence that even in the midst of these companywide convulsions, some employees were hurt more than others (the effects of layoffs and all the other changes Boeing implemented on well-being are explored in more depth in chapter 8). Those with closer personal contact to layoffs were the ones who reported the highest levels of depression and the most symptoms of poor health. So, for example, those who were directly targeted for layoffs (that is, warned) tended to report feelings of greater fatigue and burnout as well as more back pain, heart problems, and high blood pressure than did those workers who escaped any direct threats to their job security. Such effects on well-being were also noticeable among those who had not been directly targeted but who had seen friends and close co-workers laid off. This group tended to report more health-related problems than did those who had the good fortune to avoid either direct or indirect personal contact with layoffs.[16] Moreover, when we computed a scale to measure the degree of worker exposure to, or contact with, layoffs (combining, for example, getting warned and friends and co-workers being laid off), we found a fairly consistent relationship between the degree of depression and the employee's score on the scale. Knowing colleagues who had been laid off tended to make workers feel more insecure because they seemed to overestimate the likelihood that the same thing would happen to them. In psychology, this is known as "availability," whereby dramatic and familiar events have more powerful effects because they come more readily to mind. During layoffs, familiarity with layoffs seems to magnify distress.[17]

According to the logic implied by the above results, we would expect those who actually were laid off to show the greatest deterioration in their well-being. To assess whether that, in fact, had happened, we also surveyed those from our initial sample in 1997 who subsequently left the company before our 2003 survey. We asked them questions about why they had left Boeing and what had happened to their economic situation and to their well-being since their de-

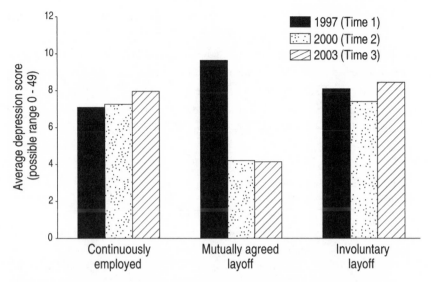

Figure 4.3 Depression scores in 1997, 2000, and 2003: comparison of continuously employed workers versus those who took "mutually agreed" layoffs and those who were involuntarily laid off

parture. We also obtained from the company the official reason for the termination. The most surprising results concerned what happened to the well-being of those laid off. Those who defined their departure from Boeing as a "mutually agreed voluntary layoff" reported lower scores on the number of symptoms of poor health, on drinking problems, and on whether they were drinking or smoking more than their scores had been when they were working at Boeing. They also reported that they felt they had more control over their lives (see chapter 8 for a fuller comparison between those who left and those who remained employed at Boeing). Particularly startling was the drop in their depression scores. As shown in figure 4.3, whereas those who remained at Boeing saw little change in their depression scores over time, those who were deemed laid off by Boeing but who characterized their leaving as "mutually agreed" saw improvements of close to 50 percent in their depression scores.[18] What's more, this improvement was sustained for several years. However, when we look at the reports of those who classified their layoff as "involuntary" or forced, we see very little sign of any significant change in their mental health. This finding offers some guidance to other companies embarking on mass layoffs: giving employees some sense of control and influence over decisions that govern their fate can sharply reduce the psychological damage they suffer.[19]

The comments made to us in 2003 by those who left a few years earlier were almost universally positive about their state of mind post-Boeing. They talked of being "much happier," "more in control of my life," and of "feeling a lot better since leaving Boeing." One put it in very stark terms, claiming that "leaving Boeing was like walking out of a cave into the light." Another told us that "even though I have been unemployed for a long time, I am not depressed. I was when I worked at Boeing." A manager who left and started his own business recounted:

> I was a manager at Boeing during my last ten years there. While I enjoyed my job and the challenges, the imposed stress was draining. Just before I left, I was facing my fourth layoff cycle in the last six years. It became apparent to me that Boeing was not being managed properly and [we] had to be the implementers of their poor decisions. I had the opportunity to do some aviation consulting so I took a voluntary layoff to pursue a dream of mine. Consulting for multiple companies has its own stress, however I enjoy my job and my personal anguish has [been] reduced considerably from my days at Boeing. I know if I had stayed, my health would have been affected. It is sad to meet with Boeing colleagues who are still there and to hear of their anguish and disappointment with Boeing's policies and direction.

Surprising as such sentiments might seem, other studies are confirming that leaving a downsizing company and getting a new job can sometimes be better for employee well-being than staying on as a survivor in an uncertain and difficult environment.[20] Our comparison of leavers and survivors tracks a particularly turbulent period in Boeing's history, encompassing as it does both the postmerger cultural turmoil and the mass layoffs following the collapse in airplane orders after 9/11. Escaping from that environment must have seemed like an immense relief and reprieve for those who left Boeing, and, of course, those who stayed had no way of knowing that a turnaround in company fortunes was on the horizon to lighten their gloom and anxiety.

In pointing out how so many who left felt better about themselves and their lives postemployment at Boeing, however, we do not mean to downplay the pain and dislocation that layoffs and unemployment cause. The evidence is clear that involuntary job loss tends to result in lowered earnings if one is able to find a new job, and sometimes it also means the loss of health insurance for varying periods of time.[21] This was certainly the case for many of the laid-off Boeing factory workers who had to take jobs in the service sector at much reduced wages.[22] A Seattle newspaper cited Washington state statistics for 2004 that showed that the median hourly wage of former aerospace workers was $20 an hour lower than of those still employed in that sector ($16 versus $36). This is a huge drop in income, and the effects of such a drop were illustrated in some of the comments made to us. An hourly worker who lost his job told us, "My family has experienced a drastic reduction in our standard of living and increased stress levels from trying to make ends meet with a negative cash flow situation." Another said, "Layoff almost cost me my house and my way of life." There were also nonfinancial consequences. Some told us they missed the excitement of working on challenging projects at a renowned company. Others missed the daily social interactions or the work friends they no longer saw. As one put it, "I miss my job and the excitement and challenge that I had to do a good job and I was appreciated. I miss the interaction with all different types of people." But there is no skirting the general impression made by the majority of Boeing workers who left the company in the late 1990s and responded to our survey: their mood seemed to have brightened, as if a cloud hanging over their heads had been lifted. It's hard not to see some resemblance to the change in mood one sees among those who have left a bad marriage.

CONCLUSION

Mass layoffs cause a great deal of turmoil. They create economic hardship for some and psychological anxiety and pain for many more. Even top executives sometimes learned the hard way how painful the experience could be. Ron Woodard, the former head of the commercial division, admitted several years later, "It's a horrible thing. Actually, I never understood how debilitating it was to get thrown off the payroll because I never was, until I was. It's a miserable thing for your family. I've since talked to lots of people; it's just a horrible, degrading, miserable way to be."

Unions put up a dogged, defensive struggle to protect their members' jobs but managed only to delay the inexorable decline in employment at their company. Individual employees were thus left to scramble and cope as best they could with the consequences of these wild employment swings. Some of those who lost their jobs or who left the company found relief and thrived in their new circumstances; many of those who remained employed rode the ten-year psychological rollercoaster ride and emerged whole but somewhat shaken. They were grateful to still have a job and determined to hold on to the excellent and comprehensive benefits they had won at one of America's flagship companies, but they were uneasy and apprehensive about what the future would portend, and their strong sense of loyalty was replaced by a more instrumental attitude to the company many had long admired. Imagine, then, how much more vulnerable millions of American private sector workers are to the effects of layoffs and downsizing without the protections, however limited in nature, of labor unions to bargain for orderly and fair layoff processes, for benefits during cyclical downtimes, and for giving priority to former workers during rehiring phases.

But if there is widespread agreement about the human cost of mass layoffs, there is no consensus on alternative strategies and policies that companies and governments could pursue in the future to mitigate the damage. Woodard, even after acknowledging the misery repeated mass layoffs cause, could see no real alternative to responding to what he called the "world business cycle" where "on the way up, if you didn't expand to sell the airplanes somebody else would. And on the way down, if you didn't cut back, get rid of people to get rid of the cost structure you couldn't survive." He went on to say, rather ruefully, "I don't like it but I don't know how you avoid it, given the system, because no company can keep an extra hundred thousand people on the workforce payroll."[23] We will return to an examination of this critical issue in the last chapter.

Chapter 5 Working in New Ways

Change was the norm at Boeing Commercial Airplanes, extending into the very ways of working. In particular, a ramp-up of teams and technology dramatically affected how work was done on a day-to-day basis for virtually all employees. These new ways of working were integral to Boeing's lean and outsourcing strategies. The ability to do more with less requires tight linkages between people and processes. Flatter hierarchies and far-flung work processes demand more of employees: more autonomy, more responsibility, more collaboration, and more creativity. Did these new ways of working help or hinder employees' ability to respond to the new demands of a new Boeing?

Early in our study, participation in teams and increased use of technology seemed to improve employee perceptions about their work as well as their commitment to Boeing. However, as time went by, the positive influence of these new ways of work diminished. The reality of the team experience often didn't match the rhetoric of teamwork, and overuse of team lingo confused and disillusioned employees, diffusing the impact of teams over time. Technology proved to be a double-edged sword, offering job challenge and flexible work schedules, but eventually escalating the pressures of the workday and blurring the boundaries between work and nonwork.

This chapter examines how employees experienced teams and technology at Boeing and how these experiences influenced perceptions of their work and their relationship with the company. We also look at how these perceptions changed over time and explore some reasons why the expected positive impacts on employee attitudes were not sustained over the course of our study. We hope the employee experience at Boeing offers "lessons learned" for other companies implementing teams and technology in their transformation efforts.

THE RHETORIC AND REALITY OF TEAMS

Implementation of teams emerged as a corporate strategy in the United States through the early 1990s as American firms actively adopted Japanese quality and lean production principles. While it could be argued that teams have been part of corporate life since the 1940s, the Total Quality Management movement (TQM) propelled the self-managed work group or "quality circle" to the forefront of managerial literature and the popular press and, to varying degrees, affected actual practice in the workplace. Teams offer essential energy for the postindustrial firm, in theory, replacing tired pyramids and hierarchies with empowered and engaged workers charged with the urgent mission of continuous improvement.

After Boeing executives returned from Japan in the early 1990s, where they had observed the Toyota processes, there was a flurry of new team initiatives on the shop floor. Literally hundreds of Integrated Product and Design Build Teams (IPTs and DBTs, respectively) sprang to life in support of Boeing's World Class Competitiveness and Continuous Quality Improvement (CQI) initiatives. The enhanced role of "team member" should have been well entrenched in the organization by the time of our first survey in 1997.

Team Involvement at Boeing

Team experience was fairly widespread when our study began at Boeing. Roughly four in ten employees reported that they were currently members of a team during our surveys in 1997 and 2000; just over a third were not currently members of a team but had been members in the recent past. Only about one-quarter of employees had never been on a team by 2000.[1]

Looking at involvement in teams in a different way, we also asked a relative membership question: Compared with two years ago, are you involved on teams much more, more, about the same, less, or much less? Over 50 percent of employees in 1997 reported an increase in their team activity over the previous two years. Boeing ramped up its team activity in the mid-1990s and many employees became involved with new teams in the years leading up to our first survey in 1997. Team involvement leveled off during 2000 and 2003, as more employees reported their team activity was about the same as in the previous couple of years. Team activity seemed to be on the upswing again in 2006, perhaps coinciding with teams formed for 787 production. Only 10 to 20 percent of employees reported a decrease in their team experience over the ten years of our study.

Given the enthusiasm for teams in the academic and popular press, we expected those who reported more team activity to also report more positive relationships with Boeing and better attitudes about their jobs. We did find a positive relationship between team involvement and organizational commitment, but only in the 1997 and 2000 surveys; those reporting more, particularly much more, involvement in teams appeared to be more committed to Boeing. Conversely, those with relatively less involvement on teams appeared to be less committed to Boeing. In the 2003 and 2006 surveys, however, there was no difference in commitment across the groups; in fact, there was a slight *drop* in commitment for those at the extreme high end of the team involvement scale.

With few exceptions, patterns for other organizational and job attitude measures were similar to these findings: involvement in teams was associated with more favorable attitudes toward Boeing and their jobs in the first two surveys, but less associated, or even negatively associated, by 2003 and 2006. For example,

- Job involvement was very high in 1997 for those with "much more" team involvement; in all later times, however, those with "much more" team involvement show drops in job involvement. Team membership no longer appeared to engage employees in their jobs or the company.
- Similarly, with respect to workers' intentions to quit the company, in 1997, 2000, and 2003, employees reporting more involvement with teams indicated less interest in leaving Boeing. There is a dramatic shift in 2006, however, with reported intentions to quit virtually the same across all team involvement groups: those reporting more team involvement were as likely to be seeking other employment as those who had less involvement.
- Employees' sense of job security had only a limited relationship with team involvement. Most noticeable, however, were rising concerns about job security in 2000 and, especially, 2003 across all groups: being on a team did not buffer team members from job security concerns.

In summary, membership on teams did not consistently contribute to positive feelings toward Boeing or jobs at Boeing. While we saw positive effects of team membership early in our study, by the end of our research in 2006 there was a noticeable drop in attitudes toward Boeing for employees with high team involvement. In fact, very high involvement in teams may have had a negative rather than positive effect on employee relationships with Boeing. The rest of this chapter will explore some of the possible reasons for this shift.

The Experience of Being on a Team

Much of the extensive research on teams has focused on the effects of readily observed elements of team structure. Structural characteristics of the team, such as the number of team members, the kinds of tasks done by the team, the frequency of meetings, and the degree to which teams are represented by a mix of skills and functional departments (generally called co-location), have been variously hypothesized to lead to better team and organizational outcomes.[2] In our data analyses, however, we found little connection between employee reports about team structure and their attitudes about Boeing and their jobs. This led us to ask about other factors that might influence team member attitudes.

We wondered in the first place if teams at Boeing subjectively felt like teams to team members or if they were a team in name only, and whether the difference mattered. Relatively few studies examine workers' own reports of how teamwork impacts their attitudes toward their job or company,[3] for example. But we were intrigued by the fact that some studies have found that subjective experiences on the job, more than the objective structural aspects of work, are what creates a link between job redesign or enrichment efforts (teams being one example) and employee attitudes.[4] So we wanted to pay special attention to employees' subjective experiences with teams. The literature on teams identifies at least two key dimensions that might uniquely characterize a subjectively "good" team compared with a traditional work group experience. The first is social cohesion, or the sense that people belong to a unified group where they are valued and respected. The second is decision-making authority, where people feel they are making a substantive contribution and having a real impact on group decisions.

SOCIAL COHESION IN BOEING TEAMS

While descriptions of teams often focus on collective responsibility around tasks, the social dimension may serve as the foundation for employee evaluation of their affective versus instrumental relationship with the organization.[5] Social cohesion, rather than task cohesion, is more often found to be associated with positive affect or attitudes toward work or the organization as well as organizational outcomes such as absenteeism and reported well-being.[6] Haskins, Liedtka, and Rosenblum (1998) go so far as to describe the "thermonuclear reactions" of energy and performance when team members experience relational rather than simply transactional (task) collaboration.

When asked to describe the most important changes at Boeing over the last several years (2006 survey), several respondents commented on their experience of team cohesion and sense of contributing to a greater good. For example, a manager with over two decades of experience at Boeing listed several team cohesion items as important in her perceived positive transformation of Boeing: "The continued focus and commitment to working together. . . . Recognizing that we must be a team, each contributing our part/role/expertise/support to the agreed to plan and common goal. By leading and supporting/participating in highly effective teams, I believe that we have achieved more as a company and regain our orders lead over Airbus. Because we are a team and not individual contributors only looking out for ourselves" (female manager, twenty-five years at Boeing).

Another frontline manager notes that "I've had the opportunity to work on the 787 program and am impressed by how focused the team members are and how much they utilize the teams to solve problems. None of us are really alone in terms of solving work problems" (female manager, nineteen years at Boeing).

This strong sense of cohesion described by these managers was not shared universally by team members at Boeing, however. In 1997, only one in ten team members strongly agreed with statements like, "The team works well together," or "Everyone feels obliged to do their fair share." Only 16 percent strongly agreed that people on their team worked well together, and over one-quarter indicated there were deep divisions in their teams. Impressions of the social dimension deteriorated slightly in 2000 on virtually all indicators. In general, the bulk of team members seemed to feel simply "OK" about the social aspects of their team rather than strongly positive or negative (for example, ratings on most team experience questions were clustered in the midrange of the scale, rather than at the extremes).

DECISION-MAKING IN BOEING TEAMS

There is a long research tradition which shows that job experiences having to do with the exercise of power and autonomy in the workplace shape job attitudes.[7] More specifically, employees in teams usually seek more participation in decision-making and report a wide range of positive outcomes from the experience, including greater commitment to work organization that provides this participatory opportunity.[8] In fact, Kirkman and Rosen (2000) describe "winning" teams as those characterized by employees who exercise freedom and discretion in decisions.

In regards to autonomy, the bulk of team participants (71 percent) reported they had been selected by management rather than volunteering to be on a team. More than half of team members agreed that employees would prefer not to work on teams and about one-third of team members indicated that team members were not happy to be part of a team. Being forced or "encouraged" to be on a team seems to run counter to team rhetoric regarding empowerment and self-management. In addition, the perception of teams being handpicked by management may result in an elitist rather than egalitarian image of the teams and team members.

In addition, while most team members reported that their teams made important decisions (86 percent), responses to other items suggest that team autonomy and real decision-making authority were relatively low. For example, only about one-third of participants said their team had access to management or had a great deal of say in how work was done on the team; less than one-third said they had a great deal of say in allocating work tasks or setting team goals. Even smaller numbers reported having a say in scheduling or team member evaluation activities. Open-ended comments in the 2006 survey often included a sense of "spinning wheels" in teams rather than action-oriented decision-making. A male engineer with twenty-six years at Boeing, for example, commented: "I think the most important change also happens to be the worst change. The growth of 'teams' to work problems and day-to-day business, the 'empowerment' of employees, and the general unwillingness by anyone except for top management to make a decision is dramatically slowing down a bureaucratic monster that was painfully slow to begin with. In order to make a decision, one has to go through as many as five teams or councils, each time presenting the facts or data in manners such that approval to get to the next level is given. In effect, no one is 'empowered.' "

RELATIONSHIP OF TEAM EXPERIENCE WITH ORGANIZATIONAL ATTITUDES

There appears to be a relationship between subjective team experiences and attitudes toward Boeing. For example, team members who strongly agreed that they were respected by other team members (a reflection of social cohesion)

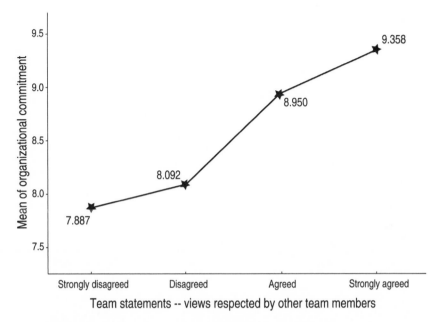

Figure 5.1 Social cohesion on teams and organizational commitment

were significantly more committed to Boeing as compared with team members who did not feel respected (see figure 5.1). Team members who believed the team made important decisions also reported being more committed to Boeing than did team members who felt the team did not make important decisions (see figure 5.2).

We see similar patterns of results for other organizational attitudes across similar measures of team cohesion and decision-making. It may be in everyone's best interests, then, for the team experience to be positive. Team members benefit because they feel better about their team, their work, and the organization; the organization likely benefits from increased productivity and the creativity of engaged workers. Unfortunately, as suggested by relatively low ratings of their overall team experience, the implementation of teams at Boeing did not always result in truly "team"-feeling teams. The benefits of teams might not have been realized because not enough team members felt they were on a cohesive team or had real autonomy regarding team membership or meaningful participation in team decisions.

Team membership, in and of itself, then, may not be sufficient to improve or solidify relationships with employees. The subjective experience of the team member, rather than membership alone, influences commitment. Positive social

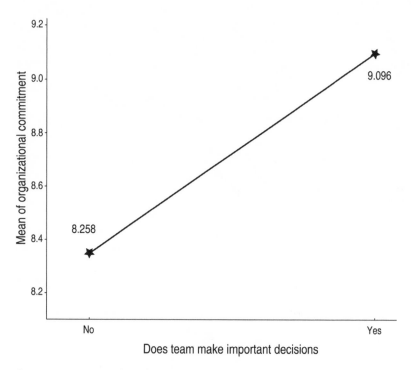

Figure 5.2 Decision-making on teams and organizational commitment

connections within the team and meaningful participation appear to contribute to positive team effects on organizational outcomes. Without a meaningful team experience, there is little reason to expect teams to have any more impact on organizational attitudes (or business results) than any other work group.

Our findings suggest further that *a poor team experience may be worse than no team experience at all.* For example, team members with low ratings on cohesion and decision-making in their teams had lower ratings of commitment (and other job attitudes) than did employees who had never had any team experience at Boeing. In addition, open-ended comments from our 2006 survey often had a "dashed expectations" feel to them, i.e., the team should have been empowering, but it wasn't, with a cynical tone that suggests employee distancing from team rhetoric as well as from Boeing. Teams have significant potential to enhance worker dignity and rebuild relationships, but they may have negative impacts on worker morale and productivity if they are implemented as ploys or pseudo-teams to co-opt or placate employees. Wholesale or casual implementation of a team strategy may backfire, then, if attention is not paid to the day-to-day experience of team members.

The Terminology of Teams: A Rose Is a Rose?

There is an assumption that labeling any group of individuals as a "team" re-sults in employees knowing and feeling they are on one. In fact, team members may not even realize they are on a team. Conversely, individuals who are not officially on a team, at least from a management point of view, may believe that they are. For example, in an exploratory study conducted with team mem-bers (membership based on a list provided by Boeing), only 56 percent of re-spondents identified themselves as members of a team. Conversely, 53 percent of nonteam employees (again based on Boeing's internal data) self-classified as team members. Objective labels or descriptions reported by managers, human resource departments, or outsiders (such as research investigators) don't always line up with the views of employees. We shouldn't be surprised, then, if stud-ies about teams sometimes yield contradictory or unexpected results; if I don't feel like or identify as a member of a team, why would my attitudes be any dif-ferent than those of someone who is not officially on a team?

Team membership, then, is not a straightforward or unambiguous classifi-cation. As noted earlier, after the early 1990s, teams became de rigueur for cor-porate America. After Boeing's executives made their trips overseas to learn the Japanese way, literally hundreds of cross-functional teams were implemented at Boeing. Further, team lingo became normative as part of the TQM/continu-ous improvement culture, replacing traditional language around work groups and functional units. This language was retained even as the organization shifted from TQM to lean production in the mid-1990s.

Our unexpected findings regarding the impact of teams on employee atti-tudes may be due, in part, to the numerous, often contradictory, uses of the word "team" as Boeing shifted its strategy and culture over our ten-year study period. Based on a casual reading of Boeing documents and press releases, we see at least five different ways the terminology of teams was used between 1996 and 2006.

"Capital T" teams, or the formal IPTs and DBTs, were initiated as part of Boeing's World Class initiatives in 1991–92. Based on both public press and employee comments in our research, these teams were high profile and rela-tively high status groups at Boeing. Composition of the teams skew towards the elite of Boeing—these teams are populated largely by professional engi-neering or technical employees and those handpicked by senior management.

Participatory or quality circle–type teams were common in the 1980s and early 1990s as companies aligned themselves with the Japanese management approaches. Perhaps because these types of teams were normative during the 1990s, there is limited mention of them in public information from or about Boeing. In the open-ended comments in our last survey, in 2006, there is evidence that workers were not particularly enthusiastic about these general production teams, perhaps because of their eventual strong linkage to lean initiatives and cost-cutting as opposed to employee empowerment. While one manager observed that "employee engagement and the team-based organization has allowed lean and cost-cutting initiatives to become realities at a faster pace," a technician with nearly thirty years of experience at Boeing reflected the less positive view regarding teams and lean organizational strategy: "Managers give lip service to team, while only worrying about the bottom line." An hourly worker commented on diminished opportunities for participation in the lean environment: "Lean manufacturing has had a 'mixed bag' effect, better competitive ability, but less opportunity for hourly employees to participate or contribute in any meaningful or substantial way."

The attitudinal benefits of production floor teams—for example, cohesion and participatory decision-making—may have been diminished as the organization shifted away from the "amae" (community, fraternalism) inherent in the Japanese implementation of teamwork and embraced the cost-cutting and efficiency goals of lean production and other short-term shareholder value strategies.

Global partner teams were increasingly visible as Boeing shifted toward outsourcing and offshoring with international partners. Team language was very common in press releases and internal communications about the innovative approaches planned for production of the 787. It is significant that these Boeing teams were not composed exclusively of Boeing employees but also included external partners. These were not teams of people per se, but a collection of international suppliers and vendors that were directly connected to Boeing's offshoring strategies of the late 1990s and recent years. So, these were not "we-teams" in the group theory or psychological sense, but were teams composed of "them": the faceless, impersonal corporate abstractions getting the jobs and projects that used to be "ours." An engineer raises concerns about job stability as a result of this shift to "them": "I have spent the last two years preparing Japanese, European, and Texan engineers to do the job I have been doing for the last twenty years. I expect that within the next five to seven years, Boeing will no longer need engineers with my skill code."

And a manager makes the direct connection between offloading teamwork and deteriorating job attitudes: "We've sent some of my team's work to

Moscow, whether it's a smart move or not (core competency loss?), adversely affecting morale and skills."

Teams closely tied to off-loading, outsourcing, and job loss, much less one that is formed of distant corporate entities rather than Boeing coworkers, likely had a less positive impact on employee attitudes than did IBTs or CQI quality circles.

"Team" used as a verb became ubiquitous at Boeing. In effect, teams and teaming became synonymous with "working together" and were embedded in the day-to-day vernacular at Boeing. Virtually every work group, including traditional departments and the senior management team, was now "teaming" together to accomplish a goal. The overliberal application of the concept of teaming or "team = working together" led to little or no differentiation between a traditional work group and a new team. With limited structural or psychological distinction between groups, it is unlikely that perceptions of one collective differed from the other. Thus, we might not expect team membership to have as large an impact on attitudes in an environment where everyone is "teaming" in some shape or form.

Team used as a label to describe the new corporate culture may have significantly undermined the effects of teams as a job redesign practice. When sorting through the open-ended material for comments relevant to this section, we were struck by the sheer number of team comments related to this culture shift rather than to implementation of, or experience on, specific teams. Perhaps no other use of a word had more impact, mostly negative, than the use of "team" to describe the new culture at Boeing. As one manager succinctly noted in her 2006 survey comment: "Going from a 'family' to a 'team' had more ramifications than our leaders recognized."

As noted earlier, one of the important psychological benefits of teams should be an enhanced sense of belonging, or identification with, the firm. Teams might be actively used after a merger to create a sense of unity in the company —a "we're all in this together" culture—to propel the troops forward with enthusiasm and renewed commitment to the cause. However, as was more thoroughly described in chapter 3, after the McDonnell Douglas merger, many Boeing employees felt forced to abandon a culture they embraced (the Boeing family) and accept an unappealing culture as a team. The new team culture, rather than building cohesion and cooperative enterprise, was perceived as cold, calculating, and uncaring. Many open-ended comments reflected an "every man for himself" view of the new culture that was not consistent with collective goal setting and collaboration of teams. "There is a new corporate emphasis on reducing familial atmosphere and replacing it with every man for himself," said a male engineer with thirty years at Boeing. A male technician who was also a thirty-year Boeing veteran said that he had noticed a "dramatic shift from family type environment to team type of setting, i.e., coaching and support (going the extra mile and effort) to just the top players, replace the 'starters or first team' with the next layer to see if they can do better. We shoot our wounded rather than nurture."

This last sentiment is probably not what team theorists and proponents had in mind. Not only did the new team culture further dilute the concept of team and the team experience, it also created a negative halo for many employees, such that the word "team" seemed to provoke a twist in the gut for several employees rather than enthusiastic support for the company. We wonder if this culture shift, initiated roughly around the same time as the implementation of our survey in 2000, is at least partially responsible for the diminishing of team influence on employee attitudes we see through the latter half of our study period.

In sum, given the multiple and not always palatable flavors of teams being served at Boeing, it is not surprising that Boeing employees not only were uncertain as to their team membership, they were unsure that teams were such a good idea in general. The indiscriminate use of this term muddied the subjective waters for employees (and researchers) and likely diluted the psychological and organizational benefits of a more focused, deliberate team strategy.

TECHNOLOGY: A DOUBLE-EDGED SWORD

Like many corporate and academic workplaces, the daily routine of Boeing office workers was transformed over our study period by the burgeoning and ultimately routine use of e-mail, the Internet, and new office production and communications technologies. In chapter 2 we describe the dramatic shifts in use of technology in virtually all phases of the manufacturing process—within a very short period of time design, engineering, and production of airplanes moved from World War II methods to computer screens, databases, and robots. So, not only were the ways of white collar work changed by technology at Boeing, the work environment for engineers, technicians, and frontline workers was transformed by moving lines, Define and Control Aircraft Configuration/Manufacturing Resource Management (DCAC-MRM), and virtual design.

Technology has been identified as a key means to greater efficiency and productivity for firms.[9] The success of lean production on the shop floor is highly dependent on transferring cumbersome, fragmented, "by hand" tasks to tightly orchestrated, computer-aided, and coordinated processes. Technology is also prominent in job redesign and enrichment initiatives intended to benefit the individual worker.[10] Automation of routine tasks, it is often argued, should improve the quality of work life of employees. Freed from time-consuming, often mind-numbing repetitive tasks, the hands and heads of employees are available to pursue more creative and interesting work.

Computer-supported work, in theory, should then benefit both the firm and its employees. We expected a positive relationship between the availability and use of technology at Boeing and worker attitudes about their work and, ultimately, their firm. However, similar to the effect of teams, the use of technology has had a mixed impact on employee attitudes. In many instances, reactions to technology were ambivalent: there were certainly *efficiency* benefits ascribed to many technological innovations, but employees were not always convinced that technology offered substantial *effectiveness* benefits. And, while productivity gains might be evident in the corporate bottom line, there were often costs to the individual employee in terms of pace of work and quality of work and home life. In this section, we'll see how the pervasive and rapid influx of technology both helped and hindered the ways of work for Boeing employees.

Use of Technology at Boeing

Technology impacted the work of virtually every employee at Boeing. In responding to an open-ended question in our final survey questionnaire in 2006, a technician wrote that the most important change at Boeing over the last several years was the "almost total dependence on computers to do our jobs." This may be only a slight exaggeration. All four of our surveys included questions regarding the degree to which the use of technology, computers, and software had increased or decreased over the previous time period.[11] For the majority of employees, across all four time frames, the answer was "increased," and for many the answer was, "increased a lot."

Perceived change in the use of technology was highest at our 1997 survey, with nearly 80 percent of respondents reporting they were using technology more or a lot more than they had been in the previous two years. Technology impacted both office and manufacturing employees as technicians, managers, and salaried office workers reported the highest levels of change. The 1997 survey coincided with the early implementation of DCAC-MRM and other manufacturing design and work flow innovations at Boeing, as well as the spread of general office automation and Internet services throughout most corporate environments. It is not terribly surprising, then, that so many employees experienced changes in use of technology during this time frame.

We saw a modest decrease in reported change in technology use in the 2000 and 2003 surveys, suggesting that the rate of innovation slowed a bit at Boeing around and immediately after the millennium. It is noteworthy, however, that nearly seven in ten employees still reported "more" or "a lot more" technology use in both time frames. The pace of change may have slowed, but technological innovation was still the norm in manufacturing, engineering, and office environments. Our final survey (2006) reflected a renewed surge in demands for "more" or "a lot more" technology.

The pace of technological change appeared to be relentless, then, for all work groups. The vast majority of employees, regardless of occupational category, reported a persistent demand to learn and adapt to new technology in their jobs. In 1997 and 2000, we asked employees if they were satisfied with their level of use of technology. In general, those employees who reported "more" technology tended to report they were more satisfied with their use of technology as compared with those who reported that they were using less technology. In 2000, we also asked if technology improved employee job performances. Again, those who reported higher levels of technology were more likely to perceive that technology improved their job performance.[12]

During the early phases of our research, it appeared that new technology was viewed as a positive thing. In the next section, we examine if this positive perception is reflected in job and organizational attitudes and, importantly, if this positive connection is sustained through all ten years of our study.

Technology and Employee Attitudes Toward Their Work and Boeing

When examining the impact of technology use, we saw a similar pattern of results as we described in the section on the impact of team involvement and work outcomes. The expected positive relationship between the increased use of technology and key outcomes such as job satisfaction, job involvement, and organizational commitment was evident in 1997, when those employees reporting more technology use over the previous two years also reported significantly more positive attitudes as compared with those reporting similar or lower levels of technology use. In 2000, 2003, and 2006, however, the impact of technology on these attitudes was limited. While those reporting less technology continued to have less favorable attitudes toward their jobs and Boeing, there was no difference at all between those reporting the same, more, or a lot more technology use. In 2003 and 2006, there is even the suggestion of a negative impact of more technology on employee commitment to Boeing; that is, while not statistically significant, those employees reporting more technology, particularly "a lot more," have slightly lower commitment levels than those reporting "the same" level of technology.

These patterns suggested a weakening of the potential benefits of technology on employee attitudes toward their work and Boeing in general. We were left wondering why the expected positive relationship between availability of technology and these attitudes was not sustained over time. As noted in chapter 2, implementation of the DCAC-MRM got off to a rough start. Some employees were still "smarting" from that painful process several years later. Technicians, in particular, were apt to include negative comments about this system in their response to 2006 open-ended questions.

> DCAC/MRM resulted in my job being much more complicated. Changes in drafting standards and bill of materials, which seems to be constant, result in older drawings being very difficult to understand, almost impossible if you're new at it. [male technician with eleven years at Boeing]

> DCAC-MRM has been the biggest impact—totally new way of doing business, new "culture." Has been stressful for us all. Has made my job more difficult. [female technician with twenty-seven years at Boeing]

Despite these types of comments, frustrations with DCAC-MRM did not seem pervasive enough to explain our unexpected results. Further, we would expect these frustrations to have a negative impact in 1997 (when DCAC-MRM was floundering), not in 2006, by which time it had become familiar and was in widespread use. The remainder of this section will explore other possible reasons for these somewhat unexpected findings.

Technology: Is More Always Better?

When looking at more specific attitudes of job challenge and job stress, we find an interesting contrast. As noted earlier in this chapter, technology has been identified as a way to minimize the tedious, repetitive, sometimes mind-numbing tasks that can dampen the intellectual and creative energy of employees. This opens the door for work that is more challenging and interesting—that is, work that utilizes more of the employee's special skills, training, or brainpower, resulting in improved quality of work life. As seen in figure 5.3, with the exception of 2003, when differences were not statistically significant, the increased availability of technology was consistently related to increased percep-

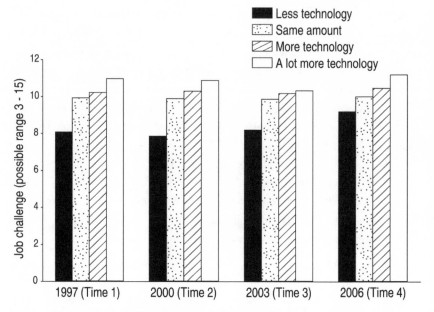

Figure 5.3 Ratings of job challenge by perceived amount of technology change over time

tions of job challenge. However, regarding other indicators of quality of work life, results suggested that this "challenge" was not entirely positive. For example, in figure 5.4, while the pattern of results is not consistent across time, we do see evidence that "a lot more technology" was typically associated with higher levels of job stress. The relationship between more technology and more stress is most noticeable in 2003, the same time period where we saw relatively neutral effects of technology on job challenge.

Interestingly, in 1997 and 2006, periods when technology was likely ramping up on the shop floor (DCAC-MRM in the latter half of the 1990s and 787 innovations in the mid-2000s), those claiming "less technology" also reported relatively high stress levels. Perhaps these employees felt left out or "stuck" in old projects or products. Or, it may be that the contrast of their older technology with new innovations amplified the perceived inefficiencies of their old ways of work. We have no data that illuminate these "less technology" patterns, but several open-ended comments allude to the mixed blessing of technology:

> The biggest most affecting change is the use of computer programs for more tasks and the loss of staff. . . . My job has become much more stressful but also more rewarding as I meet the challenge. [female technician with twenty-six years at Boeing]

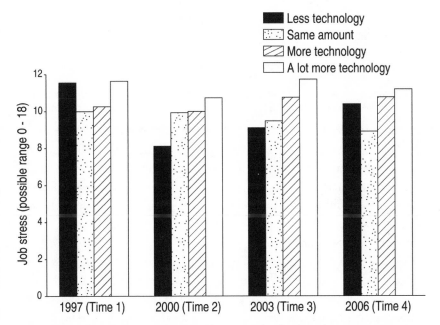

Figure 5.4 Ratings of job stress by perceived amount of technology change over time

Frustrated and engaged. Using new tools and processes that have not been perfected is frustrating because deadlines are a constant. However it does keep one learning and engaged with work. [male technician with fourteen years at Boeing]

When reviewing the open-ended comments,[13] we rarely see a uniformly positive or negative response to technology, as exemplified by these observations by a male manager:

Changes I can think of: Explosion of work and communication done by e-mail. The supply of information has increased by an order of magnitude to individuals and consequently the demand for info from individuals has increased proportionately. . . . Increased e-mail makes my job more reactive as opposed to proactive . . . [and] relaxation of personal work schedules by use of 9/80s, 4/10s, flex time, and virtual office, all of which reduced work related stress. [male manager with thirty years at Boeing]

There are often conflicting perspectives regarding the same tool, even within a single respondent's comment; a sort of "yeah, but . . ." reaction to technology that speaks to employee ambivalence or uncertainty regarding the true benefits or drawbacks of these new ways of work. The two areas where we saw this tension emerge most often are around work-at-home technologies and information/e-mail access.

WORK-AT-HOME TECHNOLOGIES

Many respondents noted the benefits of technology that allowed them to do their work from home or, at least, away from the physical Boeing offices or plants. Information technology has "untethered" many employees from the workplace.[14] Typically, this untethering applies to office workers, managers, and engineers, as work for the hourly ranks and technicians typically remains connected to materials and systems on the shop floor. "Temporal and spatial boundaries of office work are being extended" by what Towers et al. (2006) term Work Extending Technologies (WET): mobile phones, laptops, Black-Berrys and iPhones, and the like.

In effect, office workers are no longer confined to the office and many workers, particularly, but not exclusively, female workers, appreciate the flexibility and work/life balance afforded by these work extending technologies. A female manager noted that technology was a major change at Boeing and she "can do my job more easily and sometimes work from home." Similarly, a male engineer appreciated the "ability to balance family/work life and address 'firefights' without having to go into the plant." Along with the flexibility, several participants noted that work-at-home technology implied a level of trust in their abilities and dependability. A comment by a female office worker reflects the reciprocity implicit in these untethered relationships: "I telecommute three days a week. I live 200 miles from my job site! I like this arrangement. I feel trusted and do not let my job down."

Some respondents also noted that the emergence of technology allows reduction or more flexibility in their work schedules. Flextime and part-time arrangements are more manageable when employees are still able to remain connected to the firm via e-mail and communications tools. For example, another female office worker notes that, for her, "the most important changes are the allowance of part-time (for me) schedules and virtual/telecommuting office. This was not an option two years ago."

Other employees, however, were not as positive about the role of technology in creating boundary-less organizations. Participants talked about working more unpaid overtime that is "easier from home" and how laptops increase productivity but also "cut into personal time." The feeling of working "24/7" was mentioned as often as the feeling of flexibility and freedom. A male exempt worker writes of the "nostalgia for when I wasn't connected everywhere and at all times. [Technology] enhances productivity but intrudes on home life." For these employees, the boundaries of home and work were becoming increasingly blurred. A male manager describes the encroachment of work on his personal life: "I have to work between ten and twenty extra hours per week in order to get things accomplished, which included Saturday and sometimes Sundays. I also find myself working at home."

Work-at-home technologies, then, appear to elicit both positive and negative reactions from Boeing employees. They are not alone in their ambivalence. A study of thirty-three thousand Canadian office workers found similar conflicting findings about the use of work-at-home technologies. About four in ten employees said that technology made it easier to balance work and family responsibilities, while a similar sized group said technology made balance more difficult.[15] The darker side of work-at-home flexibility has been described as part of a "discourse of competitive needs": the need of the company for more productivity for less cost overlaid on the need of individuals for autonomy and control over their workday.[16]

From this more critical perspective, technology is viewed as a means to get more work out of employees without increasing salaries; flexibility is the bait, as it were, on the corporate cost-cutting hook. As the use of these technologies becomes more prevalent, the 24/7 workday becomes normative; not replying to e-mails on Saturday is viewed as an affront or, perhaps, a sign that the employee is not really dedicated to his or her job. The multitasking executive glued to a BlackBerry at his or her child's concert is obviously essential to the firm, an "in demand," indispensable person who must always be hooked into the action of the firm—or, at least, someone who wants to appear that way to others as well as to him- or herself. As more work pushes into the home domain, social connections are also at risk. We see some evidence of this at Boeing. A female office worker, for example, raises concerns about the downsides of the virtual office with its increasingly virtual relationships: "We have learned more computer skills, how to adapt at work and at home to the computer life. More and more people working from home, soon we will all be little robots in our homes losing touch with the physical and emotional contact with people. But!! The company will benefit with flexible hours around the clock to accommodate workers globally."

If work-at-home technologies open the door to more (unpaid as well as paid) work at home, we may see increasingly ambivalent views about both the technology and the organization that "offers" these flexible tools. At Boeing, the negligible, perhaps negative, impact of technology on organizational commitment in 2006 may reflect disillusionment of managers and other exempt workers when outsourcing and global partnering became more prevalent and technology intruded further into their personal lives due to involvement with increasingly global, multi-time-zone teams, vendors, and projects. While we cannot directly test this in our data, we wonder if distancing from colleagues or erosion of social relationships at home and at the workplace may have become too high a price for flexibility and work-at-home convenience.

INFORMATION AVAILABILITY

Respondents frequently noted that technology increased and enhanced their access to information about projects, human resource and benefits data, and news about corporate initiatives and events. Information was kept more current and was more easily shared with colleagues. Within the context of mergers, new airplanes, lean, and offshoring, some respondents identified e-mail as the biggest change they have seen at Boeing over the last several years.

> E-mail access and info related to Boeing suppliers and other non Boeing information. Intranet access is huge improvement over the huge binders for Boeing standards and processes. Many of these were slow to be updated with current information. [male, sixty-four years old, hourly, thirty-five years at Boeing]

> Better communication through the advent of computer software for e-mail, providing better exchange of information between related disciplines. [male, sixty-one years old, hourly, twenty-five years at Boeing]

As the knowledge intensity of work increases, information becomes a critical resource for corporate productivity, the raw material, if you will, for competitive advantage in the twenty-first century. Information is often noted by theorists and practitioners as central to employee empowerment and effective participation across levels of the organization.[17] Technology is increasingly deployed to ensure that the right information is available to the right people at the right time so decisions can be based on the best data available. The right people can be anywhere in the organization, from corner office to shop floor. As an hourly frontline worker wrote, "It is easier to get the information I need to do my job." There is an implicit sense of democracy when information is more readily available to all employees. Intranets, in particular, make it easier for employees to learn about strategic initiatives, financial data, and pending changes in the organization. No longer is information the exclusive domain of the elite ranks of managers; it is shared more equitably across employees, thereby leveling the playing field in the firm.

When access to information increases, then, we might anticipate that employees would feel not only more productive and effective in their jobs, but also more involved in and, ultimately, more committed to Boeing. Open-ended comments in 2006 about information availability often reflected this positive tone as more employees increasingly felt "in the loop" and more connected to Boeing. However, there is a potential drawback to the increased availability of information: sometimes quantity of information is mistaken for "good" information. Technology, casually applied, can metaphorically open the floodgates to a deluge of data, most of it irrelevant, or needed information can be buried in the cyber-haystack that is the company Intranet.

Like many of us, employees at Boeing often commented on feeling overwhelmed with "unimportant" information. E-mail was often viewed as a primary source of information overload. Managers seemed to be particularly burdened by e-mails. For example, two different female managers write:

> Laptops and PCs have been the major change [at Boeing]. They are good for Boeing and individuals now have a good tool but it also adds a tremendous amount of work for us, especially e-mails.

> E-mail . . . is pervading all business interactions and making focus and separation of important/urgent from less important/less urgent projects, tasks, request more difficult.

A male manager reports that he "deletes numerous e-mails without reading just due to time restrictions or they're not important to my management responsibilities." Another female manager succinctly characterizes the mixed blessing of e-mail: "E-mails are pretty much overwhelming. There is more communication but actually more than can be processed."

E-mail was originally designed to be a tool for efficient information transfer, that is, for situations where social cues are not important, immediate feedback is not necessary, and asynchronous communication is nonproblematic.[18] Instead, e-mail is increasingly used as a verbal communication tool rather than a vehicle for the transfer of information. In situations with high ambiguity or charged social dynamics, e-mail can lead to or exacerbate confusion or conflict or both. Importantly, e-mail may be used as a way to avoid difficult face-to-face interactions, which can compound workplace problems and, ultimately, reduce productivity. A male manager has already taken steps to counteract the "e-mail instead of talking" problem: "The [biggest change at Boeing is] huge increase in the use of e-mail. I have forced some of my managers not to use e-mail and meet people face to face to address critical issues."

So, even as technology makes information readily available to many, the sheer volume of information, especially via e-mail, may negate the perceived value of technology. As one manager notes, "You're always buried in e-mail." We think e-mail alone is unlikely to undermine employee attitudes regarding Boeing. It is not a universally held concern, and while managers' opinions of information overload or misuse of e-mail may spill over to their subordinates, we believe this perception is only the tip of a larger "overload iceberg" that may be a primary factor in the weakening link between technology and organizational attitudes.

"Feel always on and tied in, can't escape . . ." Perceptions of overload and stress are likely to be related, not only to information overload as described above, but also to perceived time compression as the amount of work expands to fill the time theoretically made available by more efficient systems. Towers et al. (2006) observe that the "outcome of the ability to complete tasks more quickly is not an increase in the amount of free time available to an individual, but rather an increase in the number of tasks to be completed." Not only does the volume of work increase, but pace of work accelerates as information transfer and communication occurs in real time with expectations of immediate response. Multitasking becomes an essential skill; it is not uncommon for employees to simultaneously participate in a conference call, revise a PowerPoint (online with an entirely different set of co-workers), reply to e-mail, organize their schedule on their BlackBerry, and instant-message with colleagues.[19] As a result, technology feels like it is adding to rather than reducing the burdens in the workplace.

Numerous comments in our 2006 survey suggest that technology added to, rather than reduced, the time pressures of working at Boeing. These comments reflect the emotional intensity of the "time panic"[20] noted by many respondents.

> Feel always on and tied in, can't escape, there is always more to do than time to do it, can't ever catch up much less get ahead. [female manager, thirty-eight years old, fifteen years at Boeing]

> More information—need to assimilate what is important and not. Higher workloads. Managing own career path. Total overall effect is that there is much more expected of us not only with direct work responsibilities, but we are expected to take care of all the administration responsibilities that go along with our daily work, our career and training path, travel arrangements, housekeeping (garbage, cleaning, stocking printer paper, etc., etc.). There is a lot less time to accomplish real engineering work. [female engineer, fifty-six years old, fifteen years at Boeing]

Interestingly, these types of comments were often from the younger workers in our sample, perhaps those who initially embraced technology, then found themselves too deeply enmeshed with their "efficiency enhancing tools." And, not surprisingly, hourly production employees were less likely to be impacted by these work-at-home issues given the nature of their work. The portability of office or engineering tasks may be both a blessing and curse for managers, engineers, technicians, and office workers.

In addition to the pace and volume of work, we noted earlier that technology had been introduced, or has been perceived to be introduced, at Boeing at a fairly high level over the ten-year study period. The advancing pace of information technology increased pressure to renew and upgrade skills in increasingly complex systems while simultaneously increasing expectations for productivity.[21] Wang and colleagues coined the term "technostress" to describe the "discomposure, fear, tenseness, and anxiety when one is learning and using computer technology directly or indirectly, that ultimately ends in psychological and emotional repulsion and prevents one from further learning or using computer technology" (2008). Not only does technostress inhibit acquisition of new technology, it also is associated with lower levels of productivity. Comments by a Boeing shop floor worker suggest that the sustained level of change in new manufacturing technology may have reached a point of diminishing returns for some employees.

> There seems to be an inexhaustible amount of new processes which add more work, but are nonvalue activities. With the new processes come a never ending learning curve. . . . I feel as if it is impossible to keep up and understand all the information and process changes affecting my workload.
>
> As far as the constant changes in technology it feels like you're chasing your tail and things are really much more inefficient. [male office worker with sixteen years at Boeing]

> Working faster and harder is just making me burn out that much faster. With emotional resiliency low, I'm then forced to do everything on my own from daily PC problems to trying to manage career and skills development. I feel as though no one is looking out for me anymore. The focus is all about productivity improvement and yet we are being self-helped to death having to do everything on our own while trying to actually do our jobs! [male technician, forty-five years old, twenty-two years at Boeing]

Beyond the overload of information, pace of work, and pace of technology innovation, we should remember that this innovation was occurring within a larger context of constant organizational change. Many open-ended comments regarding the "biggest change at Boeing" were simply long laundry lists of disconnected changes; new technology or computer systems was only one of the myriad changes happening at Boeing over the ten-year study period.

> Always new computer programs to learn—upgrades. The fact that change is now the norm—no more getting comfortable in a position and thinking you will be there forever. If your job doesn't change, your manager will, or the people you work with. [male technician, eleven years at Boeing]

Workers and managers were not simply learning "a" new system, they were learning multiple systems while simultaneously absorbing the impacts of layoffs, reorganizations, offloading, and teaming. Employees eventually reach a point where they are simply unable to learn, adapt, and effectively react to the unrelenting pace of change.[22] Resistance may not be a case of fear or unease regarding the technology itself, but a result of cognitive and, perhaps, physical overload due to unrelenting changes in the workplace. Employees are overwhelmed and shut down to reserve energy for what they perceive to be the most important or pressing tasks of immediate consequence.[23] When organizational change and technological innovations are out of sync, such as when a new purchasing system is at odds with new vendor management procedures, or when transformation of manufacturing systems occurs in the middle of a merger, the sense of chaos and complexity increases exponentially.[24] Under these conditions, it may not be surprising that more technology is associated with more stress and ambivalence toward innovation.

CONCLUSION

Teams and technology have often been described as instrumental in realizing the potential of transformative business strategies. It is difficult to imagine the success of lean production without the enabling support of cross-functional teams and technological innovation in manufacturing processes. Additionally, teams and technology have been identified as vehicles to improve the quality of work life of employees while simultaneously ramping up productivity and profitability for the firm.

While it would be naïve to claim that Boeing executives introduced teams and technology for the primary purpose of creating happy employees, the literature and business press certainly suggest that these new ways of work should empower and engage employees in their work. We expected that employees with greater levels of team or technology involvement would have more positive attitudes toward their work and Boeing.[25] Surprisingly, we saw deterioration or, at best, a flattening of most job attitudes over time in relation to more teams and technology. Open-ended comments in 2006 suggested a growing cynicism and frustration with the rhetoric and reality of teams and technology as well as with the Boeing management team that promoted these innovations.

Several factors may have contributed to the, at best, neutral impacts of these new ways of work over time. The subjective experiences of social cohesion and meaningful decision-making were limited for many team members. The unique experience of teams also became mired in the "teaming" of virtually every work group at Boeing, and the positive image of teams also seemed to be tarnished by the negative halo of the emerging, largely disliked, team culture. Technology certainly permitted employees to do more with less and offered substantial flexibility as the walls of the workplace dissolved into cyberspace. However, we saw that technology was a double-edged sword: productivity expectations escalated along with norms for real-time 24/7 access to work and workers. Intrusions on personal and family time increased as both paid and unpaid overtime was facilitated by BlackBerrys and laptops. The increased pace of work and innovation overwhelmed the ability of some employees to cope and adapt; cognitive and physical limits may have been reached or breached for those immersed in rapid-fire change over sustained periods of time.

We also wonder if the ends of teams and technology didn't impact attitudes toward work and commitment to the organization. Teams may have lost their vigor as the organization shifted from TQM values of the 1980s and early 1990s and more strongly toward the cost-cutting and efficiency goals of the short-term shareholder value philosophy. Teams and technology are central to lean and outsourcing strategies; a key outcome of these strategies is often job loss. We found, for example, that employees who reported using a lot more technology also tended to have a reduced sense of job security across all four survey time periods. Employees often wrote about teaming themselves out of jobs (if not their own, someone else's) or using technology to allow one person to do the work of three former colleagues.

So, despite some evidence of positive influence of these new ways of work, we also found that teams and technology at Boeing may have interfered with, rather than amplified, the passion and creativity of employees. Implemented within a context of short-term shareholder value reflected in lean, outsourcing, and downsizing strategies, the end goals of teams and technology were not always, perhaps even often, in the best interests of employees. While Boeing may have profited from these new ways of work, we wonder what potential remains untapped and what business results might have been if more employees had also profited from these new ways of work. Chapter 9 offers additional thoughts as to how these ways of work might reduce additional "bruising and battering" of employees during times of turbulence.

Chapter 6 Managing Through Change

Managers are expected to do significantly more work, handle more number of employees, and meet more business targets (with vague plan and strategy in place) with little to no administrative help. There are more tasks managers need to handle that are non-value-added. Continuous effort to reduce cost resulted in constant job security fears for employees. I have employees located in five different cities. It's difficult to keep in touch with them. The fact that I manage two distinctively different groups makes it difficult for me to get to know my customers. I feel increased level of stress due to my job and I no longer feel passionate about my job.
—*Female manager, twenty years at Boeing*

Frontline employees were not the only ones working through turbulence at Boeing. Managers—especially first-line and second-line managers who had to cope with new duties and less support, and who had to deal face-to-face with stressed and distressed employees—were not immune from the perpetual changes at Boeing Commercial Airplanes. Boeing, mirroring many other large industrial firms, was organized for most of its history like a multitiered pyramid. Thousands of supervisors or first-line managers reported to hundreds of second-level managers and directors who, in turn, reported to even fewer vice presidents. Not surprisingly, then, our survey sample was dominated by first- and second-level managers.[1] As a result, findings reported in this chapter largely reflect the opinions and perspectives of managers "closer to the ground" who interact more directly with nonmanagerial workers than do executive level managers.[2]

A manager is "an individual who is in charge of a certain group of tasks, or a certain subset of a company."[3] A manager is usually in charge of people but can also be in charge of a project or set of projects, while a supervisor is a first-line manager who monitors and directs a specific group of employees in a specific set of tasks. Despite the manager title, first- and second-line managers were fairly low on the Boeing totem pole.

As we describe later in this chapter, managing in the postindustrial era is moving away from authoritarian "controlling and directing" by the explicit exercise of power and toward a more participative model emphasizing teamwork and bottom-up decision-making. Managers are increasingly responsible for creating an environment that enables and inspires or, at a minimum, motivates workers to identify with the company and work toward common goals and objectives. In today's world of perpetual change and frequent upheaval, managers play an even more critical role as "sense-givers," defining the mental models or interpretative frames about what is important, how work is to be accomplished, and who really matters in the workplace (that is, the relative pecking order of fellow workers, superiors, customers, shareholders, suppliers, and larger community).[4]

It is important, then, to understand how managers perceive change and how these perceptions, in turn, influence their perceptions of the organization. It is surprising how little work has been done to understand the perspectives and needs of this pivotal group of employees. Not only do these lower-level managers organize work and "make real" the policies articulated by senior managers and top executives, they are instrumental in setting the stage for how employees perceive and respond to what is happening around them. No matter how carefully crafted the official message is, managerial attitudes will inevitably be communicated to subordinates. Their words of hope and optimistic demeanor are critical to rallying the troops in times of organizational stress and chaos. If managers become cynical, alienated, discouraged, or simply exhausted by change, if their commitment to the organization and engagement with work is negatively impacted by living through turbulence, their subordinates may struggle to maintain their own enthusiasm for their work or trust in the organization.

In this chapter, we explore in more detail how living through turbulence impacted the work, role, and attitudes of managers at Boeing.[5] In addition, we look at the impact of the flattening organizational structure on managerial aspirations, asking whether managers and aspiring managers continue to see meaningful opportunity for moving up the ladder at Boeing. Are the traditional pathways for success still open for ambitious workers? If not, what has replaced those opportunities? Who is viewed as best suited for managerial roles at Boeing, and what are the implications for worker (managerial and non-managerial) commitment and enthusiasm for their work?

MANAGERIAL ATTITUDES—DIFFERENT THAN OTHER EMPLOYEES?

When compared with other employees, managers usually have more favorable attitudes toward their firms.[6] This is generally the pattern we found at Boeing —managers' attitudes toward Boeing were typically more positive across all four survey periods as compared with other Boeing employees. However, their attitudes over the long haul showed the same pattern as other employees. For example, ratings for our measure of organizational commitment (see figure 6.1) were significantly higher for managers at all four time periods, but we see a substantial drop in 2000 that remains in 2003. Consistent with other employees, managers' attitudes rebounded in 2006, reflecting better times in the company, but levels remain slightly below 1997 survey ratings. Similar patterns were evident for measures such as trust in management integrity and perceived organizational support and, to a lesser degree, ratings of job satisfaction (see appendix for descriptions of these measures). Managers, then, were not entirely immune from the impact of change at Boeing; like others in the company, their attitudes toward Boeing often took the same negative track in 2000 and 2003.

Even more telling are managers' intentions to quit Boeing, a reflection of their psychological distancing or willingness to separate themselves from employment at Boeing (see figure 6.2). In 1997, managers were substantially less likely than other employees to report a willingness to leave Boeing. However, in 2000, when many of the merger, technology, and lean-related changes were in full swing, we see a strong uptick in managers' willingness to leave the company. In fact, this is one of the few instances where the distinction between manager and nonmanager attitudes disappears: managers were as likely as non-managers to be looking for or thinking about other opportunities for employment. By 2003, the gap between managers and nonmanagers returns—sub-

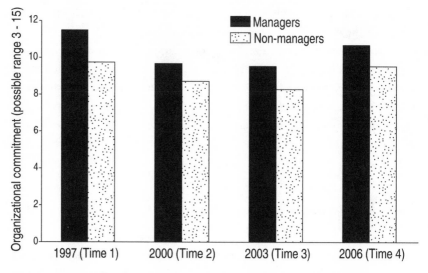

Figure 6.1 Ratings of organizational commitment: comparison of managers and nonmanagers

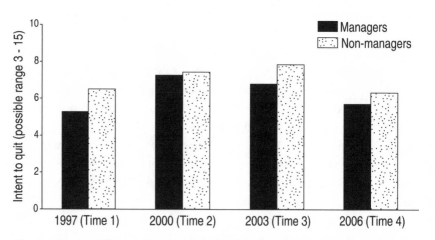

Figure 6.2 Ratings of intent to quit: comparison of managers and nonmanagers

stantially explained by the increasing likelihood among nonmanagers to quit. Finally, attitudes improve among managers in the fourth survey in 2006, but again, we see no statistical difference between the two groups. Managers were as willing as nonmanagers to leave Boeing for other employment. This may be our strongest indication that the changes over the study period took a toll on the relationship between Boeing and its managers.[7]

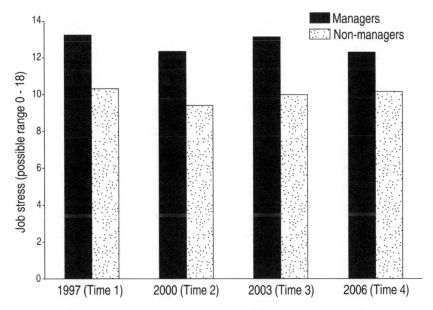

Figure 6.3 Ratings of job stress: comparison of managers and nonmanagers

The remainder of this chapter explores in more detail the possible drivers of this change, using our quantitative survey data as one input into this exploration and also leveraging the rich qualitative materials from interviews and 2006 survey open-ended questions.[8]

THE STRESS OF BEING A MANAGER AT BOEING

The role of manager was stressful during the ten years of our study. Survey results over all four time periods show large gaps between managers' and nonmanagers' perceptions of job stress (see figure 6.3). While job stress levels were consistently perceived as high for both groups across the entire ten years of our study, managers consistently gave higher ratings for job stress than did nonmanagers. Similar patterns were seen for measures such as role overload and job challenge, but the gap between managers and nonmanagers was not as dramatic. In general, then, managers reported feeling stressed, overloaded, and challenged during the ten years of our study. What was driving these perceptions? One could argue that the role of the manager is, inherently and inescapably, stressful and demanding. But is there any evidence that the myriad of organizational changes at Boeing were at least partially responsible for these sustained stress levels? Since our survey was not designed to delve into the nuances of the manager role, we turn here to the qualitative material to explore possible drivers of these perceptions.

The Expanding Role of Manager

The comment opening this chapter captures the range of pressures experienced by managers as Boeing dramatically shifted gears in the ten years of our study. Other managers also commented on the sheer volume of tasks as their span of control increased within the context of the other dramatic changes occurring within our study period.

> Boeing has made a lot of changes in organization structure and a reduction of management. This has put more responsibility on each individual manager and many things are left undone. [female manager, nineteen years at Boeing]

> My job responsibilities changed from managing a single skill [manufacturing engineering] which I was very familiar with, to managing three different skill codes, two of which I am not very familiar with. This has been a big change which has taken me out of my comfort level and forced me to learn a new job. The outsourcing of Design and Manufacturing Engineering work has caused a lot of concern and stress among the employees that report to me. This causes more stress in my job. [male manager, twenty-three years at Boeing]

"More" was a common theme across many managers' comments: more work, more employees spread over more locations, more aggressive business targets, more pressure to reduce costs, more technology, and, as result, more stress. "More" was particularly noticeable in comments about administrative tasks. Manufacturing was not the only area of the company to get aggressively leaned and streamlined via new technology; support staff in many areas had been aggressively trimmed with many tasks shifted to managers or, as one male manager described these changes, "dumping of their traditional and legal responsibilities onto first-line managers." Many respondents, both managers and nonmanagers, noted that human resource (HR) support had all but evaporated, replaced by an automated, online "Total Access" system for benefits and other personnel management tasks.

> As a first-level manager of a group of research scientists I have seen the support organizations evaporate around me (HR and finance and training) and be replaced with Web-based processes that I must execute myself, so that I have become the accountant, personnel rep, and training facilitator as well as supervisor for my group. At the same my group has expanded from 16 people to 35, so I am doing the work

of two first-line managers and a senior manager. The net effect is: my work is never done, there is always a backlog. I plug away and try to not let it stress me out. [male manager, thirty-one years at Boeing]

Lots of my time is wasted on non-value BS items that used to be easier, or used to be done by someone else. It takes way too much of my time and energy to navigate the convoluted Total Access and other HR self-help systems, then I have to fix it myself anyway because the systems are useless, help people are clueless, or my problem is a unique one. All the time I spend on non-value-added stuff takes away time from me being with my group. [female manager, eleven years at Boeing]

When employees are confused, managers and supervisors get pulled in to help problem-solve and troubleshoot the system because "the centralization of HR and other tools has hindered getting help from real people who know anything." Several comments linked perceptions of overload directly with the increased burdens of HR as "managers have absorbed the personnel function." As one manager succinctly writes: "The burden of administrative duties pushed to managers is insane!" In addition, managers are more involved in orchestrating training for their staff members: identifying needs, finding appropriate training courses, and providing follow-on coaching is handled increasingly by managers, all within the context of other time and work pressures. "Managers have an impossible assignment. We have to be everything for our employees: more time with them, career counseling, coaching and personnel, complete admin tasks (hiring, salary planning, retention, etc.), and still be involved in our business. I think we cannot be fully successful at all of those and do a good job at each. This adds a lot of pressure and time to try and be successful" (male manager, twenty-five years at Boeing).

Between a Rock and a Hard Place

As the work of the manager expanded, the feeling of being squeezed between subordinates and senior management increased. Not only was there perceived time compression (too much to do, too little time), but as seemingly endless new initiatives were pushed down the organizational pipeline by senior management, lower-level managers struggled with communicating and, frankly, selling often unpleasant changes to their employees. Being between a rock and a hard place is not an unusual position for managers, especially middle managers. Some might say this is a primary role of a middle or frontline manager: filtering and translating upper management directives to subordinates who may or may not be particularly interested in or enthused about implementing needed changes in their day-to-day work.

Open-ended comments at our 2006 survey hint at the squeeze on managers as the rock and hard place became tighter and tighter. Managers were not always convinced that senior-level decisions were sound but were nevertheless in the position of trying to sell these decisions to subordinates. A relatively young manager writes about her concerns regarding the impacts of corporate decisions on employees as well as the well-being of the company: "I watched the fabrication division, where I worked for 15 years, shrink in half. I managed organizations that downsized by 40–50 percent and I felt sad for three reasons: 1) skilled and loyal employees were forced out. 2) more and more work landed on existing employees and this has resulted in a lot of poor quality work. 3) my gut tells me there is significant risk in outsourcing so much work—which results in some anxiety."

A male manager simply notes: "I'm trying to explain what's going on. They don't believe the message." This "I don't know how to explain what we're doing to employees" theme was echoed in several comments written by managers. Another manager with nearly twenty years' experience at Boeing writes about the challenges of obtaining buy-in from her team, an admittedly easier task as corporate fortunes improved toward our 2006 survey: "As a manager I have been responsible to implement strategies, communicate the goals and vision, and engage the employees. This has been a difficult change for people to accept and lots of emotions to work through. Most people are on board and excited about the future. At least in the up cycle."

As their span of control increased, many managers had to take on functions or work groups entirely unrelated to their own areas of expertise. So, at the same time several managers were trying to establish, even sell, the credibility of unpopular corporate-level decisions, their own credibility with their employees was eroding. The shift toward "professional" rather than "up through the ranks" managers (detailed later in this chapter) also contributed to distance between some managers and their subordinates. Several comments from non-managers, as well as from managers, suggest that negotiating the rock and hard place became even more uncomfortable, and possibly less effective, as supervisors had to communicate unpopular strategies to workers who felt increasingly suspicious of or alienated from management.

> I was always very interactive with the hourly employees that worked for me and 95 percent of the time had a very good rapport with my employees. I witnessed this working relationship struggle as new managers were moved, removed or replaced with people that had a hard time communicating with a blue collar work force. [male manager, twenty-five years at Boeing]

Senior managers (2nd levels and above) have lost contact with what is going on the floor. Lean Mfg. is good but the push is way too hard. There is no buy-in from the factory personnel. It's been a long time since they have been there or not at all. [male manager, twenty-four years at Boeing]

The biggest change [over the last several years] is the amount of time management spends in meetings and not on the floor and available to employees. Total lack of direction and not addressing employee issues that contribute to the success of the company. Management has no idea what happens on the shop floor or our process. [female line worker, seventeen years at Boeing]

The Shift from Tyrant to Coach:
The Changing Role of Managers at Boeing

The structural and strategic changes at Boeing not only increased the (perceived) amount of work handled by managers, but had substantial implications for the very nature of the managerial role. As noted earlier, the traditional managerial role typically includes planning, setting objectives, managing resources, monitoring results, and, of course, controlling subordinates. Control and authority are, in fact, defining elements of the traditional manager role;[9] much of the traditional manager's work revolves around telling people what to do, when to do it, and, importantly, how to do it. These old-school managers were variously described by Boeing employees as "cracking the whip," "bossing people around," "dictatorial," "autocratic," and "tyrannical." These managers were, historically, white and male, so the term "good ol' boys" was also used in employee comments as shorthand for the traditional manager at Boeing, as we shall explore in more detail in chapter 8.

Larger managerial trends in the United States have shifted away from the tyrannical manager; the transactional manager has been supplanted by the transformational manager, authoritarian by charismatic, task-focused by people-focused, and so forth.[10] At Boeing, employees often referred to the transition away from "Theory X" managers, referring to the framework developed by McGregor in the 1960s.[11] While this model has been subsequently replaced by other management frameworks in both research and practice, the terminology of "X and Y" is clearly embedded at Boeing and influences how employees view managers and managerial styles. Boeing's move in the early 1990s into the Total Quality Management world of self-managed teams pushed managers even further away from the traditional authoritarian role, and lean production continues the emphasis on collaborative decision-making and autonomous workers.

The new world of management, then, focuses on people skills, team-building, employee engagement, and decentralization of authority. Many comments regarding the biggest change at Boeing centered around this transition, and, in general, most employees and many managers commented positively on the more relaxed environment at Boeing. As one technician observed: "The 'Theory X' managers are gone. When I started at Boeing twenty-four years ago management was strict and intimidating. I never initiated contact with my manager. Now all the managers I know are very friendly and approachable. I really like my manager. It makes coming to work stress-free and enjoyable."

In noting a reduction in yelling, screaming, and/or cussing several respondents not surprisingly tended to comment on a friendlier, less stressful environment. An office worker with twenty-six years of experience at Boeing also notes that "the positive changes have enhanced my trust and loyalty of the company attempting to 'humanize' the environment." A female manager also believes that "moving away from Theory 'X' management and empowering and engaging non-mgmt employees contributes to a feeling of being valued." Finally, and not least important, several employees also believed that this new environment was associated with greater productivity, effectiveness, and innovation, their own as well as that of co-workers.

While the general reaction to this transition to "new" manager was primarily positive, we were a bit surprised at the frequency of negative comments regarding the move away from "traditional" management. Critics of the new way often used terms such as "touchy-feely" to describe what they believed was an overly soft, overly people-focused workplace that emphasized process over production. While one shop floor worker said he actually "missed the good ol' boys," others seemed to feel that the pendulum had simply swung too far away from managers being managers, that is, being accountable for getting work done as well as supporting the needs of their employees. The term "lack of accountability" emerged in several of these more critical comments:

> I think going from Theory X to a more compassionate way of managing was a turning point. The lack of accountability and discipline has made for many lazy unproductive employees. Hourly workers where I last worked just did as they pleased with no consequences. [male shop floor worker, twenty-seven years at Boeing]

> Too much focus on soft skills. Lack of accountability, people are not pushed to perform and be responsible for actions or lack thereof. Quality of product has diminished from both Boeing and vendors. [male manager, twenty-seven years at Boeing]

Several managers seemed to feel they were constantly walking a tightrope trying to meet increasingly aggressive production goals while maintaining a "nice" environment for employees.[12] The balance between effective production and effective people management was a struggle for managers, and several mentioned feeling helpless in enforcing standards or dealing with behavioral problems because employees would "run to HR" and complain about being mistreated. One manager said he felt violated when employees abused the system.

> There is frustration when I deal with HR on employee performance issues. HR is too soft and doesn't want to take any action so this puts more pressure on managers who would like to have some recourse when an employee is not performing. [male manager, sixteen years at Boeing]

> Discipline has become too lax. Managers are not backed by the HR and are helpless (in many cases) to get an 8 hr day out of their employees. My effectiveness as a manager is lessened. [female manager, twenty-three years at Boeing]

So, while most managers and employees appreciated the new managerial approach, there were those who were concerned that the focus on empowering the workers was leaving the work behind.

At least one manager apparently became so frustrated with the balancing act that he left Boeing after twenty-seven years of employment: "We could not tell people to 'Get to work!' There is way too much about protecting person rights, rather than making them do the right thing. Way too touchy-feely."

Several other respondents also felt that the increased pressure and shifting responsibilities of being a manager at the "new" Boeing outweighed the benefits; these individuals made a deliberate decision to leave their management positions and return to the "more sane" role of an individual contributor. Ironically, not only were nonmonetary costs of their job reduced, monetary benefits were often higher than when they were in their management role.

> I have been a Boeing manager for 10 years. It used to be fun. Boeing has put more and more responsibility on the 1st level manager including the enforcement of company policy. We are liable when an employee abuses company policy. That, along with a reduction in HR support (I have to do everything thru the Web) makes the 1st level management job the least desired job at Boeing. It's usually just a matter of time before 1st levels decide it's not worth it and go back to an engineering job. The expectations are just too great. [female engineer, nineteen years at Boeing]

> It's better to be out of management and not have to deal with people issues in this day and age. Lack of incentive to stay in management is making this decision easier. [male manager, fourteen years at Boeing]

> I finally became fed up with it as a manager, and 18 months ago, requested to leave management to be an engineer again. As a SPEEA member, there are limits to how

much they can demand from me, and I'm not constantly pressured to do more with less. I am so much happier, and the pay is better! Now I just live for retirement. [female engineer, twenty-six years at Boeing]

The want to advance any further than 1st level management was taken from me. When politics is more important than results, there is no need to advance. [male manager, twenty-five years at Boeing]

The role of the manager became both quantitatively and qualitatively more demanding at Boeing. Some of the demands, such as being more people-focused and team-oriented, were generally viewed as positive, particularly by subordinates. However, even positive changes take a toll on managers and these, coupled with increased workloads and reduced administrative support, have led some to abandon the manager role altogether.

IMPLEMENTING LAYOFFS—A PARTICULARLY STRESSFUL NEW ROLE

Few managers were left untouched by the layoff drama. A small number were themselves victims of WARN notices, but many more were directly involved in executing the layoffs. In our longitudinal sample of employees who responded to all four surveys, we found that over 70 percent of managers had handed out WARN[13] and layoff notices at some point during our study period. And most of those had done so more than once. Our analysis of their survey responses and of their comments reveals that doing this work exacted a steep emotional toll.

Before we look at their reactions, it might be useful to review briefly how the layoff process worked at Boeing during the years of our study. Top executives, of course, decided on the size and timing of mass layoffs. First-line managers (that is, those who directly supervised nonmanagement employees) and middle managers (who might also supervise first-line managers) were then assigned the task of carrying out the cuts. In the case of hourly production workers covered by a union contract, the selection of who was to be targeted for layoff was largely determined by seniority, with more junior employees being the first to be let go. Workers with high seniority in positions targeted for elimination could transfer to other positions in the company and "bump" workers with lower seniority out of those positions. So although managers of hourly workers did not select the individuals who were laid off, they still met with and delivered WARN and termination notices to their unfortunate subordinates.

The process for the salaried workforce was more complicated and probably also more stressful. Specific percentage targets for cuts were provided to various committees that corresponded to particular functional areas in the organization. Managers in these committees debated and negotiated the relative importance of particular skill sets the company needed to retain. Assessments of the skills and performance of individual workers were made primarily by frontline managers, and, after extensive discussion with other managers in these committee meetings, each salaried worker was given a grade of A, B, or C.[14] These so-called retention ratings were then conveyed to each salaried employee, including all engineers and technical employees, in a face-to-face meeting with their supervisor. Employees receiving a C grade were designated "surplus" and were the ones most likely to be laid off in a downsizing. Those receiving a B grade could also be vulnerable to layoffs depending on the level of workforce reduction required. In the post-9/11 downsizing, layoffs reached high into the B ratings in some work areas. So managers of salaried workers not only delivered the bad news to employees but were to some degree responsible for selecting those who were let go.

We should also note that, according to the vast majority of workers we surveyed across the four time periods, Boeing treated those it let go "well" or "very well" (over 75 percent checked these response categories at each wave) and implemented a "somewhat fair" or "very fair" layoff process (over 66 percent at each wave). Moreover, we found little difference in these attitudes between hourly workers, who are covered by the seniority provisions negotiated by the machinists' union, and salaried employees, who are subject to the more discretionary termination process.

Still, it would be wrong to imply that the difference in the process didn't upset managers who supervised hourly workers. One expressed frustration that there was very little he could do to "show loyalty to high performers" who had "put their heart and soul into the job," whereas those with greater seniority but poorer performance were protected and "allowed to stay." Another, while acknowledging that the union contract forced Boeing to keep senior employees over high performers, was relieved that "that system gets me off the hook" because she didn't have to select who among the hourlies would be laid off.

The retention rating process also had its detractors, who complained about how politics or the buddy system sometimes influenced decisions. A female manager described how some managers got together before retention rating meetings to form alliances about how they would vote to help protect their favorite employees. She claimed to have seen "people set up and top notch people downgraded through political circumstances outside their control" and compared the process to the television show *Survivor*. She also noted that if the cuts were very deep, as was the case in the post-9/11 period, managers were forced to downgrade good performers. In fact, given the forced distribution of the retention rating system, with 40 percent of employees categorized as grade A, 40 percent as B, and another 20 percent as C, with each successive round of cuts more and more high performers ended up being reclassified into lower grades. An experienced old hand at these negotiations reported, "I am proud of the fact that I have been a manager for over 16 years and have never had to lay anyone off—[it] took a lot of work and knowledge of organizational politics."

Despite the seniority provisions for the hourly workforce and the general sentiment that Boeing tried and largely succeeded in carrying out the layoffs in a fair and caring manner, managers could not avoid the acute emotional discomfort caused by the job they had to do. Many of the managers we interviewed vividly described strong personal reactions to these painful tasks. A female manager said the recent 30 percent cut in staff she had to implement was "the most catastrophic experience of her career to date." It was "devastating" and "gut wrenching" and one she hoped never to experience again. A male manager who had to "walk six to ten people to the door" in one year talked of how difficult a task it was and how "oftentimes, the employees are crying and asking me what are they going to do." Yet another, with twenty-two years of service, who said the experience had made her an "absolute wreck," chastised herself for crying when she gave out her first notice and thought to herself, "How inappropriate and shallow for me to cry" in that situation. Tearing up as she described the anguish she felt in evaluating employees in preparation for layoffs, a woman in her thirties called the experience "just terrible . . . you take it home with you and you can never get away from it. People call you at home to see if you know anything."

Sometimes the whole process piled one tragedy on top of another. A woman manager recounted how she had to deliver a WARN notice to a woman who was on leave because her mother had cancer. She chose to call her from her home for privacy and regretted that she had to tell her by phone but felt she had no other option. She described seeing the "entire grief process" in her one-hour conversation. A senior male manager echoed this observation when he said laying people off was "like mourning a death—there is a grieving process—a realization that more than just the employee's life will be affected."

While one male manager noted that he "has never had anyone become aggressive with him," some managers noted potentially dangerous situations emerging out of WARN or layoff discussions. One told us of stories he'd heard of "spooky" behavior by those who had received WARN notices. A second manager told of a woman who apparently announced she felt homicidal and was escorted off the grounds by Boeing security. Another recounted how a man who, after receiving a WARN notice, showed pictures of his children to a manager of another department as he asked that manager if he had any openings. Fear, anger, numbness, or simply "being down" seemed to increase the perceived likelihood of unpredictable behavior on the part of employees. This, naturally, increased the tension experienced by managers as the company moved into each round of layoffs.

First- and second-level managers found little escape from these emotionally taxing face-to-face situations. Although many felt great sympathy for those they had to lay off, many also understandably adopted defensive and protective postures. Some managers talked of becoming "calloused" or "emotionally numb," and one joked that they might need to go to a camp where they "could learn to be nice and happy" and lose the callousness that had built up over the years. Another found comfort by telling himself that his employees "are pretty resourceful and will find better things after they leave." A female supervisor spoke of wanting to "tune out and shut down" during downsizing periods and of not "wanting to get close to people until things stabilized." An hourly employee also noticed many co-workers and managers distancing themselves from those about to be laid off. Such emotional detachment was confirmed by our survey results, which found that managers who had handed out WARNs were somewhat more likely than those who hadn't to report that they treated people at work as if they were "impersonal objects"; this group agreed that their jobs were "hardening" them emotionally and had made them "more callous" toward people at work.[15]

Finally, working in a downsizing environment also took its toll on managers' overall sense of job security. As noted earlier, most of the managers' job attitudes were significantly more positive than those of nonmanagers. However, as noted in figure 6.4, managers shared the same sense of job insecurity as nonmanagers at the time of the second survey in 2000 (that is, there was no statistical difference between manager and nonmanager ratings of job security). And, while not showing as dramatic a drop as nonmanagers in the third survey in 2003, managers' perceptions of their own job security had dropped. We see a strong rebound for both groups by the time of the fourth survey in 2006, as Boeing's processes and prospects improved. But the fact remains that during times of downsizing, when managers were already called upon to do the dirty work of

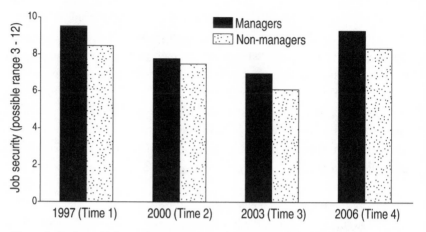

Figure 6.4 Ratings of job security: comparison of managers and nonmanagers

implementing layoffs, their own sense of insecurity was likely to increase stress levels and make them even less emotionally available to help their employees cope with job loss or the loss of colleagues and friends.

BECOMING A MANAGER—COMPRESSING
THE CAREER LADDER

While a few respondents perceived that the number of managers at Boeing was greater than in previous years, most respondents felt that there had been a constriction in management positions and, therefore, management opportunities at Boeing. This is consistent with other research that shows that management jobs, particularly middle management jobs, are declining in U.S. companies.[16] Several nonmanagers perceived that lean, downsizing, and outsourcing strategies, along with current employee rating/ranking systems, capped advancement opportunities, leaving them to wonder what there was to work for. A male engineer with forty years of service writes: "My chances of promotion are stagnated which tends to be a challenge on self motivation. Ranking in the organization kills personal incentive and morale because each person knows that unless you can all of a sudden walk on water, your status will never change and even then it probably will not. Receiving peer awards are nice but it completely removes management responsibility of having to worry about rewarding personnel under them, again where is the encouragement for improving one's self."

For the older nonmanagers, frustrations were even more acute as they saw advancement opportunities shift to younger workers. Rules had changed and

years of service and experience seemed to carry little weight, they felt, in promotion decisions. One hourly worker writes that he "witnessed many very good
first level managers forced to the hourly ranks and replaced with younger college people at a lower rate of pay." Another hourly worker with thirty-two years
of service at Boeing observed that there was not much effort "to advance the
older workers like myself. Management does not want to spend extra time on
us but puts all their effort into younger employees and managers." A sixty-
year-old office worker echoed this feeling: "Sorry to say my age has put me out
of the picture for promotion so I have taken my current job and work to the
best of my ability so that I feel some sense of success and fulfillment." In effect,
despite these employees' belief that they still have much to offer Boeing (and
would like to), they concluded there were "no points for experience" in the
new Boeing. As one technician observed: "Long-term employees often do not
have college degrees but instead have years of experience and have worked their
way up the ladder. Experience no longer counts, a degree does, even if in an unrelated field" (female technician, twenty-one years at Boeing).

So if these older, more experienced nonmanagers weren't getting the promotions, who was? According to many employees, "college boys" and "outsiders" now dominated the limited management jobs. The shift to professional
managers defined by degrees rather than by experience was clearly viewed as a
slap in the face to those who had given many years of service on the shop floors
of Boeing, an embarrassment to workers with decades of "real" experience who
now had to "clean up after all the poor decisions" made by their managers.
There was obvious frustration, even disdain, for supervisors who had book
learning but no in-the-trenches knowledge of day-to-day operations and basic
manufacturing processes.

> We continually have to spend time explaining to supervisors why things have to be
> done in a certain order or way. This takes time away from what we should be doing
> and keeps them from attending to the things that we need them to do for us. [male
> shop floor worker, twenty years at Boeing]

> Boeing management is no longer technically minded. They are supervisors with al-
> most no knowledge of the technical. Therefore, they really don't know what an en-
> gineer is doing or why things aren't going the way they should. They also lack lead-
> ership in technical decisions, which causes problems in getting things done. [male
> engineer, eighteen years at Boeing]

> I talked to a friend in that shop that said they hired someone that had never done
> electrical but took the required classes. I don't like math. Geometry is a requirement

[for promotion], but the only thing that comes close is in the job you have to use a 6 in. scale. I know how to do that. The person they hired does not. They also had no clue on how to tie the wire bundle. [female shop floor worker, sixteen years at Boeing]

Not only were these new managers and supervisors perceived to be lacking practical knowledge of "how to make an airplane" and unable to make "intelligent decisions" when faced with manufacturing or production problems, they were also often viewed as "not one of us." The schism between management and labor became wider as "manufacturing is no longer represented by manufacturing" (male shop floor worker, sixteen years at Boeing), and workers were "being managed by people who were pretty much out of touch with the reality of building multi-million dollar aircraft" (male shop floor worker, thirty-five years at Boeing). A sense of "us" and "them" often characterized comments about new managers.

The value of an employee cannot be based on a degree or piece of paper. . . . I had been a manager with great appreciation for the position and the people that made our group successful. Now I have difficulty respecting my managers who do not have technical skills nor the talent to empower the great people of Boeing. [male hourly shop floor worker, sixteen years at Boeing]

Top managers are hired from outside the company who have no knowledge of aerospace and are using Boeing for a stepping stone to something bigger. Therefore, they have no interest in employees. [female technician, twenty-one years at Boeing]

It was clear to many employees that their years of experience on the shop floor were no longer part of the equation for promotions. As fewer workers with "real" experience filled the limited manager roles, but pressures for worker autonomy, productivity, and doing more with less increase, one wonders who is really calling the shots on the shop floor and if the right people are getting rewarded for making important day-to-day manufacturing decisions. As more manufacturing and production are sent overseas, perhaps this is immaterial, for now.[17] But, the elements for labor/management friction seem to be in place as shop floor workers become increasingly responsible for managing the production of airplanes but less likely to reap the benefits in terms of promotions and movement up the ladder.

At a minimum, lack of a clear career path or upward mobility may shift workers into a "just get by until retirement" mode; the desire to generate new ideas, to go above and beyond, and to look for new opportunities for sales or cost savings diminishes for those who see little reward or recognition of their contribution. New roles of mentoring, training, and leadership on the shop floor (or in the office environment) with commensurate monetary reward might continue to stimulate enthusiasm and initiative from workers and help Boeing continue to tap and leverage the tacit knowledge of a significant portion of its workforce. It might be argued that the traditional managerial role may no longer be relevant in a postindustrial world where work and decisions are decentralized across teams, time zones, vendor partners, and countries. As new organizational forms emerge, perhaps new managerial forms need to be identified to better suit the needs and nature of the emerging workforce.

CONCLUSIONS

While some argue that the manager still holds a privileged, somewhat insulated position in American firms,[18] our data suggest that managers at Boeing were not immune from the challenges and pain of change during our study period. Though managers' opinions of Boeing were never as low as those of nonmanagers, we saw their views drop as turbulence peaked during the early years of the decade (2000 and 2003 survey periods). Importantly, at the end of our study period, there was no statistical difference between the number of managers and nonmanagers regarding their intentions to quit Boeing.

The role of some managers simply disappeared as the leaning of Boeing flattened the pyramid and their managerial work was outsourced to teams or partner vendors overseas. For many, the stress of being a manager escalated as they came face-to-face with the human side of the corporate downsizing strategy: conducting the tough meetings with subordinates and, often, long-term colleagues who were getting WARN or layoff notices. For others, the ever increasing span of control and management of unfamiliar functions stretched their time and capabilities, placing them in the sometimes awkward position of managing those with much higher levels of functional expertise and causing these subordinates to have frank disdain for a manager "who doesn't know what we do."

At the same time that emotional and time demands increased, the manager's role expanded to include more human resource tasks as the HR department shifted to online self-serve benefits and career management tools. For some managers, this was a welcome expansion of their role as coach/mentor, broadening and deepening their relationships with their employees. For others, however, self-serve and other technologies simply added to their mushrooming to-do lists, pushing more and more work into their personal lives through email, BlackBerrys, and Internet-connected laptops. Similarly, while many employees and managers applauded the more participatory environment and shift to Theory Y management style, the emotional demands of engaging and mentoring team members rather than directing and monitoring subordinates were taxing on a day-to-day basis, especially for those grounded in old-school management styles. Finally, as the organization flattened, the career ladder became compressed to a step-stool; many managers and employees felt dead-ended as opportunities for advancement seemed to evaporate.

As managers are increasingly placed in the position of enabler, inspirer, and sense-giver, we should be concerned that these individuals receive attention and support through times of organizational stress and change. The operating assumption (in research and in practice) appears to be that they are immune to or at least insulated from the harsh edges of change. Their ability to help others navigate turbulence, stay focused on corporate and individual work goals, and simply get things done may be significantly compromised, however. Little research has been conducted on this group in general and, while other managers in other organizations may show less wear and tear and require little explicit support, our data suggest that managers at Boeing would benefit from programs that help them manage the increased demands of their role. For example, as decisions are made regarding cuts in support staff, it may be prudent to explore the ripple effects on managers: is this a penny-wise, pound-foolish decision that simply shifts low-level support tasks onto higher paid managers? Is the loss in managerial productivity and creative energy worth the incremental gain on the balance sheet? Support for managers is crucial during periods of downsizing, particularly those directly interacting with laid-off employees.[19] Given the potential influence of managers on their subordinates and the overall profitability of the firm, we hope our findings will encourage others to examine how corporate change impacts the attitudes and behaviors of this important group and, critically, what can be done to support managers during periods of rampant change.

Chapter 7 Changing
Roles of Women

An attractive appearance is important and can be achieved by using intelligence in the selection and care of clothes and the use of proper makeup. . . . Don't risk embarrassment to either your employer or yourself. Invariably, the girl who is most admired by her fellow employees is well groomed but tailored, and has learned the importance of being properly dressed and immaculate in her appearance. She never arrives at work with her hair in curlers and without makeup, thereby creating the impression that the effort to be "ready for her job" is just too great.
—*Boeing Commercial Airplanes Manual, Office Instruction, Aero-Space Division; Secretarial Standard N. 901, June 28, 1961*

The movement of women into a historically male-dominated workplace represented another major transformation for Boeing and its workers. Unlike the other changes we have addressed in this book associated with Boeing's attempt to become more efficient, productive, and profitable—including lean manufacturing, broad and deep computerization, outsourcing and global partnering, and mass layoffs—the pressure to increase the numbers and broaden the role of women at Boeing came from places other than the competitive global marketplace. Some pressure, for example, came from the general change in American culture, social practices, and social expectations in favor of women's rights. Some came in the form of requirements in federal government contracts for racial, ethnic, and gender inclusion. And some came from a series of high-profile class action lawsuits filed in Washington, California, Kansas, and Missouri in the late 1990s and early 2000s, claiming gender discrimination in the company's pay and promotion practices.[1] Whatever their origins, whether marketplace, cultural change in society, or mandates from government, what these various changes have in common is that they required employees to cope with, and adapt to, a different working environment. Boeing was a different place to work, for example, before and after lean production processes were introduced; it was a different place to work after more women were hired and others were moved into positions with more authority. What we address in this chapter is how the influx of women into Boeing and their changing role in the company affected employee attitudes about their jobs and the company, as well as their perceptions concerning the role of gender in the workplace. We are especially interested in how these changes affected the outlooks and well-being of women at Boeing over the course of our study.

For most of its history, Boeing was described to us as being a male-run company, with a "macho" culture, and a highly gender-segregated division of labor. Even when our study began in 1996, the Boeing workforce was only 22 percent female. Women then were represented in very small percentages in some areas; only 10 percent of managers and 5 percent of engineers were women. On the other hand, 80 percent of clerical workers were women. From a gender equity point of view, these may seem out of step with what was going on in the country. The 2000 U.S. census reported that women made up roughly 42 percent of the category "management, business, and financial operations," up from 17 percent of the not-exactly-comparable category in the 1990 census "managers and administrators, except farm."[2] These broad categories, however, do not depict the reality for women at higher levels of management. According to Catalyst, a leading nonprofit organization that conducts research in the area of women and leadership, in 2005 women held 16.4 percent of corporate officer positions, up only 0.7 percent from 2002. At this rate of growth, they predicted, it would take forty years to achieve parity.[3] Clearly, Boeing's gender gap is not uncommon, but rather part of a much larger societal trend.

What makes the "gender story" at Boeing interesting is that our interviews and surveys capture a company in the middle of change. We see an influx of women into the company and changing roles within the company, but to something that is less than full parity in a strictly numerical sense, and a situation that left Boeing workers, both male and female, with complex and sometimes contradictory reactions to what was happening and what it meant for them. For example, while some female employees reported much improved treatment over earlier periods at Boeing, others did not see much authentic transformation. While much of the overt forms of discrimination are nearly a thing of the past, more subtle forms of discrimination persist, contributing to a glass ceiling at higher levels of management. Thus, the *process* of change is illuminated by capturing it midstream.

Moreover, because the company is in mid-transformation, the issue of gender tends to be on the minds of workers who, in turn, are aware of, and can report to us, the multifaceted nature of this change. Beyond issues of "mere" representation, equal pay, or similar work responsibilities, women, for example, also reported that they were burdened with the task of trying to disentangle their gender from work events. If her suggestions at meetings are ignored, is it because she is a woman or because she has poor ideas? If she wins a promotion, is it only because she was needed to satisfy a diversity initiative, not because she was the best person for the job?

We also found that managerial women in particular thought a great deal about what others thought of them—their work, their appearance, and their managerial style—and were exceedingly careful in trying to manage such impressions. While it is tempting to dismiss this latter form of stress (after all, shouldn't people outgrow worrying about what others think about them?), the degree to which these problems permeated the female managerial ranks was astonishing. More than anything, it points to the power of subtle forms of mistreatment and their ability to undermine the confidence of well-educated, competent, hardworking, and highly committed female employees. In short, even if the Boeing story is one of a remarkable business turnaround, gains in areas of gender equality have come more slowly and are still in the midst of being realized.

THE BOEING CULTURE THROUGH
THE LENS OF GENDER

Political Correctness Meets
the Good Ol' Boys' Club

> When Mr. Woodard issued that statement about advancing minorities
> and women, someone magnified it on the copier, highlighted it in
> yellow, and put it on my desk. I laughed it off. You have to laugh a lot
> of crap off. The snide remarks . . . it's a male bastion. If you complain,
> you can't get cooperation, or get anything done. Humor is essential
> for survival.
> —*Female manager, twelve years at Boeing, 1999*

This quote, as well as comments in other chapters, have documented Boeing's culture of the 1980s and earlier—one that was creative and risk-taking but also arrogant and macho. Many workers reported that it was commonplace to work around a lot of swearing and disrespectful treatment. Whether it was really the norm, or whether it could be found in all corners of the company, is harder to say, but it is nonetheless the comparison against which many in our study judged the current working environment. "In the past, my manager would send us letters that his poor secretary had to type where he'd say things like, 'If you all don't get your head out of your butts,' and we'd have to initial them. There were no problems with discipline in the olden days!" (female manager, twelve years at Boeing, 1999).

Against this backdrop, then, some of Boeing's first women were challenged with fitting into a "rough and tumble" good ol' boy environment. For women to work in positions that had been historically filled by men, whether those were in manufacturing or managerial sectors, was often associated with sexually harassing behavior, or general mistreatment, aimed specifically at them because of their minority status. Stated one veteran employee:

> As far as gender relations go, I've had everything happened that could happen. I've worked there so long. In the engineering organization, I was the only woman there, and I was put in compromising positions. I was young, I didn't think about it, I had no support system and no one to talk to. A lot of things happened that would never happen today. But I learned to cope with it, and I cope with some things today much better than I did at age 30. . . . Well, for example, there were men who would put their hands on me, on my neck and shoulders. I didn't know what to say, although it made me very uncomfortable. My mother never told us how to handle situations like that. Now, I've become more assertive. Some men just don't realize what

they're saying is inappropriate. In fact, recently, I had a man who put his hand on my shoulder and asked me out for a drink. And I told him, "Take your hand off me and don't you ever ask me that again!" I've become more forthright. . . . I've been put in terrific positions in Boeing, but mostly because no one else wanted to do it. Boeing has been good for me. [female manager, twenty years at Boeing, 1999]

By and large, our interviews revealed that such overt, harassing behavior had become, for the most part, a thing of the past. Workers we interviewed often attributed the shift to more professional behavior to society's larger concern with political correctness (PC), while others credited Boeing's efforts to educate people about appropriate behavior. Most workers viewed these changes as positive, but a few commented that concern over being PC had gone too far or at least had some unfortunate side effects. A male manager we interviewed described how in the past he would share books and novels with his employees and had "pretty frank" discussions with them. Now, he felt he simply must be more careful about what he says, never talking about politics or religion with anyone. He was more apt to think before he spoke, which, he told us, put more stress into conversations (male manager, twenty-seven years at Boeing, 2003). Similarly, "I can see a greater need in the last 5–10 years for diversity and dealing with people's issues. Some might feel the workplace is less open because of this; they fear being overheard. No one knows who the audience is anymore" (female manager, twenty years at Boeing, 1999).

More commonly, however, employees had positive things to say about the care and thoughtfulness expected in conversation. For example, "Boeing puts an emphasis on a threat-free environment. . . . There's a strong commitment to being ethical here. There's pride in being respected and trusted. . . . It's frowned on to lose your cool or use intimidation tactics" (female manager, ten years at Boeing, 1999).

In terms of movement of women into managerial positions or jobs that had been historically underrepresented by women, several employees noted striking changes. They also cited the attention the company had given to ensuring more equal representation, as well as the degree to which this had been made deliberately visible both inside and outside the company.

In HR, in personnel, it's way more women than men. When I first started at B[oeing], it was opposite. Women had lower-level jobs. First-level management and up was all men. That's changed dramatically. A lot of the men have retired, gone to jobs in the organizations they used to support. It seems like it's all women, except my boss is a man. I think it makes him feel uncomfortable. When we have a staff meeting, it's all women. Never heard a man say he feels discriminated against, and never seen a man not get opportunities, but I feel like opportunities are pretty even . . . we used to sit in our little lunch groups and complain that all the men got all the opportunities. [female manager, twelve years at Boeing, 1999]

Boeing was all too willing to make people aware that they had women in positions of management. There are women in management at all levels now, and Boeing is making definite efforts to look at women and other minority categories. [female manager, twenty years at Boeing, 1999]

It's like . . . well, for a long time, I was the first engineer to get promoted at all in [the] liaison [department]. And so I knew I was a spotlight on the chart. Cause I saw a guy's chart once that showed the EEO [Equal Employment Opportunity] measures and I thought, "Hey, I'm that little spike on the chart! That's me!" But I didn't see the company using me too much as a poster child until after I got named an executive potential candidate. And then my name kind of got out, I guess. So then the company sent me to Milwaukee to talk about diversity issues, and then they sent me to Texas to do recruiting. [female manager, thirteen years at Boeing, 1999]

In areas where representation had not yet achieved parity, some we interviewed implied that they did not hold the company responsible for the lack of representation of women in various positions. Larger societal trends, they seemed to reason, were simply manifested in the Boeing workforce. The implication, therefore, was that this is something for which the company could not be held responsible nor expected to impact.

There aren't many girls here because early on, girls are told that they can't do factory jobs—that they're not good at it. I'm working to change their minds. But how do you combat it? There's a 50:1 male-female ratio here. Men apply. Women don't. It's self-discrimination. [female manager, twelve years at Boeing, 1999]

How do we promote women in manufacturing as a job? The manufacturing environment is male. When we go to the schools, we don't specifically try to recruit girls, but we do keep track of the figures. They're low. We just can't get their interest. The tasks don't appeal to them—riveting, drilling. . . . They're still thinking about the office. [female manager, ten years at Boeing, 1999]

Different Tasks, Treatment, and Perceptions

Even with the reduction in overtly inequitable and offensive treatment, and with the efforts made by the company to reduce gender disparity, many we interviewed pointed to more subtle forms of bias and discrimination, manifested most clearly in different types of work tasks for men and women. "But I found that I was assigned the 'female' tasks: scheduling, typing, planning. I was the 'social person' for the whole organization. I asked, 'Am I the only person who can plan?' But if I don't do it, it doesn't happen. . . . I feel that because of gender, I was given certain tasks. I laugh it off" (female manager, ten years with Boeing, 1999).

More frequently, however, many of the women we interviewed—particularly the managerial women—said that rather than the work tasks themselves, it was the reactions they received from colleagues and subordinates that changed because of their gender. One, obviously, can never prove that another's reaction is due to gender, but this was the impression many of those we interviewed lived with on a daily basis.

I hear, "Some days she's friendly and some days she's really cold." I frequently feel as though they wouldn't say that if I were a "Dave." [female manager, fourteen years at Boeing, 1999]

I wonder sometimes whether sometimes people aren't more apt to engage in . . . give you a venting verbal tirade if you're female. I think about this sometimes. I get the venting, verbal tirade. Everybody does, but I wonder if it's just more frequent. [female manager, thirteen years at Boeing, 1999]

I had one guy who wanted to go off and do something, and I said, "Okay, here's my staffing plan. You can go and do that in June." He wanted to go in March.
"No, you're going in June."
"But I really wanted to go in March."
"Well, here's why I said June."
"But I really want to go in March."
"Well, you're not going in March, you're going in June."
"I really want to go in March."
"I'm not getting through to you—what more do you want me to do here because I've told you in writing, and I've told you verbally, and I've explained it to you, and I've given you my rationale."
"Well, I'm going to talk to your boss then."
"That's a great idea. You'll see exactly why you're going in March. Maybe he can explain it better than I can."
Then the guy stared at me, and I realized he'd just been trying to intimidate me. And I thought, "Okay. Whatever." [laughs] [female manager, thirteen years at Boeing, 1999]

I definitely feel like I'm in the spotlight. Some people want to see you fail. When I was an instructor, one guy said, "Oh here's our token." He was a peer. I said to him, "Fuck you." That silenced him. His attitude changed after that. [female manager, twelve years with Boeing, 1999]

A number of the workers we interviewed likewise reflected the difficulty they had seen men experience in trying to include women into their work groups. One managerial woman who had been with the company twenty-three years (as of 2003) told us that when she first joined Boeing, she was hired as an engineer. At that time, she felt women were not accepted as contributing team members, and she looked to leave the department when several of her male peers shared comments her supervisor would say about her such as, "She's not like my wife. She's not like my daughter. I don't know whether to screw her or what." Others seemed to struggle with the dilemma of trying to simultaneously include women without calling attention to them, thereby treating them differently.

> Even a speaker speaking to a group—"Gentlemen this is how we do this, we need your support. . . . oh, and lady"—where they'll stop their speech pattern to point out that there's a difference in gender in the group. In the situation where I had a VP who started out by saying, always including "and lady" in his comments in the first couple of meetings—after one of the meetings I talked to him on the side and said, "I'm really comfortable with—a lot of people use the term 'you guys' as a generic kind of term. Gerry, I consider 'you guys' a generic term. You don't have to say, you guys and gals you guys and ladies. You can use whatever term you want to refer to the group. I'll be more comfortable with that than you using a separate term for me." And it worked great. He was very comfortable with that. [female manager, twenty-three years at Boeing, 1999]

Individual remarks paint a vivid and compelling picture, but they do not communicate the degree to which these problems permeate all areas of the company. The 2006 survey revealed consistent gender differences in how employees evaluated their workplace treatment. When asked, "How often have the following happened to you in the past 12 months?" women reported that they had been blamed for things that were not their fault, had experienced other employees making derogatory remarks about them to others, had been humiliated at work in front of others, and had had others take credit for their ideas. Although figure 7.1 illustrates that these problems are not uniquely experienced by women, we find fairly regular gender differences with women across all job categories reporting poorer treatment on more than one occasion in the past year.

Beyond reports of differential treatment in tasks and in reactions of other employees, many of the women we interviewed revealed that they were acutely aware of what other employees thought about them. They gave great thought to how they came across, whether they would be perceived as inexperienced, callous, or thin-skinned. Many did recognize that trying to control others' per-

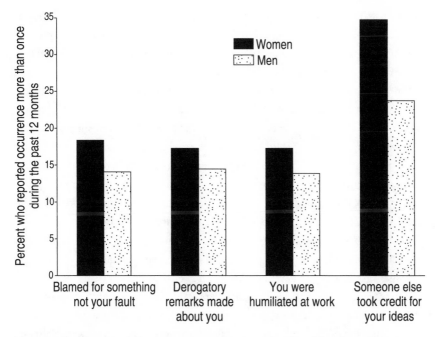

Figure 7.1 Ratings of workplace treatment: comparison of male and female employees

ceptions of them was perhaps a fruitless endeavor; nonetheless, getting to that point seemed to take a lot of soul-searching or, at the very least, a fair amount of time and energy.

> I met one of my employees in the store once. He was there with his wife, and he introduced me as his boss. It felt really strange; made me uncomfortable. I have self-doubts, and wonder if they're thinking, "Oh, she's a woman, she's young, inexperienced." So I worry about telling them my worries. [female manager, ten years at Boeing, 1999]

> I'm very conscious of team interactions; things I wouldn't do because I'm a woman, such as being a nag or being bitchy. They just shut down if you do that. Or they say, "Oh, she just has PMS." You get discredited because of your insecurities. Men can wing it and get away with it. They can do it from the hip. I don't have the luxury. I am always very prepared. I always get my ducks in a row before a meeting. [female manager, ten years at Boeing, 1999]

Respect and Women's Efforts to Gain It

For many of the women we studied, the issue of respect came up time and time again. The ways in which they were dismissed, ignored, disregarded, and left out, and the different ways in which these women attempted to gain the respect of their fellow co-workers and subordinates, were important and more specific types of differential treatment that were rarely mentioned when we interviewed men. In 2003, a woman manager with twenty-four years at the company told us that she noticed that her colleague—a man with the same position and tenure at Boeing—could say the exact same thing as she, but his comments would be accepted while hers would not. She and her male friend had developed an understanding, wherein sometimes she would tell him she needed him in a meeting because she did not "have the right body parts." In essence, she communicated her point through her friend. Similarly, a safety and health administrator told us that when she informed managers that they were out of compliance, they would question her authority to make recommendations and take the issue to a male safety and health administrator—only to get the same answer. Not surprisingly, she told us that she had grown tired of constantly having to prove herself (female manager, thirteen years at Boeing, 2002).

Again, the survey data we collected in 2006 illustrate consistent gender differences (see figure 7.2), with women reporting more frequently that they experienced the following on more than one occasion within the last year: their opinions were not valued, someone talked down to them, they were evaluated unfairly, less was expected of them, their work contributions were ignored, and they had been excluded from meetings. What these points have in common, of course, is that they all deal directly with a lack of respect and poor employee treatment. While it is possible that women might be more likely to *admit* that these experiences had happened to them—men may feel sheepish about confessing to such—these data are corroborated by the information we obtained via our confidential interviews and focus groups and are also in line with descriptions of the traditional macho culture at Boeing.

Thus, proving one's competence—making sure that one's work performance was well up and over the bar—became paramount. Demonstrating such über-competence was a theme echoed by a number of the women we spoke to.

> We have to prove ourselves above and beyond what men have to do—that hasn't changed. Maybe to a lesser extent than it used to be, but I still think that. I still think there are a lot of people with old ideas [soft, quiet voice]. And they're changing. They know women who are very capable. But you still have to prove it. With a man, they just assume he's qualified. [female manager, ten years at Boeing, 1999]

> In my area especially, your work very quickly shows if you know what you're doing or not. So, if there ever was a gender issue as to how the mechanics worked with you, or how willing people were to give you challenging work, it's rapidly destroyed by being competent. [female manager, thirteen years at Boeing, 1999]

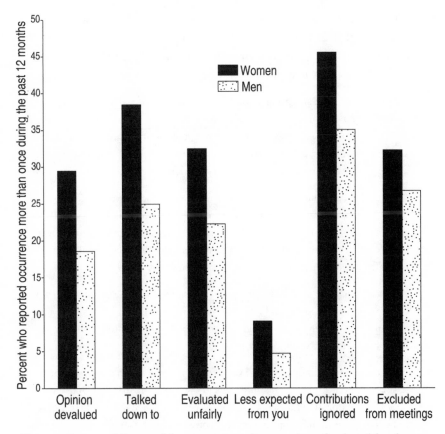

Figure 7.2 Reports of disrespectful treatment at work: comparison of male and female employees

Managing one's appearance seemed to be another way that women attempted to garner the respect of their male colleagues. Women not only reported being very conscientious about their clothing, hair style, and body weight, they also gave much thought to the tone of their speaking voices, body posture, hand gestures, and the like. One female manager with over twenty-two years at the company told us in 2003 that a male colleague said to her, "You are very expressive in the way you communicate. Analyticals really hate that." In response, she told us she had worked hard to tone down her inflection and gestures when she spoke. And another female supervisor said to us that to be successful as a manager, it was helpful to look like a man—short hair, large in stature. She believed women with those attributes had a better chance of being taken seriously (female manager, twenty-four years at Boeing, 2003). Still another woman related the tale of a female manager who could not break into upper management until she lost thirty pounds. After her weight loss, this woman's career took off (female manager, years at Boeing unknown, 2003).

Other voices reiterated this same theme.

I had a tough time accepting second-level management position. I was sent to a course taught to hourly women called "your speaking image." It made me think about how I talk. . . . It was about self-representation in language—on the phone and in person—and how the way women use inflections that take away from their authority. It weakens them. [female manager, twenty-eight years at Boeing, 1999]

I've heard other women talk about how much time they have to put into getting ready in the morning. Their husbands can jump out of bed and throw on a pair of jeans, but they have to dress just right, do makeup, create an image. Especially if you have to go to a higher level meeting on your boss's behalf. There, it's all white males over fifty. [female manager, twenty years at Boeing, 1999]

I learned quickly to stop carrying a purse. I'd be the only one coming into a business meeting with a purse and nowhere to put it. To this day, I don't carry a purse, although I was talking to my daughter about going shopping to get a new one. [female manager, twenty years at Boeing, 1999]

A lot of the women in Boeing that I've noticed who have gotten promoted, they don't have probably as much of a feminine side to them as normal as the population. The ones I'm thinking of in finance, very short hair cuts, I mean, not that they aren't feminine, but as far as their appearance, very conservative dress, high collars, short hair cuts, no makeup. Dowdy. [laughs] [female manager, ten years at Boeing, 1999]

PROMOTION AND LEADERSHIP

I think that when you want a non-dominant group—I don't care whether it's gender, race, way of thinking—to succeed, the rules have to be established and consistent because then it doesn't become any kind of personal, "good ol' boy network" for decision making. When the rules aren't clear, non-dominant groups have a heck of a time excelling. . . . Finance has much clearer rules. It's why . . . it's part of why I think I was successful.
—Female manager, twenty-three years at Boeing, 1999

This quote from a high-ranking manager reflects what many women told us about their ability to obtain and succeed in managerial positions with the company. In the absence of a level playing field, such as the one finance seemed to

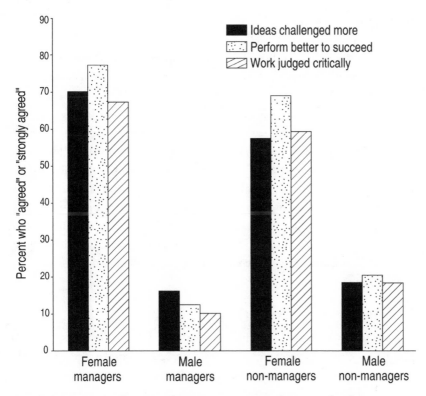

Figure 7.3 Perceptions of managerial women: comparison of managerial and nonmanagerial male and female employees

offer, women could not succeed as easily despite being competent and "reasonably" committed to the organization. Another managerial woman, commenting on the good ol' boy culture, remarked that "since a woman can't be one of the 'club,' she has to find another angle to success." She went on to tell us about a woman who rose to the level of vice president: "This woman is excellent at what she does. She simply beat the competition and gave her entire life to the company." Continuing this thought, she went on to say that a man could have hobbies and still attain a level of success, but a woman had to perform ten times better to get the respect and recognition. Yet another simply stated, "It still tends to be a man's world, and if there is a choice about who is going to be promoted, they still look to the man" (female manager, ten years at Boeing, 2003).

Our data likewise confirmed that these perceptions were held, not surprisingly, most strongly by managerial women (see figure 7.3). When asked if managerial women were more likely to have their ideas challenged than men were, if they had to perform better to succeed than did men, and if they had their work judged more critically than did men, managerial women "strongly agreed" or "agreed" with these statements at rates that *far* surpassed those of men.[4] Women who were not managers likewise shared these perceptions at very high rates; interestingly, men who did *not* hold managerial positions rated this type of discrimination as occurring slightly more often than managerial men did. Even if women's perceptions were, moreover, "inaccurate" as measured by some type of objective standard, the very fact that women have these perceptions is problematic for a company that desires to make gender discrimination an issue of the past. Furthermore, that men did not perceive such discrepancy in the way men and women are evaluated and regarded is also problematic: those who are in a position to shape Boeing culture and enforce similar performance standards are nearly always men. It is hard to imagine how they could therefore be agents of change if they fail to detect much of a problem in the first place.

Moving up the Ladder

According to the women—and some men—we interviewed, these types of problems became increasingly more pronounced as women aspired to hold higher and higher levels in the organization. A male manager with over twenty-seven years at Boeing reported that he saw "subtle misogyny" toward women in higher levels of management expressed in the forms of a higher level of scrutiny of women in executive ranks and resentment that "she is there to be an EEO statistic." Because he had not heard any overt statements to that effect, he questioned whether his perceptions were accurate (male manager, twenty-seven years at Boeing, 2003). Others, however, shared his observation about the increasing difficulties women experienced as they attempted to climb the career ladder. "Opportunities are equal to a point. At the first level manager, it's equal, but when you go up the scale, it's not equal. I know several women who have advanced, but they are so few. There are changes, but they are so few and far between" (female manager, ten years at Boeing, 1999).

Perhaps because of the perceived increasing difficulty as one endeavored to move up in the ranks, a number of managerial women told us that they didn't want promotions and were not willing to make the sacrifices needed in order to be promoted. Citing temperamental differences between women and men or the importance of family, a number of managerial women seemed to be satisfied with, or at worst resigned to accepting, their present position.

I turned the third level of management down. I didn't respect the boss who wanted me . . . but many of the men in my area could not believe it. "Are you crazy?" They would take promotion over any other consideration. The male ego can't handle demotion [during downsizing]. Status reversals are really hard for men. [female manager, twenty-eight years at Boeing, 1999]

If you don't have children, it's different than if you do. In the old organization, there was a woman named Shelby. She had no children. She wasn't the best candidate for a promotion, but the manager said, "She was promoted because she could come and go as she pleased." I don't think there was anything else going on. Inez was more qualified, and she had an engineering degree, but she didn't get the promotion because she has three kids. In my mind, that's what happened. I've turned down jobs I've been offered because they'd take me away from my little girl. I don't want that. [female manager, twelve years at Boeing, 1999]

Impact of EEO and Affirmative Action

Undoubtedly the highly publicized lawsuits affected Boeing's behavior, making the company more aggressive in seeking to promote well-qualified women into managerial positions. Without question, such practice, in addition to being required, had a number of positive effects. But it also created some resentment, or at least the perceptions of resentment, and made all workers more sensitive to the issue. A male manager with sixteen years at the company told us in 2003 that it was a widely held belief that women were sometimes promoted to meet diversity requirements. Human resources, he said, was fond of saying, "Sometimes the best candidate does not always get the job, but the best *qualified* person does." In this case, the word "qualified" meant that satisfying a diversity requirement may be one of the qualifications for the job. On our 2006 survey, several workers emphasized the negative impact such attention to diversity requirements had, noting that the company "de-rated the importance of professional white males" as it promoted "diversity at the direct expense of competence and leadership qualities" (male engineer, seventeen years at Boeing). Another remarked, "There has been company-wide promotion of women and minorities over equally or even better qualified personnel" (male engineer, fifteen years at Boeing, 2006), and a similar sentiment was expressed by a male manager who told us that the biggest change he had experienced in his thirty-six years at Boeing was "increased focus and attention on quality and diversity issues where female and non-Caucasian employees are given the benefits of any doubts" (2006).

Real push in the last couple of years to promote women because studies have shown that there are very few women managers at Boeing. So they really pushed to promote women. And of course there was a lot of resentment about that. We even hear from other women, "Oh the only reason so and so got a job is because they had to promote another woman." I mean, there's a lot of qualified women managers, and there's a lot of qualified women who haven't been promoted. I still think that that's slow. [female manager, ten years at Boeing, 1999]

To a certain degree, I feel like I've been in the spotlight, yes. There was push to promote women a few years back and that's still going on. I know that I heard in the finance area, the males say, "We can't find any qualified women to hire in our organization." I said, "When I was going to school there were lots of women graduating in finance. How come you can't find any qualified women?" [female manager, ten years at Boeing, 1999]

By contrast, not all women and men we interviewed perceived the impact of affirmative action so pessimistically, nor did they view the company's desire to promote and support women as being as disingenuous. One woman, for example, said that the statement that women are promoted to satisfy diversity requirements was probably true five years ago, and she was able to think of examples where women were in jobs as tokens and not expected to do or say much. Such is no longer the case, she opined. "Women are working at higher levels in the company and doing very well. Men are beginning to take women more seriously and working relationships are improving" (female manager, twenty-four years at Boeing, 2003). Likewise, another told us that she owes great loyalty to the company because the company has given her "every opportunity" for a successful career. The company owes and provides her with clear direction so that she knows how best to contribute (female manager, fourteen years at Boeing, 2003).

I feel like my chances for promotion are better than any of my peers. The company wants to promote women. They are self-aware; they know the ratio is low. I have the sense that if I want to advance, I can. I think this will continue to increase. [female manager, ten years at Boeing, 1999]

I have been more vocal with management—not getting paid enough, not getting promoted. And that's when things started to happen. They didn't seem to resent me. They didn't see me as a complainer. I don't know if the guys were always doing that, maybe they were more assertive. I've been more assertive with management. Sometimes managers say they can't do anything for you, but I found out that's not necessarily true. [female manager, ten years at Boeing, 1999]

Fitting into the Male Culture

The historically male-dominated work culture, a problem for many women, was especially difficult for managerial women. First, women were *particularly* a minority within the managerial ranks; as noted earlier, 22 percent of Boeing employees were women, but only 10 percent of managers were women, and this percentage dwindled rapidly as one moved above level I managerial positions. In turn, female managers often reported not having much access to other managerial women with whom they could talk over problems, receive workplace support, or develop simple friendships.

> When I was promoted to the second level of managers, I joined thirteen male second-line managers. There weren't any problems, but we never had rapport. The male managers would spend up to an hour "chatting" in his [another male co-worker's] office, socializing. I never desired to do so. I was asked to, but I didn't feel like we had anything in common. [female manager, twenty-eight years at Boeing, 1999]

> The other thing I worry about is that I don't want to develop any close friendships with men. I'm married. It's a fine line I walk, so I just don't do much socializing with them. The men do a lot more together. I'll be in their offices, and they're setting up lunches and things with buddies and stuff. [female manager, thirteen years at Boeing, 1999]

> I think that the higher you get in the organization, there is more tendency to be isolated. But most of my colleagues are male, and I do not use them specifically as support system. [female manager, twenty-three years at Boeing, 1999]

In addition to this problem, however, managerial women often told us that they sat on the horns of a dilemma vis-à-vis their managerial style. To conduct herself in a forthright, self-confident, or an assertive way—in essence, to act in a manner that many often associate with successful male leadership—was to risk incurring the hostility of her subordinates . . . and sometimes her family members.

> Women have to operate on a relationship basis. Men can operate more strongly on authority. Even in relationships with the secretary. Men can operate in a more authority role with the secretary; women need to operate in a relationship with the secretary. He can just say, "Do this, do that." He doesn't have to say "Please." I really know a lot of men who treat their secretaries very, very well, so I don't mean to imply that they don't. A man can go in and throw their authority around and be very effective and the job gets done more quickly for them than for me. [female manager, twenty-three years at Boeing, 1999]

I came home one time and said something. I don't remember what, but I do remember what my husband said: "Susan [not her name], I'm not one of your employees!" I learned I had to take the work hat off, and have two distinct roles. Men do not expect as much now, but they still domineer. My management role didn't go over very well at home. I had to remember that. [female manager, twenty-eight years at Boeing, 1999]

And yet, behaving more masculine was something that a number of our managerial women reported needing to do in order to succeed. When asked to indicate their level of agreement with the statement "Women managers sometimes must behave in masculine ways in order to succeed," some 42.5 percent of our women managers agreed or strongly agreed with the statement. Nonmanagerial women likewise endorsed the statement at about the same level (40.1 percent) whereas managerial (11.2 percent) and nonmanagerial (13.0 percent) men did not. A substantial segment of managerial women, therefore, seemed to face an undesirable choice: succeed and be disliked, or be liked but unsuccessful.

But other comments we received pointed to a more encouraging picture. A number of managerial women cited stereotypical feminine behaviors as being part of their leadership style, noting that these *were* the reasons for their success. Granted, some were quick to point out that occasionally such stereotypic feminine styles had their downside. And yet, many of the relational, nurturing communication skills—skills they saw as being "feminine"—were cited as strengths in their supervisory approach.

Nurturing is an effective quality for coaching. Women deal with management at home all the time. It falls into women's hands; getting people to places on time, balancing checkbooks, buying groceries and the necessities. . . . Women have some "natural tendencies." These pretty traditional roles make women capable. They juggle two roles, much more than men. [female manager, twenty years at Boeing, 1999]

Now I have a man manager. He's helpful, and staff [meetings] go a lot faster. He cuts to the chase and he cuts people off if they need to be. But if I call him up, needing another idea, or input, or want to vent, he's like, "Yeah." I'm just not going to get that nurturing from him. If I ask for help, he'll give it to me. He'll ask, "Do you want me to call so-and-so?" He'll just take it on, the problem gets solved. His style is because he's a man, but it's just him. He gets things done. . . . My employees are all women. They feel that I need to spend thirty minutes once or twice a week about what's going on. Over lunch sometimes, [we] talk about what's bugging us . . . goes for all of those who work for me. They want to spend the time together. We enjoy talking and spending time together, even if we don't resolve problems. [female manager, twelve years at Boeing, 1999]

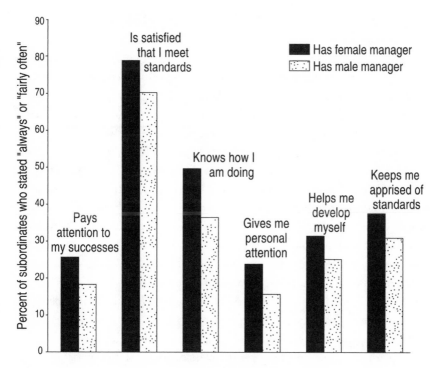

Figure 7.4 Ratings of managerial qualities of immediate supervisor: comparison of employees who have a male versus female supervisor

There are attributes that women have that definitely benefit a team decision-making situation. Women will look at the moral, social effects—to me, that means that they have a broader view than men do. Although they have the stereotype of complaining about that one little insignificant issue, it seems to me that overall, they can look at the big picture better than men. Men still compartmentalize and don't see how all the issues tie together. [female manager, ten years at Boeing, 1999]

Importantly, the subordinates—both men and women—who were supervised by managerial women also reported to us that they saw a number of these transformational leaderlike qualities come through in their day-to-day interactions with them. Whether or not these qualities are truly "feminine" behaviors, we will not debate here. They are, however, often considered to be the mark of a "good" manager, one who helps to guide and direct an employee toward achieving work-related standards.

On all questions, workers with female managers rated their supervisors more favorably, as illustrated in figure 7.4, which shows the percentages of workers who responded "always" and "fairly often" when asked if their supervisor (1) called attention to their successes, (2) was satisfied when they meet agreed-upon standards, (3) let them know how they are doing, (4) gave them attention when needed, (5) helped them develop themselves, and (6) advised them on the standards necessary to carry out their work. Although in some places the percentages differ by only slightly more than 6 percent, we do find a consistent pattern.[5]

Despite these perceived differences in supervisory style, we did not find that these styles, in turn, made a noticeable difference in subordinates' job attitudes or feelings toward the company. Those with male versus female managers, for example, did not differ in overall job satisfaction, job stress, job autonomy, work overload or ambiguity, perceptions of organizational support, number of injuries, or missed work days. This is not to say that managerial style is unimportant. Rather, it is more likely the case that many factors, in addition to supervisory style, feed one's level of job stress, illnesses, and so on. These gender differences in supervisory style shown on the graph are also not large. As with the workplace mistreatment questions, what is interesting is the consistency with which we find such gender differences. Whether these differences are "real" or not cannot be answered with our data, but at some level, what matters most here is that which is in the eye of the beholder. Even if managerial men and women were to supervise their subordinates identically, the fact that subordinates *perceive* differences in managerial styles, in some sense, becomes the reality for both them as well as their managers.

The Search for Ultra-Mentors and Work-Family Balance

In addition to difficulties associated with fitting into the male-dominated culture or balancing her leadership style in a way that was not too masculine nor feminine, managerial women noted the lack of good role models for their career development. Given the paucity of women in managerial positions at Boeing, such is hardly surprising, and yet many women we interviewed cited this as a barrier to their professional development.

> But the biggest thing lacking is mentoring for women managers. . . . In my 28 years at Boeing, I had one good mentor. Men mentor men managers; they're "thick." Women mentors are sadly lacking. They should change that. [female manager, twenty-eight years at Boeing, 1999]

> If I were advising younger women, I would definitely say, "Find a mentor." The successful managers have mentors. If you've been promoted in this company, you have

had a mentor. . . . When I first went into finance, I made this comment to one of my peers in that organization who'd been there longer. She was about my age. I said, "Women have got to stick together; there are so many men in this organization, we need to support each other." She definitely felt that I was a threat. For those years I was there, we did not bond. I look back and think, "What a lost opportunity." Taking qualified people and working with them and giving them any advice. I think men have been doing that for years. That's the old boy network. . . . Role models and mentoring are important. Women are not necessarily better at that than men. That instance, that woman, she ended up telling someone, "Katherine wants to ride my coattails. I'll be damned if she does that. I worked hard to get where I am." . . . Women can be their own worst enemy. [female manager, ten years at Boeing, 1999]

Above and beyond simply having women ahead of them, however, many of those we interviewed spoke about wanting mentors who could do more than "show them the ropes" as related to work and career. Navigating the work-home balance, particularly for employees who were also parents, came up frequently among the women we interviewed, and several expressed an explicit desire to achieve a workable, healthy balance between the work and home arenas.

Last week, my daughter was sick with the flu, and I had to stay home Thursday and Friday. I tried to juggle around. I had a laptop at home and I got a little work done. Most of the guys that are my age and younger now are dual income families, and they get that perfectly. They go through it themselves. I think that most of the managers have dealt with it enough, even the male engineers. I don't think it's a gender problem anymore. . . . My job is very important to my life. I think my kids are more central. But I guess both arenas . . . how much are you willing to compromise the kid in the work arena, and how much are you willing to compromise the work arena for the kid? 'Cause you're not going to do either one perfectly. But you want to do both. And I don't really ever want to not do both. [female manager, thirteen years at Boeing, 1999]

As this quote suggests, work-home balance is not exclusively a women's issue —indeed a number of men reported struggling with excessive demands from home and work. And yet issues related to balance were described in more vivid detail by our female employees.[6] Our survey data likewise showed that women with children reported being engaged in household tasks an average of 28.1 hours per week as compared with women without children (13.9), men with children (17.6), and men without children (11.9). Adding to this burden, many employees had lives that were teeming with activity, so much so that we were left with the distinct impression that there was very little unscheduled time; workers struggled to find time to take a vacation, exercise, or simply rest. One woman, for instance, told us that on her last two-week vacation, she returned to find 182 e-mails. To avoid a repeat scenario, she now takes a cell phone and laptop with her when she goes on vacation (female manager, twenty-four years at Boeing, 2003).

These data replicate what has been reported in hundreds of other studies of workers employed by other companies.[7] Viewed one way, Boeing can hardly be held responsible for one's family configuration, society's adoption of an increasingly accelerated and demanding work life, or traditional gender-typed expectations as related to parenting and domestic life. And yet the 24/7, historically male-dominated culture of Boeing might be especially likely to conflict with a more flexible, "family-friendly" environment.

> My child is my major stress. I want to be with him. I want to give Boeing their 40 hours a week and not more. I have a very high concentration level, so I can get a lot done efficiently. Most men I know there are willing to give much more than 40 hours. My male peers do. The career means something different to them. My struggle is with finding a balance. There's so much work. So I ask myself, "How much energy do I give the company? Should I go part-time, go for a demotion?" I feel overwhelmed. The work culture at Boeing prohibits a balance. I want to play an active role. I care about my job, but I'd really like to take it off "boil" for a while. [female manager, ten years at Boeing, 1999]

Thus, the confluence of several factors—the high level of importance of both work and home, the high levels of and somewhat incompatible demands from both arenas, the desire to be successful and fulfilled in both arenas, and the inability to see a clear and easy pathway through—seemed to cultivate a desire for "super mentors." Women we interviewed seemed to want guidance in not only work and career development, but also in areas related to work-home balance and developing healthy and fulfilling lives. One managerial woman with fourteen years at Boeing told us in 2003 that while she has worked for a female vice president, the experience was merely "okay." Although her supervisor supported her in her work, she was not a good role model—she was overworked, did not have a balanced life, and ate poorly. Eventually, the supervisor had to leave the company for health reasons. Others voiced similar sentiments: "My woman boss in the beginning said she would be my mentor, and she was. There were two men and one woman who gave me a lot of guidance; they were in touch with what I was about. My first manager gave me a lot of good advice. I had a senior female manager who helped me with prioritizing. She was very helpful through my pregnancy. But she had kids early on and then went into management. So, I don't feel she can really understand what it's like to be a manager and have a small child at home" (female manager, ten years at Boeing, 1999).

Despite their own lack of role models, however, a number of managerial women told us that they, themselves, felt as though they could be role models to others, both inside and outside of the organization.

> I never felt in the spotlight, but I did feel as a role model. Other women would say, "So glad to see you there—that's more than I could do." I think I'm a role model for my daughter. She saw a magazine with an article about women in management and it said that women in management mostly had short hair—"just like you, Mom." [female manager, twenty years at Boeing, 1999]

> My child (age five) is the most important thing in my life. I'd be a stay-at-home mom if I could. They grow so fast. And the things they say are amazing! I was reading to her one night poems of Shel Silverstein. I said to her that I didn't know who the illustrator was. And the next night, I read some more poems to her and you know what she asked me? "Mom, who's the illustrator?!" And I told her that I'm an illustrator, that's what I do. And she asked to see my drawings. [female manager, twelve years at Boeing, 1999]

CONCLUSION

As our description illustrates, Boeing's efforts, like those of many companies of its generation, to integrate increasingly greater numbers of women into its historically male culture have not come without struggle. Boeing clearly had to address issues of gender inequality, and yet these changes implied much more than simply adding women to the payroll or promoting women into positions of leadership. It also meant making changes to the male-dominated, 24/7 work culture at precisely the same point in time that other aspects of the corporate culture were transforming due to outsourcing, lean manufacturing practices, loss of the "family" identity, and increased emphasis on shareholder value. To the extent that the 24/7 macho work culture was perceived to have been responsible for the company's successes, such change was, not surprisingly, difficult.

As many of these women reported during our surveys, these increased opportunities at the company necessitated great efforts on their part to try and gain respect and fit into the not-yet-completely-changed work culture. Whether their perceptions were real or imagined, the fact remains that managerial women still believe, as recently as 2006, that their work performances are judged more critically in comparison with those of their male peers. Managerial women, particularly, saw themselves as having to jump higher hurdles and face greater scrutiny of their work. Men, likewise, had to adapt to new types of relationships with their female co-workers and supervisors. While many old-time workers reported that "things were better" where gender equality was concerned, our own data showed that there is still work to be done. Interestingly, these perceptions did not improve between years 2003 to 2006, perhaps too short a time period for us to detect change. Despite the rhetoric of equality and political correctness, and even in the face of many meaningful and authentic company shifts, the fact remains that for individual workers, issues related to gender must still be confronted, handled, and ultimately normalized.

Chapter 8 Well-Being Consequences of Workplace Change

I had a significant management role in recovering from the September 11, 2001, terrorist attacks. We were expected to work seventy to ninety hours per week to secure our airplanes. This lasted for almost two years. Lots of Boeing people developed long-term illnesses and/or ruined their marriage during that time. I had a stroke . . . during that high pressure time.
—*Male manager, thirty-seven years at Boeing, 2006*

To the casual observer of the company turmoil we have described, the question "Does living through such change affect employee health?" may seem to have an obvious answer. Workplace change and uncertainty that threaten one's livelihood, sense of "family," and sense of worth as a worker or manager unquestionably can be very stressful. Most people believe that stress is linked to poor mental and physical health outcomes, a connection that has been substantiated in the research literature for a number of years.[1] We have seen in previous chapters that employees across the board at Boeing experienced substantial change and uncertainty, and they expressed in a variety of ways how stressful it all felt to them. It stands to reason, then, that employee health must have declined significantly at Boeing during the years of our research.

But did it? Are the workplace changes to well-being outcomes so clear-cut? Might some workers emerge from the turmoil more resilient and healthy, for example? After all, we know there are many and various individual responses to stress, and some coping strategies are more effective and health-promoting than others. Moreover, stress outcomes can "present," as they say in the medical world, in different ways for different people. Furthermore, if stress is found to be associated with health outcomes, how can we be certain that company-initiated changes actually *caused* the observed health problems? Might it be the case that employees just attributed their health problems to working at Boeing rather than considering the impact of their genetic background or lifestyle habits which might have affected health directly or indirectly through stress? Or might they have experienced these problems working for *any* company undergoing change? And, even if we find workplace stress-to-health linkages, we might ask, "Just how bad were these health problems? Were they life-threatening? Did they affect day-to-day functioning? Or were they "trivial" in nature?"

At the outset of our research, we believed that employee health, with some time lag, of course, would generally track the work experience at Boeing. In looking at Boeing's history from the present, if our initial ideas were supported, we would have expected worker and manager health to roughly follow the state of affairs in the company, with financial troubles, constant change, and uncertainty marking the 1996 through 2003 period; and renewed company success, new and properly functioning ways of working, and rising employee confidence characterizing the period thereafter. By looking at things this way, physical and mental health indicators should have declined between 1996 and 2003 and improved subsequently. We will conclude in this chapter that these expectations were only partly met and that the story is much more nuanced than decline and bounce-back. In fact, we will suggest that change and uncertainty at Boeing had some long-lasting negative health effects on employees.

Our quantitative analysis that assesses the degree to which employee mental and physical health followed workplace change and conditions is based on the sample of 525 workers and managers who completed each of the four surveys in 1997, 2000, 2003, and 2006. Acknowledging that no single indicator of health can tell the whole story, we looked at a number of quantitative indices, as well as at employee comments in interviews, focus groups, and open-ended items related to psychological and physical well-being. This approach is consistent with the notion of "allostatic load," a concept which recognizes how efforts to cope with stress can tax different bodily systems resulting in varied negative health outcomes.[2]

As to whether our findings are caused by company-initiated changes, the fact that we do not have an external comparison group, or "control group," makes it difficult to answer this question. It is for this reason that we also provide data from what we call our "attrition" sample—some 170 workers who completed the 1997 (Time 1) survey but who subsequently left the company (see the appendix for a fuller description). Fortunately, we were able to survey these former employees, both in 2000 and 2003, to see how they fared once they were no longer employed by Boeing. The graphs we present throughout this chapter compare this attrition group to a matched group of still-employed Boeing workers.[3] In this way, we can see whether health improves or not, setting aside any impacts as related to age and gender, once employees left the company—something that would be expected if, in fact, the myriad of workplace changes we have described in previous chapters impacted employee health.

Our comparisons using the attrition group are important for another reason. Earlier chapters have made clear that in 1997, the year of our Time 1 survey, employees were already in the midst of a great deal of company change stemming in large measure from the multiple management initiatives and the pending merger with McDonnell Douglas. Because we were unable to capture employees before the onset of change and uncover accompanying health impacts, it may be the case that ill health increased prior to our first survey in 1997, with little subsequent change in later surveys, leading us to a false conclusion that change and uncertainty had no or very little effect on employee health. This type of "ceiling effect" in our data on continuously employed workers—those who participated in all four surveys—is somewhat akin to measuring heart rate in an athlete who has already been running for twenty minutes; detection of increased heart rate could occur only if the competitor, for example, encountered a steep hill. Although we have good reason to believe that the hill did indeed become steeper for Boeing employees in 2000 and 2003, comparison with those who left the company—those who stopped running, as it were—provides another way for us to be able to link the events at the company to worker health and well-being.

PSYCHOLOGICAL WELL-BEING

Previous research has documented numerous linkages between work stress and various forms of psychological distress such as depression, anxiety, psychological distress and fatigue, loss of concentration, and general "bad temper."[4] Remarks obtained from our focus groups and interviews, and from the open-ended comment section on the 2006 survey questionnaire, often painted a poignant picture of how employees' psychological well-being took a hit as a result of what they were experiencing on the job.

> As a result of these changes, I became discouraged and depressed. I hated getting up and going to work! [female professional worker, twenty-nine years at Boeing, 2006]

> The resources available to support me doing my job have been greatly decreased. The level of performance expected from me has significantly increased. Competition and the airline business environment have increased job performance pressures. The pressure for ever-improved performance and ever-increasing production has intensified. The level of effort necessary to keep a job, let alone prosper, has effectively eliminated any semblance of a personal life. In the past, I frequently was recognized for excellent job successes. While the successes have continued, recognition for success has been replaced by criticism for anything less than complete success. I have sought out medical assistance to manage depression. I have abandoned any hope of future career advancement and am trying to reach a financial reduction that will allow me to retire as soon as possible. [male manager, twenty-five years at Boeing, 2006]

Equally telling, leaving Boeing was associated with less depression and greater life satisfaction for a number of workers.

> [I] was laid off and now have a better quality of life. I make about ten thousand less per year but my move out of western Washington was the best move of my career. My wife and I are so much happier with our new life. [male engineer, twenty years at Boeing, 2006]

> My layoff was a good thing. I got away from a high stress work situation, and fast-paced living conditions. I now happily reside in a small town, have a rewarding job, and take care of my parents plus my family. [male hourly worker, twenty-four years at Boeing, 2006]

Of course, some workers associated their Boeing employment with improved mental health outcomes. A female engineer who had been at Boeing five years as of 2006 observed that the workplace changes had been difficult; nevertheless, she pointed to how such change can make one more resilient, stating, "Facing this uncertainty head-on can make you stronger. You realize that you will survive no matter what happens."

Likewise, some of those who left Boeing also remarked how the loss of their connection to the company had a deleterious impact on their psychological well-being: "At first, I experienced a loss of self-esteem; I hadn't realized how much I connected my job with who I was. I was proud of the years I had been at Boeing and proud of my profession and work and money. It took me about a year to settle down and be okay with the change" (female professional worker, twenty-five years at Boeing, 2003).

And another former employee who was asked how he's felt since leaving the company remarked, "I think I have been a little depressed. Also, I don't feel I am as sharp mentally and don't feel as qualified at being a quality employee" (male professional worker, nineteen years at Boeing, 2003).

Comments speaking to the psychological benefits of continued Boeing employment, however, were somewhat rare and, moreover, at odds with the trends we observed with our quantitative data over time. For example, the conviction that one is able to control his or her life, plan for the future, and have the capacity to deal with life's problems is an important component to one's sense of well-being. Typically, this is a relatively stable characteristic in people, with most possessing a moderately strong sense of this ability. Our findings from the sample of employees across the four waves reflected this tendency for personal control to be both high and relatively stable, though there was a small statistically significant uptick in 2006.[5]

Of greater interest, however, was the substantial difference in the sense of personal control between those workers and managers who stayed at Boeing and those who left and were in our attrition sample (see figure 8.1). Thus, we found some support for the assertion that leaving the bad environment—one that was riddled with change that workers were unable to control—was associated with an improved sense of personal control.

We found the same type of effect for depression. Rather than assess clinically severe or chronic levels of depression, we sought to measure more commonly experienced depressive symptoms experienced in the short-term. Employees were asked, for example, to report the number of days in the past week they experienced various symptoms such as loneliness, sadness, or difficulty concentrating.[6] Within the group of employees who completed all four surveys, we found that depression tracked what was happening in the company—2003 levels of depression (average 7.9) were greater than those reported in 2006 (average 6.4).

But again, it is the comparison with those who left the company, as illus-

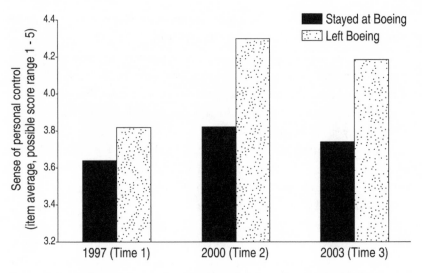

Figure 8.1 Sense of personal control: comparison of workers who stayed at Boeing versus left Boeing

trated in figure 8.2, which provides the more striking result for the measure of depression: As we found with sense of personal control, those who left the company benefited from a significant improvement as compared with continuously employed workers who were similar in age and gender.

In addition, a number of workers commented that they had started taking antidepressants, or had heard that other employees were taking antidepressants, as a means of controlling depression and anxiety they attributed to work stress. A female manager who had been employed at Boeing for twenty-three years is illustrative of such a case. In 2003, she told us that she recently had been experiencing some "weird" reactions such as feeling angry and nervous, and crying for no reason. She wasn't sure whether it was the result of menopause or stress. Her doctor prescribed a minimal dose of an antidepressant, and she said the medication helped immensely, calling the drug "a miracle." Another managerial woman who had twenty years with the company reported in 2003 that she saw a "huge" increase in absences during the reorganization. She said that she was aware of many colleagues who suffered "nervous breakdowns" and went on medication.

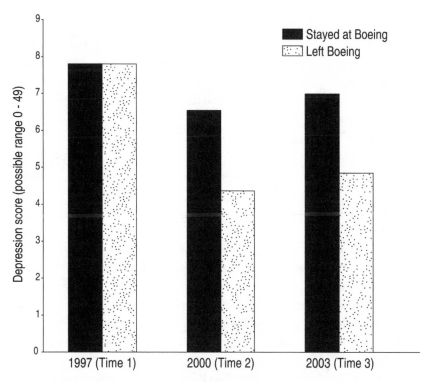

Figure 8.2 Depression symptoms of the past week: comparison of workers who stayed at Boeing versus left Boeing

COPING WITH PSYCHOLOGICAL AND
PHYSICAL HEALTH PROBLEMS

Use of antidepressant medication was but one way employees reflected the toll that workplace change had on their psychological and physical health. As is clear from reviewing other studies on workplace stress and health, employees are likely to have some type of reaction to work stress: few people are content to do nothing when they experience something as unpleasant. These responses range from cognitive reappraisals of the situation to instrumental efforts to gain control of the situation, to avoidance of the stress, to diversionary tactics to escape the negative feelings.[7] As varied as the problems themselves, Boeing employees likewise pointed to a myriad of coping strategies—some positive, some not as positive—they used to offset the pressure they experienced from so much change and uncertainty.

Devaluing Work

One way to deal with the work-related uncertainty and stress Boeing workers mentioned was to devalue work's importance relative to other important areas such as family, friends, or religion. One managerial woman with fourteen years at Boeing noted in 2003 that being a parent was a "blessing in disguise," as it offered her a built-in reason to force herself out of the office when other people continued working. As she was unwilling to compromise time with her family, work was therefore contained and could not assume a disproportionate amount of her time or energy. Another similarly said, "People feel they're just putting in their time till it all goes away. . . . My refuge has been the return to my Catholic faith after a thirty-five-year absence" (female hourly worker, nineteen years at Boeing, 2006).

Our longitudinal survey data substantiated these types of remarks, revealing significant and meaningful shifts in the degree to which workers had decided to invest in their work and family following our 1997 survey. As described in the chapter on Boeing's changing work culture, employees reported significant decreases in their work ambitions and the amount they were willing to work as well as marked increases in the amount of time they reported spending with their families. Changes were most dramatic between 1997 and 2000, and, importantly, they had not returned to 1997 levels when we surveyed employees in 2006.

Changes in Eating Habits

Other forms of coping mentioned by workers had more direct, negative effects on health. Either in addition to, or instead of, more healthful ways of coping, a number of workers reported dealing with their work-related stress by changing their eating patterns, typically marked by increased eating, but occasionally by decreased eating. Higher body mass indices (BMI) and obesity rates, for example, have been associated with higher levels of job strain,[8] but others have noted poor appetite as one of a number of reactions experienced by workers with high job stress.[9] Statistically removing the effects of age, education, and income, our own quantitative data showed that lower job security was related to higher BMI, but the impact was small, perhaps owing to the fact that some percentage of the workers had an opposite reaction (such as eating less) that offset the effect to some degree. For that reason, we considered all changes in eating patterns as one of the many possible reactions.

For example, "In the past ten years, Boeing has cared less about the value of

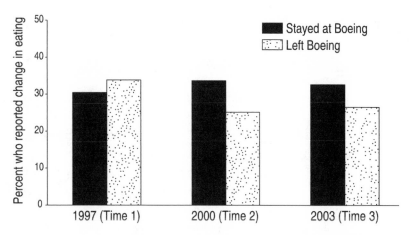

Figure 8.3 Change in eating habits, past twelve months: comparison of workers who stayed at Boeing versus left Boeing

long-time employees. They have given our work to other outside companies. They have laid off experienced workers like myself and others that have worked for Boeing over twenty years. I have gained weight and smoke more in the past 2 years" (female nonexempt worker, twenty years at Boeing, 2006).

And again, sometimes leaving Boeing enabled employees to change their habits and to adopt healthier lifestyles. A former employee reported: "I have lost forty pounds and am able to exercise four to five times a week. My time and my life is my own. I'm broke, but I'm happier" (male professional worker, thirteen years at Boeing, 2003).

Our quantitative data for the panel of workers across the four surveys did not show a dramatic or statistically significant change in habits—either in eating more or less in the past year. Although the least amount of eating fluctuation occurred in 2006, eating changes did not show the same type of pattern (that is, peaking in 2003) we saw, for example, with depression or sense of personal control.

Again, however, comparisons between those who left Boeing to a matched sample of those who stayed revealed a different pattern: as shown in figure 8.3, leaving Boeing was associated with a greater stability (that is, less change in the past year) in eating patterns. This type of pattern also may suggest that eating habits were already affected by the company's changes by the time we administered our first survey in 1997. The declines we see within the group who left the company may reflect a return to stress levels that existed before the major workplace changes that began in the mid-1990s, though we cannot know for sure.

Alcohol Use

Rooted in the notion that high levels of workplace stress "spill over" to home life and that workers seek to reduce such tension by using alcohol, many researchers in the social sciences have sought to affirm this connection,[10] or at least find the specific contexts or subgroup of workers who are more prone to drink when work stress is high. Certainly, the notion that "my job drives me to drink" is a phrase one might hear used jokingly or otherwise: whether or not it is truly a common reaction is another story.

Using alcohol as a means of coping with work-related stress was cited by several workers, some of whom had recognized the problem and sought help specifically for alcoholism. Other employees still reported using alcohol in an effort to cope with work stress. One managerial woman with sixteen years at Boeing told us in 2003 that she reacted to the stress by getting short with people at work and having a glass of wine every night after work—something she never used to do. She also said it worried her that she had become dependent on alcohol to relax. Another told us, "Yes, I'm becoming an alcoholic. In the past, I would have a glass of wine, beer, or scotch three to four times a week. Now I'm up to about 10 glasses a week" (female manager, twenty-four years at Boeing, 2003).

Our quantitative data did not reveal changes over time in the overall percentages of workers who reported drinking. In the full longitudinal panel study, roughly 80 percent of employees reported consuming alcohol at some point in the past year at each of the four survey periods. This percentage was somewhat lower for the attrition and matched counterpart groups at 75 percent, most likely owing to the fact that these workers were, on average, some five years older.[11] Both these rates were remarkably stable over time.

By contrast, drinking *motivations* did fluctuate over time. As compared with drinking alcohol for reasons that are socially oriented or merely as a "beverage," drinking as a means for changing one's emotional state, such as to feel more powerful, more in control, or to forget about one's job—termed "escape reasons" in our study—has been linked to poorer health-related outcomes in the scholarly literature for a number of years.[12] Not surprisingly, a substantial percentage of our sample (40 to 45 percent for full sample, 47 to 50 percent for attrition/matched sample) had the lowest possible scores on this measure, showing that they did not drink as a means of escaping. Thus, keeping in mind that these findings are set within a context of very low levels of escapist motivations

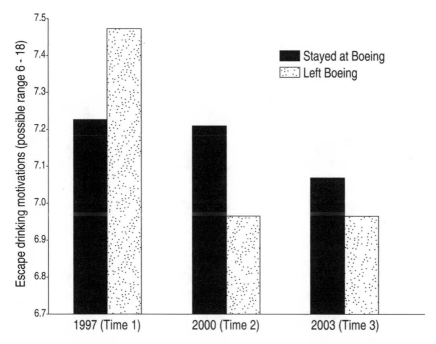

Figure 8.4 Escape drinking motivations: comparison of workers who stayed at Boeing versus left Boeing

for using alcohol overall, we found that such reasons peaked significantly in 2003 (average score of 7.6) and fell to their lowest levels in 2006 (average score of 7.3) among the group of workers who participated in all four surveys.

Between the matched and attrition subsamples we found that the slight differences seen in 1997 were not significant; however, our findings revealed some suggestion that such escape drinking motivations declined once workers left the company (see figure 8.4).

Furthermore, binge drinking, another measure of problematic alcohol use, revealed some increase in 2003 among the matched subset of our sample. Somewhat different from more moderate or steady consumption, binge drinking is associated with interpersonal violence, drunk-driving, lost economic productivity, and cognitive impairments.[13] Examining the percentage of workers who said that they consumed eight or more alcoholic beverages in a single sitting at least once in the past six months (various cutoff levels have been used to define binge drinking—eight drinks is a high threshold), we found that binge drinking picked up for the matched sample of current Boeing workers in 2003, de-

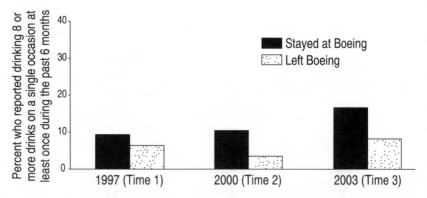

Figure 8.5 Binge drinking: comparison of workers who stayed at Boeing versus left Boeing

picted in figure 8.5. (The difference between the two groups in 1997 is not significant.) Significantly, the attrition sample's fluctuations, by comparison, remained low and did not change very much over time.

PHYSICAL HEALTH

Work absences and physical health problems provide another window into the health effects experienced by Boeing workers. For example, we recorded a significant increase in the average number of missed work days between 2000 and 2003 that failed to recover by 2006, even after the company's future brightened, employment levels stabilized, and many of the substantial work processes became more routine (see figure 8.6).

Why absences increased in our sample is open to speculation. It could be that employees were ill more frequently, were withdrawing from the company or avoiding work, or using time away to "recharge their batteries." On the basis of their meta-analysis, Darr and Johns (2008) suggest that in response to workplace stress, absenteeism early in one's exposure to stress before it has taken its toll may be viewed as a more positive coping technique. Later on, however, absenteeism may be a result of avoidance or increased health problems that have resulted from prolonged exposure to work stress. We believe that the latter interpretation is more likely given the number of years the company was in active turmoil. Importantly, Darr and Johns comment that the overall summation of many studies on work strain and absenteeism renders a relatively small statistical effect; nonetheless, they emphasize that it is costly when one con-

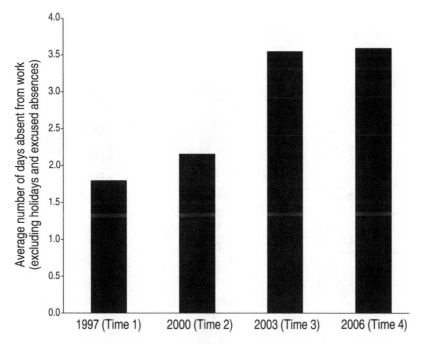

Figure 8.6 Number of workdays missed in the past twelve months

siders the impacts on lost productivity, increased health care premiums, or over-time wages.

As to physical health symptoms, we asked workers to indicate whether they had experienced the following problems in the past twelve months: headaches, back pain, heart problems, high blood pressure, and ulcers. Given what we noted earlier about allostatic load and the varied ways stress can affect well-being, we reasoned that the summative index of these items, all of which have been linked to work stress in previous studies,[14] would provide a reasonable, though necessarily partial, measure of the overall health effects of living through so much company change. As seen with many of the other well-being indica-tors in this chapter, Boeing employees' self-reported health problems were low-est in 1997 (average of 1.4), reached their highest point in 2003 (average of 1.7), but did not decrease significantly in 2006 (average of 1.7), indicating the exis-tence of lingering effects of Boeing's bad performance, multiple changes, and constant uncertainty. Especially telling, once again, are the comparisons be-tween those who left and those who stayed with the company: despite the fact that the sample was aging, figure 8.7 shows that those who left Boeing reported improved health outcomes.

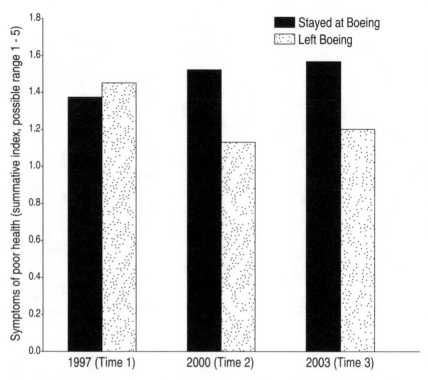

Figure 8.7 Poor health symptoms: comparison of workers who stayed at Boeing versus left Boeing

Further examination of the five items in our physical health index measure clarifies what is going on behind the overall trends for the continuously employed sample. Headaches, ulcers, and heart problems followed the pattern of peaking in 2003 and recovering in 2006, whereas blood pressure continued to climb into 2006. Back pain reflected consistently high rates that did not show significant change over time for the sample of employees who completed all four surveys (see figure 8.8).

Because of the very low base rates for ulcers and heart problems, we were not able to make meaningful comparisons at the item level between our attrition and matched comparison subgroups. We did find, however, that reports of headaches (see figure 8.9) showed a significant improvement for those who left the company after our 1997 survey. Back pain,[15] on the other hand, stayed steady at a fairly high level among continuously employed employees, but decreased for those who left the company (see figure 8.10), perhaps supporting our earlier assertion that some measures of health were probably already elevated

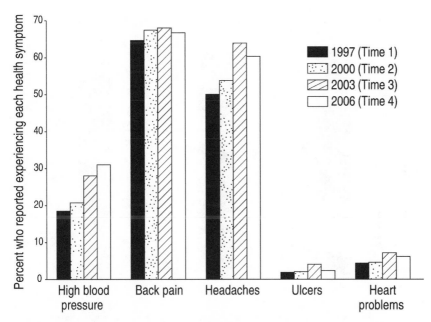

Figure 8.8 Percentage of workers reporting various health problems in the past twelve months over the four survey administrations

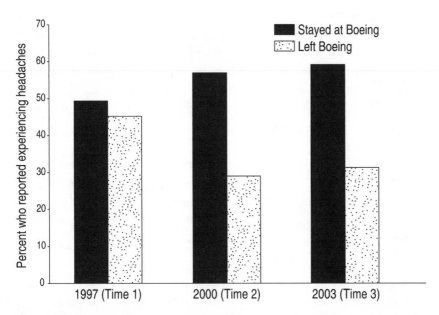

Figure 8.9 Percentage of workers reporting headaches, past twelve months: comparison of workers who stayed at Boeing versus left Boeing

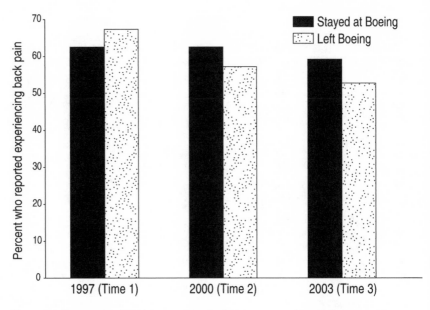

Figure 8.10 Percentage of workers reporting back pain, past twelve months: comparison of workers who stayed at Boeing versus left Boeing

when we did our first survey in 1997. Regarding blood pressure, the continuously employed and those who left Boeing showed nearly identical readings on this health indicator in 1997 (see figure 8.11). Upon leaving the company, the attrition group experienced a significant decline in 2000 and then rose in 2003, though not to the level of those who stayed with the company. By contrast, the continuously employed group experienced a steady increase in blood pressure from 1997 to 2003, suggesting once again that leaving Boeing was good for one's health.

In other research studies, investigators have studied health impacts beyond those we listed above, such as sleep disturbances, fatigue, cholesterol, hormone inflammation markers, and coronary heart disease.[16] Responding to the full set of company-initiated changes, employees often mentioned these additional types of deleterious health impacts as well as those that were part of our physical health measure.

> Feel very bitter. Tired all the time. Not the same person as I was 20 yrs ago, but, I still think I can make a difference and give 210% everyday. Silly me. [female hourly worker, nineteen years at Boeing, 2006]

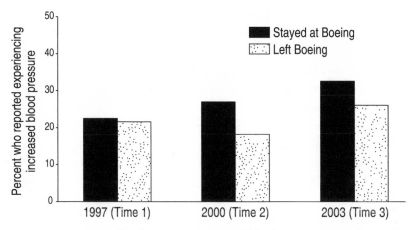

Figure 8.11 Percentage of workers reporting increased blood pressure, past twelve months: comparison of workers who stayed at Boeing versus left Boeing

The workload for everyone has increased. Jobs that used to get done are no longer performed. There is less oversight. Some people are checking out. Others are trying to do it all. Lean production techniques are increasing the amount of knowledge of other people's process issues. Improvements are being made; however, bosses are launching multiple efforts with inadequate resources and overlapping goals. Increased pressure to perform. More trouble sleeping. [male manager, twenty-nine years at Boeing, 2006]

And as we saw in our quantitative data from the attrition sample, leaving the stress-filled work world of Boeing was associated with improved health for some workers.

I do not have headaches anymore. I exercise more and feel calmer and feel very happy most days. I spend time with my grandbabies and feel like we are making a difference. [female exempt worker, twenty-five years at Boeing, 2003]

I retired as soon as I turned fifty-five. The last three years I was at Boeing, I had at least three headaches a week—sometimes they lasted all week. Since I left Boeing two years ago, I don't believe I've had more than half-dozen headaches. [male employee, twenty-seven years at Boeing, 2000]

Notably for a number of workers, work-stress-induced health problems resulted in a broad set of related health problems. A managerial woman with twenty years at Boeing told us in 2003 that she mentally and emotionally took work home every night. As a result, her sleep habits were "horrible": she was agitated and constantly tired. She tried taking antidepressants but couldn't tolerate them, and she suffered from stomach ailments and took several medications for these symptoms as well. The stomach problems continued to the point that she planned to see a specialist. To relieve stress, she said she should exercise, but didn't. She gained about fifteen pounds and felt tired all the time. She acknowledged that she did not appear grossly overweight but knew the weight impacted how she felt.

The most powerful testimonies, however, often came from those employees who linked workplace change and stress to more chronic, dramatic, and devastating medical conditions. Even though these remarks were much more infrequent, they illustrate the potential power of the workplace to impact employee health in a way that no bar chart can ever convey.

For a number of these employees, exposure to the work stress exacerbated preexisting medical conditions, resulting in serious, debilitating outcomes. One forty-two-year-old managerial woman with twenty-two years at Boeing, interviewed in 2003, noted that her group faced intense pressure when situations came up that delayed an airplane delivery. During those times, she said, the "weight of the world" was on her shoulders and she had on occasion needed to work twenty-hour days for up to six weeks in a row. She had a mild, inherited heart condition that recently elevated to a more serious level. Her father, who also had the same heart condition, did not experience this elevation until age sixty. Toward the end of this intensive six-week period, she had a routine doctor appointment and her doctor ordered her to take six to eight weeks of rest. He would not allow her to go to work the next day even though she protested. The doctor said that the cause of her ailment was not physical in nature, but rather the result of the increased stress on her heart.

Another female employee similarly linked changes in her preexisting health problems to increased stress at the job. She told us, "I went to work for Boeing in 1991 as an office administrator, the equivalent of a secretary. I was also an executive office administrator assistant to management at an executive level. Since the mid to late 1980s, I began having symptoms of fibromyalgia/chronic fatigue syndrome, but wasn't diagnosed until 1999 (while I worked at Boeing). The onset cause was determined as stress—job stress. Due to my workload at Boeing, the warp speed pace and the pressures and stresses of my job, these issues, I believe, greatly exacerbated the illness to the point that I had to retire early because of it in the spring of 2004. In the end, I was at the point of collapse" (female nonexempt worker, twelve years at Boeing, 2006).

And another commented, "I live with constant pain in my back. My hands are shot and need medical attention again. I feel less alive each year I put in here. If I had been smarter I wouldn't have given my all for Boeing, because in the long run it doesn't matter. There is someone else out there ready to take your place when you physically can't do anymore and [I] become an emotional mess from trying to hold it together at home and giving your all to Boeing at the same time. Yes, the pay is good but is my life worth that little?!" (female hourly worker, seventeen years at Boeing, 2006).

Other workers mentioned having to take time off or having to be hospitalized due, in part, to health problems that were either caused by, or aggravated by, work-related stress. For those who are looking for clear cause and effect relationships between work stress and health, it is obvious that these types of testimonials leave room for the skeptic to point to other root causes. And yet, these testimonials also make clear that the reality for many employees is that multiple forms of work stress, psychological difficulties, and physical ailments are interwoven, each contributing to, and being made worse by, the presence of the other. "Our organization has 'integrated' several engineering functions and reorganized more than usual (and that's saying a lot for Boeing). After 'integration' I've had very little choice about my new role in the integrated organization. I now pretty much hate my job and very little was done to prepare us for the new role and every day I have to find someone to explain or learn from. Very frustrating. I recently took a full month off, partly to address medical problems (diabetes and kidney stones) and partly to really think about what I wanted and could afford to do about my future and career" (female manager, twenty-seven years at Boeing, 2006).

And similarly, "Less workers—more work. No one to train to take over as we retire. Boeing is a team now, not a family (you can 'cut' team members, not family). More work for each person, cut in pay, health benefits, etc. . . . 'contracts.' More subcontracting, seeing our jobs leave the U.S. (outsourcing work). Loss of confidence in Boeing leaders. Promotions going to 'qualified' folks instead of 'best qualified' folks over and over and over. More stress. More tense. More pushed. Not happy—effects home life. Poor health. Emotionally drained. Can't sleep thinking of work. Since 2001, get six weeks vacation, take only one off per year. No time off. In the hospital two times this year. In the hospital two times last year" (male hourly worker, twenty-six years at Boeing, 2006).

Sudden and serious health effects were cited by a handful of workers who directly linked work stress to life and death itself. Even if these incidents are not common, and even if we are not able to *prove* that the work stress was the direct cause of the health problem, they illustrate the power of, and the intensity with which workers experienced, work stress.

> If things keep going the way they are going right now, I visualize a special garage right next to each building which will house a special cardiac unit. . . . I had a heart attack back in November, and I know a lot of it was attributed to the stress I was going through and the programs going on. . . . Because of the cutbacks, because of the new programs, all the other stuff they're throwing at us, all the basic pressures we have to deal with on a daily basis, I'm surprised they're not hauling people out on stretchers left and right because it's a pressure cooker. [focus group participant, 1996]

> Since leaving I have had quadruple heart surgery within a year after leaving. If I would have stayed, I would have had a heart attack on the job from stress. [male hourly worker, eleven years at Boeing, 2003]

> I found myself trapped and unable to transfer after 9/11/01. My boss was a bully who used his military intelligence background to bully and intimidate his employees. I went to the HR director and told him I was being sickened by this supervisor. The HR director did nothing. I found these events to be so disturbing that I suffered two heart attacks, chronic heart failure and internal bleeding. The incompetency of Boeing management has very nearly cost me my life. And ironically has done so because I care. [male professional worker, twenty-six years at Boeing, 2006]

CONCLUSION

Taken together, what do these numerical comparisons and individual employee comments tell us about the connection between workplace change and worker's health? How serious and widespread were bad health outcomes at Boeing over the course of our study?

Before taking on these questions, we must recognize some realities about social science research that this chapter has illuminated. First, it is unlikely that any single measure, such as "depression" or "sense of personal control" will, on its own, paint a full picture of the health impacts of change and uncertainty in the workplace. As obvious as it may seem, we must remember that people react to stress in a wide variety of ways. When all such stress symptoms are combined across all the participants in the study, no one measure is likely to show a dramatic shift—this would require the vast majority to have the same health reaction. Second, some health problems, such as heart problems (fortunately), do not occur all that often in the general working population and will not, by their nature, show large changes that rise to the level of "statistical significance."

For these two reasons, consideration of a broad set of health outcomes and behaviors gives us a better reading of the degree to which employee health suffered as a result of the myriad of changes Boeing workers and managers encountered. Moreover, many other variables make it nearly impossible to draw clear, causal connections between workplace experiences and health outcomes: some health problems may take a while to develop; some forms of workplace change were disruptive for some employees and not for others; and multiple changes happened in the company at the same point in time, making it difficult to disentangle the impact of a particular variable. Equally important, it is likely that Boeing workers and managers were already experiencing some ill effects from multiple changes in the company by the time we conducted our first survey in 1997, making it difficult to use 1997 as a true baseline against which to measure health changes through 2006. For this reason, as mentioned at the outset of this chapter, we may have failed to capture a more dramatic rise in health problems within our four surveys because the big changes in health may well have taken place before we came on the scene. The striking improvements in several indicators of well-being for those who left the company substantiate this claim and also reveal the often hidden well-being costs of workplace change.

So to answer the question "Did employee's health suffer during the ten-year period under study?" we must conclude "yes." There is evidence of some harmful consequences. While some employees fared better and others suffered only slightly, some reported that serious damage had been done to their health. As we have mentioned in earlier chapters, a sizable number of employees emerged bruised, battered, and resilient as a result of living through the ten-plus years of workplace change. The individual comments alone graphically illustrate this point, even if they do not tell us the degree to which these were pervasive problems across the entire employee pool.

To the question "Did Boeing-related change and turmoil *cause* employee's health to suffer?" we must also conclude, "Yes, to some extent," recognizing, of course, that all health problems are likely a function of multiple factors. We conclude this for several reasons. First, many of the changes for the full sample we saw from 1997 through 2006 are consistent with changes that took place within the company during the time of the study. In some cases, well-being appeared to mirror the stability of the company—sense of personal control, for example—whereas in other cases a more permanent, deleterious impact was observed (for example, the number of bad health symptoms reported). Furthermore, when we compare surviving employees with those who left the company, the data are particularly compelling in pointing to how working for the company affected certain health measures such as depression and reported poor health symptoms. Last, employees themselves in their individual remarks and, they reported, sometimes their physician's, linked their levels of work stress to various types of health problems. Although we cannot substantiate these claims and fully recognize that any single piece of evidence might not paint a convincing picture, the combination of these sources of information makes the link more compelling. While we readily concede that working for another company undergoing such change might not have been any easier, we do believe that work stress triggered by constant change and uncertainty was a partial cause for many of the aliments reported by employees, both on our surveys and in our interviews.

As to whether these health effects are "dramatic" or "consequential," we must also qualify our answer. While the quantitative data are not as remarkable, perhaps, as some of the individual stories of severe, life-altering health problems, we must consider what we mean by "consequential" or "dramatic." Heart attacks by anyone's definition are consequential, but so perhaps is feeling a depressive symptom one more day per week than in the past. "Consequential for whom?" is probably the question that should be asked. To the employee or his family it most likely matters a lot. For the company, the answer is less clear and involves many broader issues such as health care costs, lost work days, and costs associated with turnover.

If, as we have argued in earlier chapters, Boeing is emblematic of many large American manufacturing organizations confronting pressures that, on the face of it, can be solved most effectively via downsizing, outsourcing, merging, going lean, and adopting new technologies, what do these findings bode for the well-being of today's workers and managers in the United States more broadly? What can an employee do for him or herself to meet and cope with the realities of this new workplace? What can companies do to help employees as they undergo change, and is there a role for government in reducing the ill effects of workplace change? It is to these questions that we turn our attention in the next and final chapter.

Chapter 9 Navigating
Through Turbulence

TURBULENCE: BOEING AND THE STATE OF
AMERICAN WORKERS AND MANAGERS

Our study of Boeing from 1996 through 2006 enabled us to capture a company in transition, at the cusp of change, pushed by powerful social, technological, and competitive forces to change its business strategy and operations. Boeing employees had no choice but to adjust, though the costs were high for many of them. But it is not Boeing alone and its employees who have been going through these changes. Across the board, corporations in a wide range of manufacturing and service industries are confronting a hypercompetitive global and domestic environment which forces continuous innovations in products, services, and processes, attention to efficiency and cost-cutting, and a scaling back or even termination of the postwar model that combined high wages and benefits with reasonable expectations for long-term job security.[1] The Boeing story we tell, then, both demonstrates and portends a fundamental transformation in the relationship between employees and the firms in which they work.[2]

What we have in the United States in a larger sense, then, are corporations, employees, and a national economy all also at the cusp of change.

This does not mean that Boeing, or other large companies, are now so different from what they were in the past as to be unrecognizable to inside or outside observers. It does imply, however, that we are heading in a different direction, perhaps one that requires some reevaluation of what employees can realistically expect from companies and what they should ask of themselves, their unions, their companies, and their political leaders. Fleshing out the implications of this new reality for workers, and asking what might be done to accommodate needed changes while protecting the well-being of present and future employees, constitute the focus of this chapter.

Did Boeing Have a Choice in Doing What It Did?

It is reasonable to ask whether Boeing needed to change so fundamentally, given the turmoil and pain it caused many of its surviving employees—to say nothing of the pain caused to those who lost their jobs or who were encouraged to take early retirement, or to the many local communities where these former employees lived. Our short answer to this question is a qualified "yes." Even as they turned around the company between 2003 and 2006,[3] however, Boeing leaders made more than a few missteps and often behaved badly toward their employees during the years of our study as they instituted multiple and sweeping changes.

They were stunningly insensitive at times to the needs and wishes of their employees, for example. Boeing leaders might have created a more consistent strategy, better explained the reasons for decisions, and done much more to soften the impact of changes on their employees. They might have been more honest with their employees and investors about problems, including those that led to the seizing up of manufacturing in 1997—problems which Boeing top executives tried to explain away and deny until the disaster became obvious to everyone.[4]

More deliberate and careful calculation of medium- and long-term employment needs might have led to less dramatic swings in head count—the "fire and rehire" swings at Boeing are legendary—lessening the toll on employees. Boeing leaders, moreover, might have paid more attention to, and been more appreciative of, Boeing traditions and the sensibilities of its long-term workforce during the merger with McDonnell Douglas. They could have invested more in the development of new airplanes and less in stock repurchases to pump up share prices. They might have been more careful, moreover, about over-outsourcing and more honest about the financial drivers of company policy. They most certainly could have reduced employee cynicism by being more circumspect in making claims about the value to the company of long-term employees—"employees are our most important resource"—even as they were planning massive layoffs. And Boeing leaders might have behaved more ethically and avoided institutional embarrassment, financial penalties, and damaged employee commitment.

If Boeing leaders can be faulted on several of their most important strategic and tactical decisions and the manner in which some of the changes were introduced and managed, we nevertheless believe that many of their decisions for repositioning the company to make it a stronger competitor in the commercial airplane market were appropriate and necessary. In the final analysis, we believe Boeing had to change, and had to do so in essentially the ways it did.

For example, it needed to modernize design, engineering, and manufacturing processes whose main features were not much different from those used to build bombers during the Second World War. It needed to improve the quality of its talent pool, given the aging profile of its workforce, and it made sense to do some outsourcing both to American-based companies and to foreign ones where new talent was to be found. It needed to gain access to foreign markets by shifting some of its operations to the countries of its principal customers; these offset agreements, sometimes formal and sometimes implicit, were and remain part of the cost of doing business in the global airplane market. It also probably was prudent to find investors, often in those same countries, to share in the financial risks of launching an expensive new airplane model when it finally did so with the 787.[5] And, inevitably, with dramatically improved productivity achieved through process innovations, IT improvements (particularly computer-aided design and computerized tracking and ordering of parts), and workplace reorganization (cross-functional teams, more supportive supervisory styles, and the like), fewer employees were required per airplane produced than in the past. Downsizing of some sort was probably unavoidable, though Boeing may have overdone it, as suggested by the several occasions during our study when they had to rapidly ramp up hiring to replace the skilled employees they had let go. Finally, it needed to respond to social, cultural, legal, and public policy pressures to increase the representation of minorities and women in their employee ranks, which happened slowly but with significant improvement by the end of our study period.

A powerful piece of evidence supporting our claim about the necessity of many Boeing changes comes from examining the direction Airbus has taken recently. Though it operates in a very different political and regulatory environment than Boeing, being on the surface more protective of employee job security and (until very recently) of its core competencies, Airbus's behavior on head count and outsourcing has begun to mimic its rival to a surprising degree.[6] For example, EADS, the parent company of Airbus, has announced an initiative called Power8 that aims to cut costs and make Airbus more efficient so as to better respond to the challenge of its Boeing competitor.[7] The plan envisions cutting the Airbus labor force by ten thousand, including five thousand full-time, regular employees; selling manufacturing plants while maintaining a subcontractor relationship with the new owners; cutting cycle time for new planes from seven and a half years to six years; spreading lean production across the company; and building a network of Tier 1 Risk Sharing suppliers to take on most of the responsibility for designing and manufacturing sections of Airbus airplanes. (The arrangements for Airbus's latest offering, the A350, are remarkably similar to the global partnering system used by Boeing for the 787.) This leaves Airbus to focus on overall airplane specification, system integration, and final assembly. This is, of course, the strategy Boeing adopted for the 787 and may be used as the template for future projects.

There also are signs that the borrowing has been going on in both directions. Boeing is adopting practices long used at Airbus to flatten the wild employment cycles caused by market fluctuations in demand. For example, as with Airbus, Boeing is increasingly relying on temporary contract labor to respond to increases in airplane orders, thus avoiding the costs and bad publicity of having to lay off thousands of permanent employees. Of course, this and other strategies used by Airbus merely displace some of the pain caused by the layoffs of permanent workers onto workers on temporary contracts and those employed by subcontractors and suppliers.

Though it is hard to tell who is copying whom in all of this, it is clear that Airbus and Boeing are moving in the same general direction, becoming more similar in every respect, in spite of the substantial differences between American and European political systems, regulatory regimes, and labor unions. This suggests either simple faddishness or recognition of what is necessary in a globally competitive market by the leaders of each company. We suspect it is the latter.

While the commercial airplane sector is fairly distinctive—the cost of entry is high, a duopoly is in place, and national governments are deeply concerned about the health and vitality of the leading firms—many of the trends and developments we have described, including vigorous cost cutting, process improvements, outsourcing and downsizing, emphasis on shareholder value, and deploying IT to coordinate supply chains, have become common in globally competitive firms. This suggests that Boeing and Airbus faced strong pressures from global markets to move in the directions described above.[8] The pressures to shorten cycle times, cut costs, seek partners, and outsource a wide range of activities will not lessen in most industries, including the commercial airplane sector. Expensive projects will still require risk-sharing partners—Merck and Company, for example, has several such partners in China doing pharmaceutical research with it. Complex products will still need to tap into the world's top engineering and manufacturing talent, and countries with the largest and fastest growing markets—China and India in particular—will continue to insist that significant portions of the design and manufacture of products take place in their countries as a condition for selling there.

The Emerging Employee-Company Relationship

The forces creating a more uncertain and riskier environment for globally competitive companies and their employees are powerful and probably unstoppable, something that American workers, companies, unions, and political leaders must come to grips with. Among the most important things that are happening to increase uncertainty and risk for workers is the rapid erosion of the "welfare capitalist" model that was found at many large companies in the United States: high pay; comprehensive benefits, including health insurance and pensions; and lifelong job security.

The company as an "extended family," as Peters and Waterman put it in their book *In Search of Excellence,*[9] is becoming a wistful memory, as has been happening at Boeing. Sanford Jacoby, a leading scholar of this form of employment relationship, claims that predictions of the end of company welfare provisions such as generous health and retirement benefits and long-term job security are premature because many companies still value firm-specific skills and will do all they can to retain skilled workers for the long haul.[10] However, the process of outsourcing all but the most high-end design, engineering, and systems management work at Boeing suggests that it and other companies are quite prepared to move to a more fluid and "market-like" relationship with their employees even when engaged in the production of highly sophisticated and complex products. Our sense is that the security and stability of the old model will apply to fewer and fewer privileged core workers and, perhaps, only in companies where suitable skills cannot be found elsewhere or where powerful labor unions are able to forge collective bargaining agreements that slow the outsourcing process.

The most recent authoritative studies of what is happening across the wider economy also reinforce the view that long-term job security is eroding, even for those with high seniority and college degrees. Between 1976 and 2006, for example, average job tenure in the United States fell by around 34 percent for men between the ages of thirty-five and sixty-four. Henry Farber, an economist who has conducted some of the most rigorous work in this area, finds that this erosion in job tenure is accelerating, with successive birth cohorts of males less likely than previous generations to enjoy long-term job tenure, and warns young workers that they should not expect to have similar career patterns as those of their parents.[11] He speculates this is occurring because companies may feel increasingly shackled by stable workforces as they face increased global competition. Highly competitive environments may compel more frequent changes in business strategy, such as a greater reliance on outsourcing, as Yahoo did in fall 2009, for example, when it announced that it was shifting all software and Web site development of Yahoo News to Taiwan (keeping only editorial operations in the United States) in a move to reduce costs. But the option of sending work outside the company reduces not only head count but also the need on the part of companies to work hard at cementing the loyalty and commitment of its employees. We saw indications of this at Boeing, with the growth in outsourcing of high-skill-level work, producing the fastest growth in job security fears among college-educated engineers, employees that companies would normally be expected to do their utmost to retain given the investment companies make into their training and tenure.[12]

This more market-based and fluid employment relationship has real economic, social, and psychological costs for American workers and for their families and communities. As we discuss below, companies can do many things to improve the conditions of work for their employees and soften some of the painful consequences of their actions, if they are so inclined. We hope and trust that many will be so motivated, especially in light of the fact that attending to these things generally improves company performance. Nevertheless, it seems inescapable that most large companies will more or less behave as Boeing has done, because structural forces in the global economy, including competitors, potential competitors, and investors, have changed the terrain on which they operate.

Even companies as large and seemingly impregnable as General Motors (which entered and emerged from Chapter 11 bankruptcy in 2009) or AIG (bailed out by the federal government on several occasions in 2008 and 2009), as well as Hewlett-Packard and Microsoft, are vulnerable to the risks posed in the new, hypercompetitive global market economy. Companies cannot, even with the best of intentions of being good corporate citizens, guarantee they will provide job security and comprehensive benefits for life for their workforce. The postwar conditions that made the high-security, high-pay, and high-benefits social contract possible are rapidly disappearing, a point made forcefully and accurately by Robert Reich in his book *Supercapitalism.*[13]

What is therefore needed is a new arrangement that acknowledges this change and finds a sensible balance between providing more stability and security for workers and their families without sacrificing the flexibility that companies must have to survive and succeed in the new economy.

WHAT IS TO BE DONE?

Most of the changes our Boeing study participants experienced are broadly typical of what has been happening to employees of other large American manufacturing companies, whether International Harvester, Ford, General Electric, or Caterpillar, to name but a few, as well as to those of many companies outside of manufacturing, including those in business services, finance, software design, and the like. For example, Cisco Systems, Unilever, DuPont, and Marriott use IBM, Genpact, and Accenture to outsource, computerize, and administer their human resource, payroll, and information technology functions. In some respects, though, what we have uncovered among Boeing employees may significantly *understate* the disruptive impacts of job and workplace changes on most American workers. Boeing may be as good as it gets for American workers, because Boeing employees were better protected than employees in other companies against the ill effects of the multiple and continuous changes we have described in this book. After all, the vast majority of Boeing employees, unlike the overwhelming majority of private sector workers in the United States, are represented by relatively strong and active unions and, as a result, retain higher than average salaries and a wide range of company-provided benefits, including health insurance, retirement accounts, and support for continuing education.

Boeing is also in a more favorable position than many other firms in the United States because it is the largest (by dollar value) manufacturing exporter in the American economy, makes products and systems (such as avionics) that are important for American competitiveness, and has many assembly and fabrication operations in the United States. The company is, therefore, essential to the economic health of many local communities. This gives it important access to political and community leaders who cannot help but be attentive to the health and vitality of the company.[14] Additional political support comes from the fact that Boeing is an important component of the larger Boeing Company, one of the nation's most significant space and defense contractors, and that many of the designs, production procedures, and systems in commercial aircraft have dual-use potential, meaning they can be adapted for use in military aircraft. The Boeing Company, it is safe to say, can be confident that many of its needs will be attended to by government officials,[15] something not all firms and their employees can count on.

So what lessons can be drawn from the experience of Boeing employees, knowing that employees in other large firms probably don't enjoy so many of its advantages? Are we helpless in the face of larger forces in the global economy or are there ways to adapt, adjust, and improve employee prospects? We take an optimistic stand. We believe that firms can do better by their employees even as they remain competitive, and that employees can do more to protect themselves and prepare for taking advantage of change. We believe, however, that companies and their employees can thrive in an intensely competitive global marketplace only if government provides adequate safety nets to help protect and sustain American workers and to help prepare them for future employment. This will require a role for government that is historically far more expansive than ever before. The obstacles to public policy changes will be formidable. But the time may be ripe for new ways of thinking.

What Companies Can Do
for Their Employees

There are many things that companies are doing or can do to help cushion their employees against some of the ravages of change and give them the opportunity to thrive. They need only to be convinced it is important to do so. There is plenty of evidence that having engaged and committed workers who are freed up to use their talents as individuals and in collaboration with others is a central element in firm performance.[16] Firm performance generally is affected by the degree to which employees "buy in" to the overall mission of their company and the changes the company attempts to make. Employee resistance to, or confusion about, workplace reforms often undermines what top executives are trying to achieve. And unhappy employees can damage relationships with customers where timely, competent, and courteous service is essential to firm profitability. The 2000 SPEEA and 2005 IAM strikes at Boeing that caused significant production delays, bad feelings with customers and suppliers, and financial losses are examples of what can happen.

This is important in many economic sectors, including obvious cases such as retail sales, but also at large manufacturing companies like Boeing, where airplanes are first sold to airline customers, then serviced for a thirty- to forty-year period, with Boeing and Airbus providing parts and technical assistance. Even as many large companies find themselves under pressure in the global market economy to stay competitive by becoming leaner and more efficient, there are good reasons for them to keep the welfare of their employees in mind as they introduce changes. They must take care not to "over-steer," such as over-outsource or over-WARN, and to be more thoughtful about what changes are really necessary and how they should be introduced into the workplace.

STEPS TO IMPROVE MORALE AND COMMITMENT

Companies can do things to keep their employees committed and engaged even as they make major changes to meet market competition and please investors. Companies could, for example, do a much better job of sharing the gains and pains of company performance with their employees, something that demonstrates in tangible ways rather than in trite slogans—"we're all in this together" or "winning together"—that employees are valued and respected stakeholders.

Profit sharing is one obvious way to share gains. Typically, this takes the form of bonuses or stock distributions based on company profitability. This has been done for a long time by many companies, with good results for employee morale and commitment and for firm performance.[17] More companies could initiate profit sharing schemes or expand existing ones without much fuss; both employees and companies generally gain by it.[18]

Sharing pain is another matter entirely. For the most part, the pain from downsizing is borne entirely by employees, either those losing their jobs or survivors worried they might be next. Top executives should feel some of the effects as well, we believe. At a minimum, corporate boards should not vote bonuses for top executives when the company is not performing well and employees are losing their jobs, nor should top executives accept bonuses under these circumstances. If matters reach the level where companies impose on their employees pay freezes or mandatory furloughs with loss of pay, top executives, either voluntarily or under board guidance, should have their salaries and bonuses frozen or have their pay decreased by a similar magnitude to that of their employees. More than a few companies, including Nucor Steel, did this during the deep recession of 2008–9. To the argument that, during hard times, top executives may well be making tough decisions that are good for their firms and their employees over the long run, and therefore should be rewarded, we suggest that their reward will come when growth and profitability return. We favor these steps to share pain not on moral grounds of fairness—though that may be reason enough—but because sharing hard times with employees helps their morale, engagement, and commitment, which is imperative for firm performance.

And it behooves top executives to show some restraint in their lifestyles, or in exercising their stock options, especially when layoffs are happening or when employees are enjoying few tangible gains from company success. Several Boeing employees told us in interviews, for example, how angry they were at the lavish living of former president and CEO Phil Condit, who, in the midst of the disastrous and costly manufacturing meltdown of 1997, used company money to remodel rooms in the elegant Four Seasons Hotel into a grand apartment for himself. Employees were also upset at the gains made by him and other top executives when the company introduced its stock repurchase plan which drove up share prices. Corporate boards can rewrite rules on executive compensation and bonuses so they better reflect company performance, something that many already are doing in response to popular outrage at bailouts during the economic troubles in 2008–9.

Most companies could also do a better job of treating their employees with respect and dignity. They might, for example, include employees more in deliberations about the company's future and share with them the reasons why it is introducing changes in work processes, what the company's finances look like, and what its competitors are doing. This might mean holding regular meetings where employees could question top executives. Or this might mean distributing to employees reasonably candid reports and recommendations from company consultants, or opening the books for employee representatives. It could mean, as well, forming a substantial part of company operations around semiautonomous teams in which employees help define team objectives, refashion work processes to meet these objectives, create metrics to measure success and failure, and are rewarded in part by team performance and contribution to the company's success.

There is reason to believe that employees want to be proud of the products and services their companies make and provide. Pride can come from a number of directions. Some companies gain their reputation and employee buy-in by producing cutting-edge products or services. Apple and Google have done so, with each having gained iconic status. There have been times when Boeing produced at the cutting edge, before 1994, for example, when the 747, the 757, the 767, and the 777 were produced. Some Boeing employees told us they were still proud of working for Boeing, even during the bad years of 1996–2004, because they were part of building great airplanes they could see flying overhead every day. We are convinced that the turnaround in morale and some elements of well-being among Boeing employees we reported after 2003 were because of the launch of the path-breaking 787 Dreamliner, about which Boeing workers were understandably proud, something that was evident in our respondents' open-ended answers on our fourth survey.

Not every company can be at the cutting edge. But there are many other paths leading to the affections of employees. Producing the best goods or the best service, even in less glamorous industries, can do the trick, we believe— see Kimberly-Clark in the paper products sector and Nordstrom in the retail sector.[19] We recommend that companies try to make continuous innovation a central element of who they are as a firm, with innovation directed at not only improving efficiencies and cutting costs in operations, but creating new and better products and services. This is not easy, to be sure, and there is no clear path to make this happen. But the goal cannot be ignored.

STEPS TO LESSEN THE PAIN OF DOWNSIZING AND LAYOFFS

It goes without saying that the policy that would most directly address employee anxieties about layoffs is to avoid layoffs in the first place. Though some firms have tried, it is exceedingly difficult to do over the long run. We say this for three reasons. First, any gains in productivity, whether through improvements in work flows and processes or technological innovations, mean that the same number of commodities or services can be produced with fewer workers or that the same number of workers can produce more. The only way to maintain employment levels in the face of productivity improvements is to sell more —a desirable but not necessarily realistic option. Second, if a company were to stop or slow the pace of productivity increases, rival companies enjoying productivity gains would inevitably take a larger share of the market—certainly a losing strategy for any company to follow.

Third, a company might choose not to outsource, whether to other companies in the same country or to companies abroad, keeping all work in-house and maintaining employment levels. This might work in some economic sectors where a firm may not have market rivals—as in regulated electrical generation, to take one example—or where it enjoys market domination and costs of entry to new firms is high (perhaps Intel for computer chips during a period in the 1990s). For the most part, however, especially among globally competitive firms, all players outsource to one extent or another, either for market entry reasons, for access to skills, or for sharing investment risk. To eschew outsourcing for most firms in most situations is a strategy fraught with risk, allowing rivals to gain advantages on multiple fronts. Alas, it is hard to see how a "no layoffs" policy could be sustained, though Nucor Steel and Southwest Airlines, among others, managed to do this even in the face of the deep 2008–9 recession. It is worth pointing out that "no layoff" companies often address bad economic times by getting rid of temporary workers and instituting mandatory furloughs, with resulting contraction of employee paychecks (many employees at Nucor, for example, saw their pay cut 40 percent in 2009). The former solutions mean that layoffs are happening, even if not to the regular full-time workforce; the latter solution is a serious hardship for employees.

So outsourcing, downsizing, and layoffs seem, to some degree, to be inevitable. These practices are costly for employees, both for those who are laid off and for those who survive, as we have shown. They are also sometimes more costly than it first appears for companies, as morale suffers among those who remain, as some tasks are done less well as people with less experience take over or surviving employees are asked to do more, and as customers are sometimes inconvenienced or suffer a loss in the quality of service.

However, though unavoidable, the pace and extent of layoffs might be better controlled and the ill effects of layoffs mitigated if certain practices were put in place. For example, companies ought to allow employee teams or departments to bid on work that is targeted for outsourcing, something that GE agreed to in a recent contract with the IAM (machinists') union. If outsourcing work proves to be more expensive than keeping it in-house under an employee bid system, there would be no reason to ship work out, all other things being equal. Boeing did, in fact, enter into an agreement with the IAM for such a bidding process after its strike in 1995, but the company kept full control over the process, with Boeing and Boeing alone authorized to make the final decision on internal bids. The very first time the contract clause was exercised—to build pressurized doors for a number of models—Boeing turned down the union's bid in 1997 with no explanation and shipped the work overseas. Needless to say, this result angered and dismayed Boeing employees and the employee bid system was mostly forgotten. This suggests that companies who choose to enter into such employee bid arrangements must treat proposals from employees seriously or risk further alienating those who work for them.

It is important as well that companies not over-outsource. To over-outsource, that is, to send outside the company more than is optimal, not only hurts current and future company employees who see work and jobs leaving, but creates the risk that companies will lose control of their supply chain. Boeing eventually came to realize that it had over-outsourced under the global partnering arrangements for the design and production of the 787 Dreamliner. As of this writing in spring 2010, the first customer delivery of the new airplane is roughly two years behind schedule, with most of the delay attributed to inadequate coordination by Boeing of global partners and the less-than-expected abilities of second-tier suppliers (such as those who supply parts to and do contract work for the major global partners). To solve the problem, Boeing has been bringing oversight and coordination responsibilities back to the Puget Sound region, rehiring or newly hiring additional people with the skills to do these jobs, often pulling people off other important projects, including the 737, 747, and 777.[20] Boeing acted to gain even more control over its supply chain in 2009 by buying the 787 division of one of its global partners, Vought Aircraft, and dispatching people from Renton to take charge.

Another strategy that companies might pursue to both protect employee jobs and keep company access to talent is to support the creation of new start-ups by employees who have tangible and doable plans for products or services that are potentially useful for the company. The company would take an equity share in the new venture. If the new venture is successful, the parent company makes a profit on its equity position, maintains a working relationship with its talented former employees, and has privileged access to needed products and services. There is some financial risk in such a strategy, to be sure, but it has been done with considerable success already by firms in the software industry, including Microsoft and Google. Of course, it is not reasonable for a large manufacturing company such as Boeing or Ford to invest in start-ups that do large-scale manufacturing—this would require far too much money in risky ventures—but specialized tooling, software development, and the like seem to be likely candidates.[21] Companies in IT or business services would have even wider scope for employee start-ups.

Finally, if layoffs cannot be avoided, then companies should ease the pain as much as possible. The least painful options are to allow natural attrition to decrease employee head count. If attrition is too slow, companies could offer buyouts to employees who choose to leave early, as GM and Ford did on a massive scale in 2008 and 2009. Even Southwest Airlines turned to a large-scale buy-out program to weather the economic crisis in 2009. Giving workers some control over their departure seems to be associated with better psychological outcomes,[22] though companies do risk losing their best workers. This happened at Boeing in 1995 and, by all accounts, helped contribute to the collapse in its manufacturing process in 1997. Indeed, Boeing turned to retirees to help fix the manufacturing bottlenecks and get the production lines moving again. So companies need to be extremely careful on how such buyouts are structured.

STEPS TO MAKE THE INTRODUCTION OF NEW WORK INITIATIVES AND TECHNOLOGIES MORE TOLERABLE

We have shown that continuous change contributes to employee stress and anxiety and makes it harder for workers, at least in the short run, to complete their tasks. Our respondents told us in interviews and focus groups that they were simply overwhelmed by the number of changes in work processes, work organization, and new technologies that they had to adapt to and incorporate in their jobs.

One way to soften the impact of such change is to avoid running after every fad that sweeps the business community. To be sure, precisely how to do this is more easily assessed in hindsight; each innovation probably seemed like a good idea at the time. They were no doubt done with the best of intentions, and with the health and vitality of the company in mind. What will help companies avoid running down blind alleys is to make sure that each initiative lines up with or is consistent with the articulated goals and vision of the company. Also, changes are more likely to work when they make sense to employees, when they see that there is a "rhyme and reason" for what they see going on around them.[23]

Moreover, changes are more likely to be accepted by employees when company leaders allow employees to be part of the process of planning, introducing, and assessing the effectiveness of workplace innovations, and the policies themselves might prove to be more effective from the point of view of the firm. Political scientists have suggested, when comparing democracies with authoritarian regimes, that the superiority of the former regime type is based in large part on the existence of both popular consent and pooled knowledge.[24] As with the citizenry in political life, employee involvement in decision-making, a form of popular consent, is likely to increase the legitimacy of policies that arise from such a process in firms as well. Just as pooled knowledge improves public policies, greater employee involvement means that companies can tap into and acknowledge the tacit knowledge of their workforce. In many circumstances, consulted workers may bring more to the table by way of deep experience, knowledge, and engagement than can hired consultants, who drop in and out of the organization.

STEPS TO HELP FRONTLINE MANAGERS

Frontline and middle managers are essential to the success of many companies but are located in particularly difficult positions within organizations. These employees are the bridge between top executives, who set general policies for their companies, and the hourly and salaried workforces, who must translate these into daily work routines. They "get it," as it were, from both directions—those on top often wonder why change is not happening at an acceptable pace, and those whom they supervise sometimes bristle at what is being demanded of them. Implementing layoffs is an especially painful experience for most managers, particularly frontline supervisors who directly interact with employees. Managers who implemented layoffs at Boeing, for example, were more likely to report health and sleep problems as well as burnout. Emotional exhaustion was evident as "people work" increased during downsizing periods, when their own supervisees needed them the most and when their own jobs may have been at risk.

Senior leadership can play a pivotal role in supporting managers as they help either to implement change or to oversee layoffs in their units. For one thing, companies can better support the human resource functions and retain human resources staff, especially during times of organizational stress. Employees, during these times, need somewhere to turn for counseling, employee assistance services, assessment, benefits explanation, career advice, and the like, and their ready availability might reduce the burden on managers. Ironically, the human resources function, usually a source of support and information for managers and company employees, has been downsized and outsourced in many companies, including Boeing, at the same time that needs for HR services have increased dramatically.

Company leaders can try to be more aware of signs of excessive stress and strain in managers, moreover, especially during times when major new process innovations and technologies are being introduced or when layoffs are occurring. Company leaders might create more outlets for stress reduction, providing passes to local gyms, for example, establishing support group–type meetings for managers, or having an open door policy so managers can talk over problems with their own supervisors. At Boeing and other companies, top executives could do a better job of acknowledging the human cost of many of their decisions, particularly regarding long-term downsizing, and letting managers know they understand how tough their job is and how much the company appreciates them.

We found at Boeing, as well, that manager teams in face-to-face meetings consulted with one another and bargained over who was to be let go—something that, one might argue, led to more considered decisions (based on the notion of "pooled intelligence"), provided social support from managers' peers, and served to insulate them as individuals from the hostility of the people they supervised. Companies should consider creating manager teams for planning and implementing big changes in operations and doing layoffs, should this last resort option be implemented.

We have seen that career paths for managers at Boeing have altered dramatically. This is true at most large companies. The traditional ladder is now a step stool with fewer rungs. Most moves, in fact, go in a lateral direction, from project to project, rather than to a higher job title with more authority and higher pay. Companies need to do more than institute "flattened" organizations; they must recognize and reward managers and other employees who add to their skills and gain a broader understanding of the organization and its goals and operations as they take on a wide range of roles such as team leaders, subject matter experts, project managers, and cross-functional coordinators. Companies must do more to support a redefinition of careers as being one of multidimensional functions, enhance the status of these new style contributors, and reward them accordingly.

What Workers Can Do for Themselves

It seems to us that the first thing workers must do is recognize and better understand the new reality. Forces let loose by globalization, technological innovation, and regulatory reform have ratcheted up competitive pressures on globally engaged firms to change, adapt, and innovate. These processes always are disruptive. Workers in all manner of private companies are discovering that instability and uncertainty are now the norm in job markets and workplaces. In this environment, it is increasingly apparent that many jobs in the future will not come with long-term job security or generous company-provided pensions and health insurance. In the face of this, what are individuals to do?

One option is for employees to disengage from their firms by questioning the efficacy of looking to the corporation as an appropriate institution for fulfilling their need for community, meaning, and careers. With their voracious demands for workers' time and energy, these "greedy institutions," as Coser calls them,[25] squeeze the time people have for their families, friends, and civic participation. As we have seen, one outcome of the changes at Boeing over the duration of our study was that more workers told us they had shifted their focus away from their work and toward family, friends, and leisure activities. If this happens on a large enough scale, one might imagine an overall enrichment of family life and community relations.

Taken too far, however, emotional distancing can turn into self-defeating outlooks and behaviors. We saw earlier that many Boeing employees reported they did the bare minimum on the job or withheld extra effort in their work. Often anger and cynicism accompanies such sentiments. While understandable, such attitudes and behaviors may not only hurt the company but also diminish the sense of empowerment, meaning, and purpose work can provide for workers. A much healthier response is for employees to find a group—whether it be project team, work group, department, or union—that they can identify with, and make the hours they spend at work productive and meaningful. Detached, passive, and disengaged workers may not only be detrimental for companies; such toxic mental states are likely to damage employee well-being over the long run.

Another thing that workers can do is to position themselves for alternative jobs or careers as their job security becomes more tenuous, as many Boeing employees did during the years of our study. They did this by taking advantage of in-house training opportunities and by taking courses in their nonwork time to enhance their skills or earn the credentials for new careers. (For many years, Boeing was a leader in this regard, subsidizing college costs for employees, even if the planned course of study was unrelated to work at the company, and cooperated with its unions on career development programs; these now have been scaled back.) This is a wise strategy for employees in many of America's large companies because it acknowledges the uncertainty surrounding their employment relationship with the company they work for, and increases their own ability to respond to or even anticipate layoffs or other disruptive organizational change that they might want to escape. Human resource specialists have endorsed this strategy, arguing that employees must now think in terms of their own employability rather than a fixed employment relationship centered on firm-specific skills, so that they can be more flexible and mobile in response to changing workplace conditions.[26]

With skills properly honed and improved, workers might leave companies where work is unfulfilling or not properly rewarded, and even be resilient after layoffs. Recall that the people we interviewed and surveyed after leaving reported improved mental and physical health, even when they suffered income losses. For some nearing retirement, it gave them more time with their families or to pursue hobbies. For others, it forced them to change careers or locations and seemed to freshen up their lives. As we have said before, we do not in any way mean to imply that leaving a job or losing a job is painless or desirable; we merely point out that for some it loosened the bonds that tied them down, sometimes to a job they did not enjoy but were too enmeshed in to leave. Indeed, we have been surprised at the number of people who, after hearing presentations where we show the improvement in mental and physical health outcomes among those who left Boeing, told us that the same thing had happened to them and that in some ways their job loss had helped them make a more rewarding career move.

However, the fact that some individuals are able to find some benefit from adversity cannot obscure the central point: living with constant insecurity and losing a job in difficult economic times is damaging to many employees' well-being. Moreover, the effects are likely to be more acute on workers with low skills and during tough economic times. Given this, individuals who are in companies where there is a labor union remaining would do well to press their union to bargain hard for job security protections in their contract. While the unions at Boeing were able to gain a promise only that they would be consulted on outsourcing issues and downsizing, and were unable in 2009 to keep plans for Boeing to establish a second 787 assembly line in South Carolina from going forward, these are not reasons to give up the fight for more guaranteed security in other unionized companies. Indeed, it would be prudent for employees to redouble their efforts to move their unions in this direction.

In the end, these individualistic responses seem unsatisfying and paltry in the face of the big churn and rising uncertainty that workers must confront. Certainly, not putting all of one's emotional and material eggs in one basket is wise, as is making oneself more employable. Certainly, joining or organizing a union would have some benefits for workers so that individuals are not left alone to bargain with and gain concessions and rights from one's firm, but we know that in this emergent global economic system, private sector unions are increasingly having a tough time of it and are hemorrhaging members. In light of this, we believe that employees also can and should exercise their power as citizens to change public policies, the issue we tackle in the next section. One of SPEEA's longtime leaders and a participant in several collective bargaining negotiations with Boeing conveyed to us via a 2009 written communication the need to press into the political area:

In the '90s, it became clear to me that collective bargaining and contract language provided only "so much" leverage on the problems you describe. Ultimately, businesses and their employees operate in a political and economic environment, where the rules are set by public policy. Employees have some leverage with respect to employers, through unions. The labor movement also represents employees' interests in public policy for international trade, economic development, and education, among other areas. Other institutions of civil society promote similar community interests in terms of environmental policy, electoral reform, taxation, human rights, immigration and public health. Employees need to become more active and more organized in the way they project their interests into the political process.

How Government Can Help

If, as we argue, even the most economically successful companies are likely to become less able in the future to provide long-term job security, careers with steadily increasing wages and generous health care and pensions for their employees, then we face an important public policy choice as a nation. If firms are less able to provide these things, then someone or something else must. In the past decade, as pieces of company-provided safety nets have eroded, individual workers and their families have been faced with figuring out how to shore up or fill in that which their jobs had previously provided. There is no sign that things will improve. For example, a survey by the *Wall Street Journal* in late 2009 revealed that two-thirds of companies that cut employee health care benefits during the recession would not fully restore them in better times, while 10 percent said cuts in retirement benefits would be permanent. Firms large and small reported an acceleration in switching from pensions to 401k's, and there is a growing tendency among firms not to offer an employer contribution to these plans. Moreover, the pace of using private contractors and temporary workers escalated; contractors generally do not receive benefits from firms that employ them, and both contractors and temps are easy to let go if firm finances require it.[27]

This is the shape of the emerging world of work and employment. Either we will continue to expect individuals and their families to cope with the increased insecurities alone, with minimal help from government, or we will decide to pool the risks that more and more people are facing and provide a much sturdier and generous safety net for those subjected to those forces.

Expecting individuals and their families to face the insecurities alone will only exacerbate the widespread anxiety and increased economic volatility that already characterize our economic times.[28] The most pressing issue, in our view, is to find a way to ease the hardship and anxiety produced by business strategies that sacrifice job security in the pursuit of more efficient and profitable production—something firms must do—and to do so without creating excessive rigidities or counterproductive outcomes in the labor market that will cripple the ability of firms to compete.

Several European countries have sought to strengthen job security by labor legislation that makes it very cumbersome and difficult for companies to lay off workers. In France, Spain, and Italy, for example, the process of conducting mass layoffs is often long and costly and is sometimes delayed or stopped by judicial or administrative appeals and intervention. While this form of labor-management regulation can protect insiders or those who already have regular or "permanent" jobs, they also tend to inhibit the hiring of additional regular workers and, in particular, decrease permanent employment opportunities for younger job seekers. Many countries with strict employment protection regulations have seen companies increasingly rely on temporary or fixed duration contracts to meet their changing employment needs.[29] There is suggestive evidence that such regulation may also negatively affect productivity and other measures of economic efficiency.[30] For these reasons, a strict regulatory strategy for dealing with increasing job insecurity seems neither particularly equitable nor fruitful from a societal perspective.

Nor do these regulatory regimes necessarily calm worker anxiety about possible job loss. A study of perceptions of job insecurity among workers in the private sector in twelve European countries, for example, shows that strong employment protection legislation is surprisingly not associated with greater feelings of job security. Rather, it seems to produce increased job insecurity, possibly because workers with regular jobs suspect that a job loss would mean severe difficulties in getting another permanent job, and those on temporary contracts know that to be the case from their current experience.[31]

In the policy space between leaving individuals largely on their own to deal with the greater risks of the new economy and adopting an overly rigid legal framework to regulate company behavior, there is no shortage of policy recommendations for government action; in fact, there is a plethora of them. The suggestions include universal health insurance (with cost controls that protect government and company finances); increased pension portability and incentives for more 401(k) plans; extended unemployment insurance linked systematically to job retraining and job placement;[32] and instituting a wage insurance system against sizable drops in income due to job loss.[33] Other ideas that have garnered attention include a layoff tax levied on companies so that some of the costs that now tend to be borne by laid-off workers and communities when companies engage in mass layoffs are internalized by firms.[34] Proposals abound, as well, for a broad program of public investments in education, infrastructure, and research and development, especially in new information, medical, and energy technologies, to enhance American competitiveness and create jobs for the long term.

The advantages and disadvantages of these various prescriptions are open to debate, and we claim no special expertise in these areas. However, we believe the key elements of a better safety net program are to protect workers but not particular jobs; to de-link employment in specific companies from employment security and access to a range of benefits; and to provide safety net programs based on pooled-risk insurance principles with premiums subsidized by government, rather than on a vastly larger federal bureaucracy directly delivering services. We believe that such an approach would neither negatively affect the competitiveness of American companies nor significantly reduce choice for individuals. Indeed, we believe that such an approach would relieve American companies of some burdens that presently adversely affect their competitiveness and would allow labor markets to work more efficiently.

Take the example of the Danish "flexicurity" system. It shifts the focus of public policy away from protecting the jobs of employees to providing broader employment security across the entire society. The program maintains flexibility in the economy by allowing companies to hire and fire as they please, dictated by business considerations, while providing security for workers with substantial though time-limited income support from government and generous retraining and job search assistance for those laid off.[35] To be sure, like every other social safety net system, the Danish one involves tradeoffs. The high taxes on companies and employees to fund the system and the risks of disincentive effects of high income replacement rates, particularly for low-paid workers, are two features that might create opposition from important constituencies in the United States. But the principles underlying the system are ones we believe might help shape the policy debate, especially in light of the impressive economic performance of the Danish economy.[36]

CONCLUSION

Our study has documented how rapid and sometimes ill-conceived or badly implemented workplace change created turbulence in the lives of employees at Boeing Commercial Airplanes. Workers and managers at Boeing, like most people confronting difficult situations, showed admirable resilience. But they were also deeply and often adversely affected by the buffeting they endured. We see few signs that the forces producing this turbulence at Boeing or at other large globally competitive firms will disappear. If anything, they may very well intensify. The economic logic compels more and more firms to abandon job security and guaranteed benefits for their employees, introduce labor saving technology, and tap world markets for customers, suppliers, production partners, and capital. Going forward, we wonder how long individuals, families, and communities can withstand and cope with the repeated battering that is often the consequence of decisions made by corporate leaders trying to respond to increased global competition. Indeed, how long can corporations remain successful when relationships with their employees become strained and distant? And what are the implications for our social and civic life if employees and companies shift further into "everyone for themselves" attitudes and behaviors? No doubt, there is much that companies and individuals can do for themselves to better weather the turbulence, but neither companies nor employees can thrive on their own in an intensely uncertain and competitive global environment without public programs to help protect, sustain, and enhance the lives of working Americans.

Appendix: Details of Research Methodology

The overarching focus of our research study was to examine, over time, a diverse set of effects and reactions employees had to the many organizational changes described in chapter 2, including outsourcing, global partnering, lean manufacturing, downsizing, and technological innovations in engineering and manufacturing. Although our primary interest was to examine the effects on health and well-being, we also measured a broad range of work attitudes, some work performance indicators, and patterns of participation in outside work activities. We further examined many employee background characteristics and work experiences to see if, in fact, they mitigated or exacerbated the relationships between workplace changes and their impacts. These data were collected over a ten-year period, primarily via four surveys sent to randomly selected current Boeing Commercial Airplanes employees. Across the years of the study, we also conducted many interviews and focus groups, obtaining a rich source of qualitative data to add to our more quantitatively collected evidence. Table A-1 provides an overview of our major research activities from 1994 to 2006 in the context of what was happening at Boeing and its Boeing company parent.

LONGITUDINAL DESIGN AND
SAMPLE CHARACTERISTICS

A number of factors make it difficult to study the interrelationships between variables in real organizations over time. In this research especially, we were challenged by the fact that:

Table A.1 Timeline of research activities alongside major Boeing events

Phase	Year	Research activities	No. Boeing employees	Boeing events
Prestudy TQM period	Late 1980s			• Quality Improvement Teams introduced
	1990		64,409	• 777 production starts • Computerization of design and parts ordering (DCAD/MRM) initiated
	1991		83,450	• World Class Competitiveness Program introduced
	1992		86,751	
	1993		84,256	• Make-buy program introduced
	1994	Initiate project	73,527	• First commercial flight of 777
	1995	Preliminary discussions with Boeing	72,020	• Layoffs begin • Ninety-six-day machinists' strike
Short-term shareholder value emphasis	1996	First interviews and focus groups	64,206	• Airbus market share grows to 37 percent • Lean principles officially announced as central to Boeing operations • Acquisition of Rockwell Aerospace and Defense
	1997	Time 1 survey	81,570	• Production shuts down in Everett and Renton to deal with backlog • Merger with McDonnell Douglas
	1998		109,523	• Condit fires top executives
	1999	Interviews— female employees	106,381	
	2000	Time 2 survey, focus groups, first attrition survey	85,465	• Forty-day SPEEA strike
	2001		80,580	• HQ moves from Seattle to Chicago • 9/11 results in mass layoffs

Table A.1 (*cont.*)

Phase	Year	Research activities	No. Boeing employees	Boeing events
	2002	Interviews— male and female managers, female nonmanagers	72,239	• Nonunion suppliers deliver parts to assembly line
	2003	Time 3 survey, second attrition survey	56,457	• Boeing executive indicted for Lockheed Martin document thefts • CFO fired for Pentagon-767 refueling contract scandal • Condit leaves • 787 announced
Revival/new products (R&D)	2004		48,067	• First order for 787 (fifty by All Nippon Airways)
	2005	Interviews and focus groups for Time 4 survey design	Data not available (DNA)	• Stonecipher affair and resignation • Twenty-eight-day machinists' strike • Small increases in hiring for 787 • Lean processes introduced in 747 and 777 Everett lines • Last delivery of 757
	2006	Time 4 survey	DNA	
	2007		DNA	• Last orders for 767
	2008		DNA	• Fifty-eight-day machinists' strike; limits on role of nonunion suppliers • SPEEA strike threat

(1) these changes were occurring simultaneously, and (2) we did not have a second organization that could act as a control against which to compare our findings. The gold standard for demonstrating causal effects in research (that is, did these workplace changes *cause* the subsequent health effects or attitude changes) requires random assignment to a control and experimental condition and manipulation of one variable at a time. As a somewhat imperfect means of addressing these two problems, our study employed a very large sample as well as a longitudinal design. The large sample allowed us to find adequate numbers of participants who had had particular combinations of experiences, but not others, so that cer-

tain comparisons were possible. For example, we could compare managerial employees who had issued WARN notices with those who had not, removing the effects of one's own personal WARN-ing experiences. Although not the same as a pure control condition, this type of analytic strategy served as a reasonable alternative to random assignment. In addition, the longitudinal panel design was a decided strength of our research, for it permitted us to examine the timing, or "temporal patterning," between certain workplace events and various employee reactions (one component of a causal relationship), as well as to investigate the long-term impacts of such workplace changes. We also followed a subset of those employees who left the organization (explained later) as another way to examine temporal patterning.

Funded on two separate occasions by the National Institutes of Alcoholism and Alcohol Abuse (NIAAA) of the National Institutes of Health (NIH), we conducted a four-wave longitudinal panel study, measuring employee reactions in years 1997, 2000, 2003, and 2006 via a survey that was mailed to the employee's home. Beginning with a randomly selected group of 3,700 workers in 1997, employees were mailed an introductory letter that explained our independence from the company, asked them to complete the survey, promised them confidentiality of responses, obtained informed consent, and paid them for return of the survey ($25 in 1997 and 2000, $35 in 2003 and 2006). To boost the number of women and managerial employees in the total sample, we asked an additional 1,409 employees to participate in the research in 2003 (Time 3) and invited them to continue their participation in 2006 (Time 4). At each of the four administrations, participants mailed their consent forms back to the researchers and their surveys to an off-site data entry vendor that was responsible for entering the data, paying respondents for their participation, and printing and mailing the surveys. A unique ID number was created as a means of tracking participants' responses over time, and this number, linked to the mailing address, was kept secure with the off-site vendor. In this way, it was not possible for us or Boeing to link individual-level responses to any given participant.

Before the addition of extra participants in 2003, demographic characteristics of the remaining sample in 2000 closely approximated that of the larger organization in terms of the sample's gender (78 percent male) and age (mean = 46 years, SD = 8.06 years). Our sample was, however, proportionately less likely to work in production than Boeing's pool of employees (36 percent in sample, 50 percent in entire organization). Unless otherwise noted, the results we provide in the book come from the 525 workers who completed all four surveys: these employees were 80.8 percent male, 33.7 percent production workers, with a mean age of 42.70 years (SD = 7.8) at the time of the 1997 survey. Approximately 46 percent had graduated from college or had earned a more advanced degree. Table A.2 provides the response rates over time, and table A.3 provides the final sample sizes for the different combinations of survey completion.

SURVEY CONSTRUCTION

To develop the initial survey, we reviewed the scholarly literature to identify measures of various work attitudes (for example, job stress, job security) and health and well-being measures (for example, depression, physical health symptoms) that were of relevance to the larger

Table A.2 Response and attrition rates across the four surveys

Time	Left company since previous survey	No. of mailed surveys	Responded	Response rate (%)
1997 (Time 1)	NA	3,700	2,279	62
1999 (Time 2)	319	1,960	1,244	63
2003 (Time 3)	198	2,455 (1,406 continuing + 1,046 newly added)	1,409 (773 continuing + 636 newly added)	57 (74% from continuing; 45% from newly added)
2006 (Time 4)	313	2,142*	1,103	51

*At Time 4, we mailed surveys to all participants who had completed Time 1 and Time 2 as well as those who had been asked at Time 3, regardless of whether they completed Time 3.

Table A.3 Number of participants who completed various combinations of surveys

Surveys completed	Frequency
Time 1 only	1,035
Time 1 and Time 2	374
Time 3 only	295
Time 4 only	130
Time 3 and Time 4	344
Times 1, 2, and 3 (not Time 4)	241
Times 1, 2, and 4 (not Time 3)	104
Times 1, 2, 3, 4	525[a]
Total number of employees who completed at least one survey	3,048[b]

[a]Unless otherwise noted, the panel survey findings we present come from the subset of workers who completed all four surveys.
[b]A total of 5,109 employees were asked to participate in the survey component of the research, 3,700 beginning in year 1997, and 1,409 beginning in year 2003.

research objectives and that met various psychometric standards for internal consistency and validation. A thorough scan of the literature revealed dozens of scales; from these, we selected those whose content most closely captured the salient employee issues. After drafting the survey, we conducted a number of focus groups where employees reviewed the survey to ensure that the meaning was clear, that all relevant issues were included, and that Boeing-specific jargon for work experience questions was appropriately used. Based on employee feedback, we made a number of modifications to the survey. In limited cases, we developed measures specifically for the survey; once data were collected, we conducted a number of analyses with appropriate hold-out samples for cross-validation purposes to examine internal consistency and validity of the items and scales.

For subsequent survey developments (2000, 2003, 2006), we interviewed and conducted focus groups to understand more fully the meaning of various findings and, based on this information, made modest modifications to the next scheduled survey. For example, after the 2000 survey and follow-up interviews, issues related to how managerial women perceived themselves by others in the organization came to the fore. From this, we developed a scale of "stereotyped threat." Likewise, we added many questions related to the types of downsizing-related experiences employees experienced, expanded the set of questions dealing with employee health, and included an open-ended section in 2006, again drawing upon previously validated measures when available. By contrast, some questions that did not yield significant group differences or changes in responses to workplace interventions were dropped over time. In the end, approximately 70 percent of the initial survey items were included on all four surveys. A list of the items and scales cited in this book may be found in table A.4.

ADDITIONAL INTERVIEWS

In addition to the approximately sixty interviews and twenty focus groups we conducted over time to aid in survey development and interpretation of findings, we conducted two separate sets of more focused and longer interviews (approximately two hours each) in 1998–99 and 2002–3. The 1998–99 interviews were conducted with approximately twenty female employees, and the 2002–3 interviews included twenty-five male managers, female managers, and female nonmanagerial employees. Both sets of interviews focused on gender and managerial roles as related to the impact of workplace change. Letters were sent to randomly selected employees from within the designated gender and managerial status group (approximately one hundred letters in both 1998 and 2002), asking if they would be willing to be interviewed by a member of the research team; participants were assured of confidentiality and offered a small amount of compensation for their time ($30 in 1999, $40 in 2003). In 1999, a female university faculty member with training in the social sciences and extensive interview experience conducted the interviews; in 2003, a female master's-level therapist with a prior history of management in large organizations similar to the one studied interviewed all male and female participants. In only a few cases did the participant decline to permit the researcher to audio-record the interview. Written consent was obtained prior to each interview.

The interviews followed a semistructured format that addressed general themes including work history and environment, organizational changes, impact of organizational changes, impact of organizational changes on well-being and life outside work, management issues and stressors, questions specific to each demographic group, and suggestions for continued study themes. As a means of fostering a comfortable conversational setting, interviews were conducted at a mutually agreed-upon venue, at either the participant's office or home, or a local coffeehouse. The interviewer followed an outline of questions but allowed room to digress and explore relevant topics at greater length. A number of the quotes presented in the

Table A.4 List of scales with descriptive information reported in the text

Name of scale	Example item	No. of questions and (α)	Response format	Source
Absenteeism	Excluding holidays, vacations, and other excused absences, about how many days of work did you miss during the past year?	1 (na)	Write in two-digit number	Written for study
Binge drinking	In the past six months about how many times at a single sitting have you had the following amounts of alcohol, either beer, wine, wine coolers, or liquor, or some combination? . . . 8 or more drinks	1 (na)	7-point scale (from never in past six months to every day)	Written for study
Depression	On how many days during the past week have you . . . felt you just could not get going?	7 (.90)	8-point scale (from zero to seven days in past week)	Mirowsky and Ross (1989)
Eating change	Please indicate to what degree each of the following has increased, decreased, or stayed the same over the past year . . . your eating	1 (single item from a seven-item measure of health behaviors)	4-point scale (more, same, less, does not apply)	Modified from Moos et al. (1986) and Quinn and Staines (1977)
Escape drinking motivations	How important would you say each of the following is to you as a reason to drink? . . . drinking helps me relax	6 (.74)	3-point scale (from not important to very important)	Fennel et al. (1981)
Focus on work versus family/friends	Compared to the past, in the last two years have you devoted more time to your family?	7 (.70)	2-point scale (yes or no)	Written for study

(*continued*)

Table A.4 (*cont.*)

Name of scale	Example item	No. of questions and (α)	Response format	Source
Future vision of company[a]	In the last five years, Boeing has increasingly become a company that creates an atmosphere of trust and respect among its employees.	4 (.89)	5-point sacle (SA to SD)	Written for study
Intent to quit	I often think about quitting my job.	3 (.82)	5-point scale (SA to SD)	Cammann et al. (1983)
Job challenge	On my job, I seldom get a chance to use my special skills and abilities. (R)	3 (.72)	5-point scale (SA to SD)	Cammann et al. (1983)
Job-at-risk factors	In your opinion, how likely is each of the following to put your job at risk in the future? . . . overseas outsourcing	6 (NA— not additive scale)	4-point scale (from very likely to very unlikely)	Written for study
Job security	At the present time, how worried are you about your job security?	3 (.84)	4-point scale (from extremely worried to not worried at all)	Armstrong-Stassen (1993)
Job stress	Think of your job in general, all in all what is it like most of the time? . . . tense	6 (.82)	3-point scale (yes, ?, no)	Modified from Stanton et al. (2001)
Managerial qualities of immediate supervisor[b]	My manager lets me know how he or she thinks I am doing.	4 subscales, each with 3 items, .45, .79, .85, .92.	5-point scale (from frequently if not always to not at all)	Modified from Multifactor Leadership Q, Avolio, Bass, and Jung (1999)
Organizational commitment	I feel very little loyalty to Boeing. (R)	3 (.74)	5-point scale (SA to SD)	Lincoln and Kalleberg (1990)

(*continued*)

Name of scale	Example item	No. of questions and (α)	Response format	Source
Personal control	I have little control over the things that happen to me. (R)	7 (.85)	5-point scale (SA to SD)	Pearlin and Schooler (1978)
Poor health symptoms	Have you experienced any of the following in the last year? . . . high blood pressure, . . . back pain, . . . headaches	5 (.50)	2-point scale (yes, no)	Modified from Moos et al. (1986) and Quinn and Staines (1978)
Psychological work contract[b]	When first hired, I believed that Boeing owed me . . . rapid advancement.	8 (.81) when first hired; 8 (.82) beliefs now	5-point scale (SA to SD)	Based on Robinson et al. (1994)
Stereotyped threat—women managers[a]	Women managers have their ideas challenged more often than do managerial men.	6 (.91)	5-point scale (SA to SD)	Written for study
Team statement[d]	Team makes important decisions about how work is done.	1	2-point scale (yes, no)	Written for study
Team statement[d]	Views of team members are respected by other team members.	1	4-point scale (from agree to disagree)	Written for study
Technology change	To what extent have you been expected to do the following things in your work over the past two years . . . to use your skills in new ways.	3 (.76)	5-point scale (from much more to much less)	Written for study
Views of top management —competence	Top management doesn't know what's going on.	5 (.89)	5-point scale (SA to SD)	Dunham et al. (1999)

(*continued*)

Table A.4 (*cont.*)

Name of scale	Example item	No. of questions and (α)	Response format	Source
Views of top management —integrity	I have complete trust in top management.	5 (.82)	5-point scale (SA to SD)	Dunham et al. (1999)
Workplace abuse[c]	During the last twelve months at Boeing, how often have you been in a situation where someone in your work setting . . . took credit for your work or ideas?	5 (.76)— isolation subscale; 9 (.80)— disrespect-ful treat-ment subscale	3-point scale (never, once, more than once)	Richman et al. (1999)

Note: SA to SD = "strongly agree" to "strongly disagree"
[a] Included only on the 2003 and 2006 surveys
[b] Included only on 2006 survey
[c] Included only on the 2000, 2003, and 2006 surveys
[d] Included only on the 2000 survey

chapters, especially chapter 7, "Changing Roles of Women," were obtained from these interviews.

ATTRITION SURVEY

As an additional means of studying the impact of organizational change on employees, we followed a subset of workers who left the company. Between the first survey administration in 1997 and the second in 2000, 310 of the 2,279 workers who responded to the 1997 survey left the company, entering into retirement, prolonged unemployment (due to downsizing, termination), or reemployment at another company. These former employees were mailed a much shorter version of the 2000 survey to their home that included a few questions related to the terms of their leaving Boeing. One hundred seventy-one former employees responded (55 percent). Because it was outside of the NIH-funded initiative, we did not have the financial backing to pay these participants as before. As a token of appreciation, one dollar was enclosed with the survey. Responses were received from all pay categories, but a greater percentage represented white collar positions relative to their representation in the company. Women were also slightly overrepresented in our sample (29 percent) relative to their representation in the company (22 percent). In 2003, these 171 respondents were again sent a shortened version of the survey mailed to those who were part of the large, main study. As before, they were paid a dollar for their participation and were assured confidentiality of responses; ninety-five responded (56 percent). Demographic information again showed that the sample from the attrition group comprised more women (28 percent versus 18 percent) and was slightly older (mean age fifty-five years versus forty-nine years) as compared with the full sample of continuously employed workers. With respect to the age difference, such was not surprising given that a sizable number had retired from the company.

As explained in the chapter on "Well-Being Consequences of Workplace Change" (chapter 8), a matched comparison subsample was drawn from the larger sample of continuously employed workers for use in a number of analyses. To create this group, we identified the number of men and women from the attrition sample who fell into age categories divided into ten-year intervals (for example, number of women aged 30–39, men aged 30–39, women aged 40–49, and so on). We then identified the same subgroups for the continuously employed sample who, like the attrition sample, had completed the 1997 and 2000 surveys (though not necessarily the 2003 survey), and selected at random the same number of employees so that the matched and attrition groups each had the same number of men and women within each of the various age categories. In this way, the matched and attrition groups were equal in terms of gender, had the same age distributions within each gender, and, as of the year 2000, were equally likely to have completed the 2003 survey. Importantly, the two samples did not differ statistically on any of the quantitative measures at Time 1. Creating such a matched sample of still-employed workers allowed us to perform analyses that were uncontaminated by the effects of age or gender, two characteristics known to be related to many of the outcomes we studied.

Although we had planned to study the effects of reemployment and retirement within this attrition sample, the subgroup sizes quickly became too small to conduct meaningful analyses due to the fact that the work trajectories of these former Boeing employees were more varied than we had anticipated. Some workers left the company and retired; others, however, sought full-time employment, part-time employment, or further education, or remained unemployed. Still others entered and exited the workforce multiple times or became contractors.

RELATIONSHIP WITH COMPANY, UNIONS, AND RESPONDENTS

As mentioned, initial funding for this research came from the NIAAA, and its rules, as well as those of our universities, bound us to confidentiality regarding individual responses, whether gathered in surveys, interviewers, or focus groups. We informed Boeing executives and representatives that our work was scholarly in nature and that we were not gathering information for Boeing to use for its own purpose. Though we made presentations to, and wrote short reports of some of our findings for, company executives on several occasions, we also made similar presentations and gave the same reports to union representatives.

At all stages of data gathering, we informed respondents that we were scholars interested in the effects of workplace change and were not seeking information on behalf of Boeing or any other government or private agency. We also informed them that we had discussed our research with IAM and SPEEA leaders and had gained their approval for their members to cooperate in our study. We also told potential respondents that, in addition to sharing our general findings with Boeing and their unions, we would also share the same information with any Boeing employee who wanted us to do so. More than a few took us up on our offer.

Boeing provided the initial list of randomly selected employee names and mailing addresses and also supplied updated mailing address information before each survey. We would like to think this was because the company believed our research would be useful in some way, even though it had no say in the general direction of our research or in the design of the survey questionnaire.

Notes

CHAPTER 1. STUDYING A COMPANY AND WORKFORCE IN TRANSITION

1. Cappelli (2008); and O'Toole and Lawler (2007).
2. Lazonick and Sullivan (2000).
3. Several recent books highlight similar changes across large sectors of the U.S. economy. See, for example, Cappelli et al. (1997) and O'Toole and Lawler (2007).
4. For exceptions, see Greenhouse (2008) and Gosselin (2008).
5. Collins and Porras (1994).
6. We took great pains to assure workers, frontline and middle managers, union officials, and shop stewards that we were scholars interested in understanding how changes in American companies were affecting employees, and that we were funded by federal research grants and completely independent from Boeing.
7. In presenting data on health and well-being outcomes, we will also report results from our study of a sample of respondents who left Boeing after participating in the first survey. We do this to minimize the impact of possible selection bias (that, for example, the 525 employees who remained in the study for the whole period were the healthiest or hardiest), and to bolster our claim that it was working at Boeing that likely produced the health effects we report. Fuller descriptions of the attrition survey and how we used it in analyzing health effects can be found in chapter 8 and in the appendix.
8. For links to the many scholarly articles published over the years from this research project, see the Workplace Change Web site at the Institute of Behavioral Science at the University of Colorado, Boulder: www.colorado.edu/ibs/PEC/workplacechange.

CHAPTER 2. HOW AND WHY BOEING CHANGED EVERYTHING ABOUT
THE WAY IT MAKES AIRPLANES

1. Lawrence and Thornton (2005) and Wallace (2009).

2. Jim Collins argues in his best-selling book, *Good to Great* (Collins 2001), that all too often "the good is the enemy of the great," with only a handful of companies having managed to make changes in normal times that propelled them to greatness.

3. Black (2009), 1.

4. Of course, Boeing continued to change, with ongoing implications for Boeing employees, as we pointed out in Chapter 1.

5. Goldfield (1989) and Wheeler (2002).

6. Kusnet (2008), 238–240.

7. Wallace (2009).

8. *Business Week* (1996).

9. Lazonick and O'Sullivan (2000) and Rappaport (1986). To be sure, all publicly traded firms must attend to shareholder value as a matter of course. We want to distinguish here, however, between short-term shareholder value—meaning a concern for quarterly performance and stock prices—and long-term shareholder value, or the performance and stock value of a firm over a span of years. When leaders in companies such as Boeing were trumpeting shareholder value during the 1990s, they almost invariably were talking about the short-term variety. For a discussion of the increasing attention of corporations on finance and capital markets, see Muellerleile (2009).

10. Our attention in this chapter is on Boeing leaders' response to market pressures and the need to attend to issues of costs and revenues. Market pressures were not, however, the only external source of change in the Boeing parent company and in Boeing Commercial Airplanes. Cultural changes in society, federal and state statutes, and lawsuits, for example, compelled Boeing and other American companies to pay more attention to issues of race and gender in the workplace than they might otherwise have done. During the period of our study, for example, Boeing began to increase the proportion of women in its workforce and expand the ranks of female managers, though it was slow to advance women into top executive positions and, according to its own internal documents, systematically discriminated against women on wages and salaries. See Holmes and France (2004). In chapter 7 we examine various aspects of women's experience working at Boeing, a male-oriented and dominated environment for most of its history. There were too few self-identified racial and ethnic minorities at Boeing (and in our random sample in 1996) to allow for a separate analysis of their experience in the company.

11. Happenheimer (1995), 314–15.

12. Kusnet (2008), 170.

13. Buchanan and Gordon (1975); Lave (1981); Weidenbaum (1978); and Yergin and Stanislaw (1999), 345–347.

14. Capelli (1999), 75–78, and Newhouse (2007), 97.

15. Interestingly, Ron Woodard, president of Boeing Commercial Airplanes until 1998, was never impressed, saying the A320, the plane that provided much of the cash for the rising Airbus company, "was a very slow plane" (interview, March 12, 2007).

16. For example, it used common cockpits across a range of planes to make pilot training eas-

ier and less expensive. This practice of making systems similar across airplane models is called "commonality" and is much sought after by airlines.

17. Moving control surfaces on the wings and tail by electrical signal running along wires rather than moving them by using cables and pulleys, a system of steering as old as the first airplanes.

18. Aris (2004); Lawrence and Thornton (2005), 63–74; and Newhouse (2007), 98–99.

19. Though Boeing still led on the dollar value of orders because of its lead in the pricier and more profitable wide-body passenger airplanes, the 767, the 777, and the 747.

20. Dempsey and Gesell (1997) and Reuters (2004).

21. We address Boeing employee reactions to the widespread use of computers in the workplace in chapter 5.

22. Later he became president of Boeing Commercial Airplanes, then left in 2006 to become head of Ford.

23. The software system created by Boeing engineers was an amalgamation of two existing ones, CATIA (Computer-graphics Aided Three-dimensional Interactive Application) and EPIC (Electronic Preassembly in the Computer).

24. For the most authoritative telling of the 777 story, see Sabbagh (1996).

25. For a full description of the design, engineering, and manufacturing software for the 787, and some of its drawbacks and perils, see Duvall and Bartholomew (2007).

26. Womack, Jones, and Roos (1991).

27. Cort (2006), 2.

28. Kemp (2006), 142–147.

29. Aris (2004), 193–195.

30. Sabbagh (1996), 40.

31. Holmes and France (2002), 8. The breakdown proved to be very costly to Boeing. One estimate has it that delayed sales, costly production changes, and penalties owed for late deliveries to airline companies meant that the 737 NG made its first dollar in profits only after eight hundred airplanes were sold rather than four hundred to five hundred, the number that is the normal break-even point for a single-aisle derivative aircraft. See Lawrence and Thornton (2005), 132.

32. This story of the "multinationalization of production" and its natural corollary, outsourcing, has been told by many people. For relatively comprehensive examination of the issues involved, see Dicken (2007); Karoly and Panis (2004); and Reich (2007).

33. These companies sometimes have partnered with others. GE, for example, partnered with SNECMA of France to build engines for two versions of the 737.

34. On this new model of production see Cort (2006).

35. Newhouse (2007), 213–214.

36. One Boeing manager told us in a confidential interview on February 2, 2009, that the company had over-outsourced, stripping the company of critical skills needed for coordinating partners and keeping a closer eye on second-tier suppliers (those subcontracting to global partner firms).

37. Lawrence and Thornton (2005) and Newhouse (2007).

38. Madslien (2009).

39. Lawrence and Thornton (2005), ch. 6. Also see Kusnet (2008), 183–184.

40. The 777-LR, in fact, set the long-distance record for a passenger airplane in 2005—13,422 miles flying westward against the prevailing winds from Hong Kong to London without refueling.

41. According to a former SPEEA officer and longtime Boeing employee, sales of the 757 were cannibalized by the expanded version of the 737 (written communication, August, 2009). Boeing hopes to salvage the 767 by making it the basis for a new military transport. The Department of Defense (DOD) originally chose EADS, parent company of Airbus, to build the transport. Congressional opposition to the award forced the DOD to reopen the bidding process, however, which, according to EADS, favors Boeing. At this writing, the second round of bidding is under way, with a final decision yet to be made.

CHAPTER 3. BOEING'S CHANGING CULTURE

1. Cole (1998a).
2. Serling (1992), 443.
3. WCC = world class competitiveness; DCAC/MRM = define and control aircraft configuration and manufacturing resource management; five S's = sort, straighten, scrub, systematize, standardize; JIT = just in time parts delivery; DBTs = design build teams; and IW = accelerated improvement workshops.
4. Micklethwait and Wooldridge (1996).
5. Sabbagh (1996).
6. Newhouse (2007), 139.
7. Baumgarner (2001).
8. Callahan (2004).
9. A SPEEA official and longtime former Boeing employee remarked that Stonecipher had also "ruined McDonnell Douglas." He described the cultural transformation in stark terms, as a process whereby a "virus or bacteria that infects a new host, sucks out the resources needed to survive, then moves on to a new host. In business school terms, this new culture was perfectly consistent with a 'harvest strategy.' If aerospace was not attractive in economic terms, then the interests of the shareholders would be served by deferring investment, extracting the maximum value out while withdrawing from the industry."
10. Quoted in Cole (1998b).
11. All subsequent quotes, unless noted otherwise in the text, are from employee comments in the 2006 survey.
12. For fuller accounts of the 2000 strike, one of the longest white collar walkouts in American history, see Sorscher (2009) and Kusnet (2008). It is interesting that in his first public comment as the new head of Boeing Commercial Airplanes in 2009, Jim Albaugh reaffirmed Boeing's engineering tradition when he said, "In its soul Boeing has always been and remains an engineering company. As an engineer I look forward to learning from and working with you."
13. Newhouse (2007), 202.
14. Newhouse (2007), referencing a *Seattle Times* article.
15. Newhouse (2007), 169.

16. Some scholars are also concerned about the negative effects on America's intellectual capital of Boeing's outsourcing and global partnering strategy (Lawrence and Thorton, 2005; MacPherson and Pritchard, 2007).

17. These questions were not asked in the first two surveys.

18. Denise Rousseau (1998) characterizes this kind of identification with an organization as "deep structure identification" such that one thinks of the organization as being part of one's self concept. An engineer might thus answer a question about who he or she is by including in the answer, "I'm a Boeing engineer" rather than an "engineer working at Boeing." An extreme example of such deep identification is given by the office worker quoted earlier who said, "I am Boeing."

CHAPTER 4. LIVING THROUGH LAYOFFS

1. In the 2000–2005 period alone, 17 percent of our sample had been laid off and rehired, 19 percent had received a WARN notice, 55 percent had seen a close friend laid off, 77 percent had seen a close co-worker laid off, and 24 percent had been "bumped" from their position. "Bumping" is when a worker with greater seniority takes the position of someone with less seniority, a process that was quite common among hourly workers covered by the union contract between the machinists and Boeing.

   Not surprisingly, some two-thirds of our respondents also reported that this turmoil had disrupted their social relationships and had led to a loss of contact with work friends or colleagues. Over 50 percent said the disruptions had increased the level of tension between them and remaining colleagues and friends.

2. On the health and well-being effects of being laid off, see, for example, Cobb and Kasl (1977) and Winkelmann and Winkelmann (1998). On the impact on the well-being and health of "survivors," see Grunberg, Moore, and Greenberg (2001) and Kivimaki et al. (2000).

3. Kets de Vries and Balazs (1997).

4. Velocci (1995).

5. Holmes (1995).

6. *Aeromechanic* (March 2000).

7. Lunsford (2002).

8. Lunsford (2008).

9. Gates (2008). A top SPEEA negotiator pointed out in a communication to us that in the settlement of the 2000 strike, Boeing and SPEEA had agreed to set up high-level partnership meetings between top executives and union officials, which in principle could have discussed outsourcing decisions. In reality, however, these partnership meetings "never really brought high level executives and top union leaders together."

10. An ingenious experiment by Gregory Berns (2008), a neuroeconomist at Emory University, dramatically illustrates how anticipation of something painful, such as an electric shock or the loss of a job, is deeply troubling to the human psyche and can lead to impaired decision-making. In the experiment, participants' feet were attached to electrodes and they were told they would receive a slightly painful shock but they would have to wait between one and thirty seconds for it. As Berns reports, "Given a choice, almost everyone preferred to expe-

dite the shock rather than wait for it." Indeed, the stress associated with the anticipation was so uncomfortable for participants that almost a third chose to get a bigger shock straight-away than to wait for a smaller shock a few seconds later.

11. Moore, Grunberg, and Greenberg (2003). See also chapter 8 for a fuller discussion of what happened to levels of depression and symptoms of poor health.

12. Grunberg, Anderson-Connolly, and Greenberg (2000).

13. See Cappelli et al. (1997) and Robinson and Rousseau (1994).

14. Pfeffer (2006).

15. The concept of "employability" implies that employees need to prepare themselves for flexible and mobile careers rather than expect employment for life with one company. Employers, unable or unwilling to offer lifetime security, are then expected to help their employees become more employable by assisting in the development of their skills.

16. Grunberg, Moore, and Greenberg (2001).

17. See Tversky and Kahneman (1974).

18. An Australian study comparing voluntary and involuntary layoffs also found that em-ployees who chose to take the voluntary option had lower levels of depression and en-gaged in more job search activity than did those who were subject to involuntary job loss (Waters 2007).

19. An encouraging development is that the two main unions at Boeing, SPEEA in 2008 and the machinists' local in 2009, have managed to obtain "voluntary layoffs with benefits" for their members. Employees can volunteer for layoff and get one week of pay for each two years of service.

20. See, for example, the study by Kivimaki et al. (2003) and by Devine et al. (2009).

21. Farber (2005).

22. Gates (2005).

23. A senior SPEEA official reacted to reading the Woodard quote by writing to us: "I bet he can, actually. For example, our contracts provide that all contractors must be let go before any direct [permanent] employees can be laid off. Also a lot of outsourced work could be brought back in house. During layoffs, we ask if any work will be brought back from the Moscow Design Center. No, of course not; [they say,] 'We have a commitment to Russia.' So what are we, chopped liver?"

CHAPTER 5. WORKING IN NEW WAYS

1. After analyzing results at Time 2, it became evident that team membership was not sub-stantially affecting employee well-being or organizational attitudes. Because other top-ics had emerged as potentially fruitful, we reduced the number of detailed questions re-garding teams in subsequent surveys to create space for new lines of questioning. All four surveys, however, do include a question regarding degree of involvement on teams; and this is the question that is used to describe trends over the four time periods of the study.

2. Fisher (1993); Hackman (1987); and Katzenbach and Smith (1993).

3. Belanger, Edwards, and Wright (2003).

4. Hodson (2002) and Niehoff et al. (2001).

5. Devine (2002); Glassop (2002); Goodman et al. (1988); Katzenbach and Smith (1993); Carron et al. (2003); and others (e.g., Mason and Griffin, 2003).

6. Dion (2000) and Grant and Parker (2009)

7. Andrisani (1978); Grant and Parker (2009); Karasek and Theorell (1990); and McLagen and Nel (1995).

8. Applebaum et al. (2000); Freeman and Rogers (1999); Greenberg (1986); Greenberg and Grunberg (2003); Levine (1995); Mason (1982); and Pateman (1970).

9. Sweet and Meiksins (2008) and Towers et al. (2006).

10. Hackman and Oldham (1980); Sinha and Van de Ven (2005); and Tafti et al. (2007). It is important to note that there are dissenting voices here. See Wright et al. (1997) for an excellent summary of these contrasting perspectives.

11. Composite score adding together results for three items: technology, computers, and software. Other items were added later in the study (e.g., Internet use, e-mail), but we included only the three items used across all four surveys for this analysis.

12. The questions regarding satisfaction with technology and technology's impacts on performance were not included in Time 3 or Time 4 surveys due to space limitations and addition of new research topics to the questionnaire.

13. Since our quantitative survey included very few questions directly addressing technology, we turn primarily to patterns in the open-ended responses at Time 4, as well as suggestions raised by other investigators working in this field, to shed more light on how technology may both help and hinder employees and impact organizational attitudes. These ideas are therefore exploratory and will, we hope, provide fodder for future investigations of technology implementation in corporate settings.

14. Golden, Veiga, and Dino (2008).

15. Duxbury and Higgins (2001).

16. Barker (1993) and Deetz (1992).

17. McLagan and Nel (1995); Spreitzer (1996); and Tafti et al. (2007).

18. O'Kane and Hargie (2007).

19. This is no exaggeration. One of the author's typical work days as a consultant was characterized by these patterns.

20. Towers et al. (2006) and Wang, Shu, and Tu (2008).

21. Wang et al. (2008).

22. Sikora, Beaty, and Forward (2004).

23. Dooley (2002).

24. Sikora et al. (2004).

25. While empirical findings are mixed, the operating assumption for most practitioners and academics is that restructuring of work improves morale/attitudes, which then improves productivity and profitability. Variable findings are often attributed to inadequate measurement or, increasingly, to an awareness that context matters (Offerman and Spiros 2001). Corporate outcomes such as profitability and stock price are multidetermined: corporate history, culture/climate, competitive landscape, and larger political/economic context interfere with or amplify the effects of job enrichment efforts.

CHAPTER 6. MANAGING THROUGH CHANGE

1. While varying somewhat over the four time periods, roughly 70 percent of our managers described themselves or were labeled as first-line managers, another 20 percent were second-level managers, and the remaining 10 percent were distributed across level 3 and higher. The higher the level, that is to say, the fewer the respondents.

2. Full discussion of differences across levels of management is not feasible due to small sample size, particularly in our panel sample of 525; specifically, we had inadequate numbers of managers at level 3 and above to draw strong conclusions. A more qualitative review of the data indicates, however, that managers higher up the ladder were healthier and had more positive attitudes than did managers closer to the trenches. While we do not have evidence regarding why this might be the case, we suspect that day-to-day interaction with workers, especially during strikes and/or layoff events, took a toll on these lower-level managers.

3. Businessdictionary.com (2009).

4. Bartunek et al. (1999); Gioia and Chittipeddi (1991); and Weick (1995).

5. This chapter focuses on differences between managers' and nonmanagers' work and organizational attitudes primarily due to the likely linkage between these attitudes and the successful (or not) implementation of business strategy. In addition, our review of the data from all four time periods found virtually no health differences between managers and nonmanagers. That is, managers reported as many health problems, health behavior changes, sleeping difficulties, depression, problems with alcohol, and so on as did nonmanagers. This "null" finding indicates that managers were not immune to or insulated from the health impacts of working through turbulence. Because there were no unique patterns for managers, we leave the discussion of health outcomes to chapter 8.

6. Armstrong-Stassen (1993, 1998); Katz and Kahn (1978); Luthans and Sommer (1999); and Martin, Jones, and Callan (2006).

7. We will not report on any well-being outcomes here as our analysis shows no statistically significant differences between managers and nonmanagers for any of these indicators (e.g., health symptoms, sleep difficulties, alcohol use) across any of the survey time periods. This lack of difference—managers having similar well-being outcomes as nonmanagers—also suggests, though, that managers were not insulated from the impacts of organizational change. If they were somehow immune or buffered from these impacts, we would anticipate seeing "healthier" managers as compared to nonmanagers.

8. See appendix and chapter 1 for full descriptions of these sources.

9. Shead (2007).

10. Bass (1985); Bass and Avolio (1993); Deetz, Tracy, and Simpson (2000); McLagan and Nel (1995); and Osterman (2006).

11. Briefly, Theory X management, as originally conceptualized by McGregor (1960), assumes that employees are inherently lazy, not to be trusted, and require management with "a heavy hand" to ensure corporate goals are met. Conversely, Theory Y management assumes workers want to do a good job, are self-motivated, and want to take ownership of their work. The job of a manager in the Theory Y model is to create the conditions to

unlock the energy and potential of workers: building trust, open communication of goals, shared decision-making, and comfortable rather than conflictual relationships between managers and subordinates.

12. Interestingly, it wasn't just the "good ol' boy" managers wishing for a return to the old days. Younger female managers also commented on lack of discipline and frustrations with being helpless to deal with employee problems.

13. Notices required by the 1988 WARN Act that gave employees sixty days' advanced notice that they were candidates for layoffs.

14. Or 1, 2, 3, depending on the scale used in a particular year. Scale labels varied over the years, but the basic idea of high, medium, and low performers was maintained through most of the years of our study.

15. It is worth noting that there were no overall differences between managers and non-managers on such burnout measures as emotional exhaustion or detachment. Managers directly involved in the WARN/layoff process did express more symptoms of burnout than did other managers/employees per Grunberg et al. (2006).

16. Osterman (2006).

17. As one of our manuscript reviewers notes, as difficulties emerge with 787 production, more street-smart expertise may be needed than is currently available in the managerial ranks, and more pressure will be placed on nonmanagerial "experts" for problem-solving and rework.

18. For example, Osterman (2009) notes that managers typically earn twice the hourly wage of the people they supervise and, as of 2007, had a 1.7 percent unemployment rate as compared with 4.9 percent for all workers—often leaving the firm with generous severance packages in the range of months' worth of salary.

19. Grunberg, Moore, and Greenberg (2006, 2009).

CHAPTER 7. CHANGING ROLES OF WOMEN

1. Gender discrimination lawsuits against the company at this time alleged that Boeing failed to compensate, promote, and make available other employment opportunities (e.g., job training) for women and men equally. For descriptions of these events that appeared in the press, see: http://www.allbusiness.com/legal/legal-services-litigation/5885301-1.html, "Hagens Berman Announces Proposed Class-Action Lawsuits Against Boeing" (2002); http://community.seattletimes.nwsource.com/archive/?date=20040515&slug=boeing15, "Financial Settlement Reached in Boeing Gender Bias Lawsuit" (2004); and http://www.komonews.com/news/archive/4169196.html, "Boeing to Pay $72.5 Million to Settle Sex-Discrimination Lawsuit" (2005).

2. Additional details may be found at http://www.census.gov/prod/2005pubs/censr-20.pdf, page 11.

3. For the full report, the reader is directed to http://www.catalyst.org/file/207/2005%20cote.pdf.

4. The concept of stereotyped threat (Steele 1997) posits that one's own beliefs about the negative stereotype he or she believes others hold about the racial, gender, age group, etc., to which he/she belongs can impact performance on a relevant task. For example, if a

woman believes that others hold the negative stereotype that "women are poor at math," it is more likely that her math performance will suffer even if, by other objectively collected measures, her math performance is good. On this basis, we developed a scale to assess stereotyped threat for the category of managerial women.

5. A number of authors have argued that adoption of a transformational leadership style has been one means by which women can resolve the dilemma they report facing when holding supervisory positions. To be directive and task-focused is viewed by some subordinates as being at odds with a stereotypic feminine role that emphasizes nurturing and cooperative interactions. Thus, a transformational style—one that encourages, assists, and mentors—is both consistent with a stereotypic feminine role as well as with effective leadership. See Eagly and Karau (2002) and Eagly et al. (2003).

6. There is a vast literature that has examined issues related to work-life balance, with the preponderance of the scholarship focusing on the difficulties working women have in achieving and maintaining a balance. For additional details, the reader is directed to Aryee, Srinivas, and Tan (2005); Bartley, Blanton, and Gilliard (2005); Beatty (1996); Burke and McKeen (1994); Eby et al. (2005); and Wharton and Blair-Loy (2006).

7. See, for example, Byron (2005) for a recent review.

CHAPTER 8. WELL-BEING CONSEQUENCES OF WORKPLACE CHANGE

1. See Beehr and Newman (1978); Quick, Horn, and Quick (1986); and Rice (1992) for examples of some of the earlier studies on this topic. The scholarly community has proposed a number of mechanisms by which stress and health are linked: a physiological response to stress which wears a body down over time; ineffective efforts to cope with stress due to limited decision-making ability or limited support at work; and adoption of overtly health-damaging behaviors. Kuper and Marmot (2003); Karasek (1979); and Johnson et al. (1996) offer basic descriptions of such linking mechanisms. It is likely that multiple factors are implicated. See Sun et al. (2007).

2. Sun et al. (2007).

3. To create a matched group of workers who had not left the company, we identified the number of men and women from the attrition sample who fell into age categories divided into ten-year intervals (e.g., number of women aged 30–39, number of men aged 30–39, number of women aged 40–49, etc.). We then identified the same subgroups for the continuously employed sample who, like the attrition sample, had completed the 1997 and 2000 surveys (though not necessarily the 2003 survey), and selected at random the same number of employees so that the matched and attrition groups each had the same number of men and women within each of the various age categories. In this way, the matched and attrition groups were equal in terms of gender, had the same age distributions within each gender, and were equally likely to have completed the 2003 survey. Importantly, the two samples did not differ statistically on any of the quantitative measures in 1997.

It was not possible to examine the effects of reemployment within this attrition subsample due to small numbers of former employees with common post-Boeing experiences. Some returned to school, some worked part-time, some had a series of unstable full-time reemployment experiences, a number entered full-time retirement, and so on.

4. For example, see Beehr and Newman (1978); Klainin (2009); and Tian and Wang (2005).

5. A description of the personal control scale and all other scales used in this chapter and other chapters in the book, as well as their psychometric properties, can be found in the appendix.

6. Thus, a score of "5," for example, could mean that a worker might have experienced five of these symptoms (out of seven possible symptoms), one each day, or a single symptom on five days in the last week, or some combination thereof.

7. In one of the first reviews of the literature to link workplace stress and health, Beehr and Newman (1978) identified the following common responses to work stress: mediation; mastery of the environment; seeking social support; increased religious activity; changing one's diet; physical activity; seeking medical, psychological, or other professional help; and reduction of the psychological importance of work. In the intervening three decades since their review, other scholars have amassed a fair amount of empirical support for these strategies.

8. See, for example, Sun et al. (2007) and Nishitani and Sakakibara (2006).

9. Tian and Wang (2005).

10. See Ragland and Ames (1996) for one such example.

11. Alcohol use tends to be inversely related to age. See, for example, Chen, Dufour, and Yi (2004/2005) and NIAAA (2004). Percent reporting alcohol use in the past year by age group and demographic characteristics: NSDUH (NHSDA), 1994–2002 (http://www.niaaa.nih.gov/Resources/DatabaseResources/QuickFacts/AlcoholConsumption/dkpat3.htm).

12. See, for example, Abbey, Smith, and Scott (1993) and Cooper, Russell, and George (1988).

13. Courtney and Polich (2009).

14. See Beehr and Newman (1978); Johnson et al. (1996); Kuper and Marmot (2003); or Sun et al. (2007).

15. See Bigos et al. (1992) for an earlier study that found back problems among Boeing employees to be predicted by job dissatisfaction and distress. The authors concluded that "nonphysical" factors played an important role in the reporting of back problems and employee responsiveness to treatment.

16. Johnson et al. (1996); Kuper and Marmot (2003); Sun et al. (2007); and Tian and Wang (2005).

CHAPTER 9. NAVIGATING THROUGH TURBULENCE

1. On the nature of the postwar system and its passing see Chandler (1990); Dicken (2007); Gosselin (2008); Hacker (2000); Jacobi (1997); Lazonick (2005); Reich (1992); and Reich (2007).

2. See especially Cappelli (1999).

3. See Lawrence and Thornton (2005); Newhouse (2007); and Aris (2004).

4. Holmes (2003).

5. One top union official told us in a written communication in 2009 that Boeing would have had sufficient funds to finance the development of the 787 on its own had it not spent so much on repurchasing its own stock in order to drive up share values. Whether or not this is true, it remains the case that shouldering the costs of developing and manufacturing an entirely new airplane (at least $10 billion) represented a very big risk.

6. Even as Boeing has mimicked Airbus's innovations in airplane design, engineering, and manufacturing improvements and flight systems.

7. Wall (2007).

8. See Cappelli (1999), 5; Karoly (2004); O'Toole and Lawler (2007), ch. 2; and Reich (2007), ch. 2.

9. Peters and Waterman (1982).

10. Jacoby (1997).

11. Job tenure increased for women aged thirty-five to fifty-four, however. Researchers conjecture that it reflects voluntary behavior by women (taking less time off to care for children, for example) but for men reflects involuntary job loss. See Farber (2007).

12. This change in the employment relationship has prompted two social commentators to make some bold predictions about long-term societal effects. Richard Sennett, in *The Corrosion of Character* (1998), fears that the development of fluid, "no long-term" employment relationships will change workers' characters and hence their behavior in other domains. The social fabric that holds people together and makes individuals care for others may gradually erode as employees seek to take care of their own needs, as we saw in the reactions to layoff uncertainty among some Boeing employees. Jacob Hacker, in *The Great Risk Shift* (2006), worries that the "individual responsibility" ideology that has developed in the United States around the accelerating trend of companies offloading employee health care pension responsibilities onto the shoulders of individuals will not only undermine the well-being of most Americans but destroy the cultural foundations for sharing responsibilities for the welfare of others. These are certainly bleak but plausible outcomes from the changes in the employment relationship we have documented.

13. Reich (2007).

14. The classic statement of the structural power of business based on its role in the economic health of communities and the country is Charles Lindblom's *Politics and Markets* (1977). Also see Greenberg and Page (2009), ch. 7; Mitchell (1997); Wolfe (2006); and Vogel (1989). Consistent with this view, note that the state of Washington gave Boeing a subsidy of $2 billion to ensure that the final assembly of the 787 would happen in the state. Unfortunately for Boeing employees in the Puget Sound area, the agreement between Washington and Boeing committed the firm only to a single production line. Boeing decided in 2009 to put its second 787 production line in South Carolina, which offered not only a large subsidy but a less-union-friendly environment as well.

15. One anecdote is telling. When the Department of Defense awarded its massive $35-billion midair refueling tanker contract in 2008 to EADS, the parent company of Airbus, Congress forced the DoD to reconsider and rewrote the contract to split the work be-

tween Boeing and EADS (which was partnered with the American company Northrup Grumman). None of the parties found this solution to its liking, so the DoD decided to reopen the bidding process for fall 2010. At this writing, the DoD has not made a final decision on who will do the work on the tanker.

16. On the empirical link between employee engagement, morale, commitment, and firm performance, see Meyer and Allen (1991); Meyer et al. (2002); Podsakoff et al. (2009); and Solinger, van Olffen, and Roe (2008). On these linkages, Peter Cappelli and Jeffrey Pfeffer, two prominent and respected workplace scholars, draw different conclusions from their reading of the research literature, with Cappelli somewhat skeptical and Pfeffer strongly convinced that engagement and commitment matter. See Cappelli (1999) and Pfeffer (1998).

17. Florkowski and Schuster (1992) and Kruse (1993).

18. Boeing's Share Value profit sharing plan failed when company share prices twice collapsed just before the scheduled payout period. It does have a small Employee Incentive Plan that has consistently paid bonuses to employees.

19. Collins (2001).

20. In an interview with us in early 2009, one Boeing insider (who must remain anonymous) claimed that the company has since recognized that it over-outsourced and has a better handle now on what sorts of activities must stay in-house and what can be safely off-loaded. The company, he further claimed, now better appreciates its most skilled employees and is trying to better recognize and support them. When Jim Albaugh, an engineer by training, was brought over in 2009 from the defense side of the Boeing Corporation to run Boeing Commercial Airplanes, he paid special tribute to Boeing's engineers and technical workers and promised to make the firm an engineering company again and not simply a sales organization. See Gates (2009).

21. Boeing tried to do this with a program called the "Chairman's Initiative" under Phil Condit, but none of the efforts launched under the initiative achieved commercial viability. The company has not provided enough information about these efforts to enable us to analyze the reasons they fell short.

22. See our several graphs in chapters 3 and 8 comparing well-being outcomes for those who were forced to leave Boeing and those leaving voluntarily.

23. Gioia and Chittipeddi (1991); Weick (1995); Mills (2003); and Deetz, Tracy, and Simpson (2000).

24. For an introduction to the vast literature on these topics see Dahl (1989) and Lipset and Lakin (2004).

25. Coser (1974) and Deetz (1992).

26. Hall and Moss (1998); Cappelli (2002); Arthur and Rousseau (1996); Colby (2009); Waterman and Collard (2001); and Hall (2002).

27. Dvork and Thurm (2009).

28. Hacker (2006); Sweet and Meiksins (2008), ch. 7; and Gosselin (2008), ch. 12.

29. For these assertions, see Blanchard and Tirol (2003); Heckman and Pages-Serra (2000); and Botero et al. (2004).

30. Bassanini, Nunziata, and Venn (2008).

31. Clark and Postel-Vinay (2009).

32. Blanchard and Tirole (2008).

33. Gosselin (2008); Hamilton Project (2008); Cappelli (1999); and Hacker (2006).

34. Blanchard and Tirol (2009); and Blanchard and Tirol (2008).

35. Wilthagen and Troos (2004).

36. Kuttner (2008).

Bibliography

Abbey, A., M. J. Smith, and R. O. Scott. 1993. The relationship between reasons for drinking alcohol and alcohol consumption: An interactional approach. *Addictive Behaviors* 18(6):659–70.

Aeromechanic. March 2000. Our new voice in job security, http://www.iam751.org/Web mainhtml/Aeromechanic/Mar_00/WTC.html.

Andrisani, P. J. 1978. *Work attitudes and labor market experience: Evidence from the national longitudinal surveys.* New York: Praeger.

Anonymous. 2007. The giant on the runway—The Airbus A380. *Economist (US)* 385(8550): 79–82.

Applebaum, E., T. Bailey, P. Berg, and A. Kalleberg. 2000. *Manufacturing advantage: Why higher performance work systems pay off.* Ithaca, NY: Cornell University Press.

Aris, S. 2004. *Close to the sun: How Airbus challenged America's domination of the skies.* 1st American ed. Chicago: Agate.

Armstrong-Stassen, M. 1993. Survivors' reactions to a workforce reduction: A comparison of blue-collar workers and their supervisors. *Canadian Journal of Administrative Sciences* 10:334–43.

———. 1998. The effect of gender and organizational level on how survivors appraise and cope with organizational downsizing. *Journal of Applied Behavioral Science* 34:125–42.

Arthur, M. B., and D. M. Rousseau. 1996. *The boundaryless career: A new employment principle for a new organizational era.* New York: Oxford University Press.

Aryee, S., E. Srinivas, and H. Tan. 2005. Rhythms of life: Antecedents and outcomes of work-family balance in employed parents. *Journal of Applied Psychology* 90(1):132–46.

Avolio, B. J., B. M. Bass, and D. I. Jung. 1999. Re-examining the components of transformational and transactional leadership using the multifactor leadership questionnaire. *Journal of Occupational and Organizational Psychology* 72(4):441–62.

Barker, J. R. 1993. Tightening the iron cage: Concertive control in self-managing teams. *Administrative Science Quarterly* 38(3):408–37.

Bartley, S., P. Blanton, and J. Gilliard. 2005. Husbands and wives in dual-earner marriages: Decision-making, gender role attitudes, division of household labor, and equity. *Marriage & Family Review* 37(4):69–94.

Bartunek, J. M., R. Krim, R. Necochea, and M. Humphries. 1999. *Sensemaking, sensegiving, and leadership in strategic organizational development. Advances in Qualitative Organizational Research,* ed. J. Wagner. Vol. 2. Greenwich, CT: JAI Press, 37–71.

Bass, B. M. 1985. *Leadership & performance beyond expectations.* New York: Free Press.

Bass, B. M., and B. Avolio. 1993. Transformational leadership: A response to critiques. In *Leadership Theory and Research: Perspectives and Directions,* eds. M. M. Chemmers and R. Ayman. San Diego: Academic Press, 49–88.

Bassanini, A., L. Nunziata, and D. Venn. 2008. *Job protection legislation and productivity growth in OECD countries:* IZA Discussion Paper No. 3555. http://papers.ssrn.com/sol3/papers.cfm?abstract_id=1150744.

Baumgarner, J. 2001. Harry Stonecipher's linchpin role in U.S. aerospace. *Aviation Week Spotlight,* October.

Beatty, C. A. 1996. The stress of managerial and professional women: Is the price too high? *Journal of Organizational Behavior* 17(3):233–51.

Beehr, T. A., and J. E. Newman. 1978. Job stress, employee health, and organizational effectiveness: A facet analysis, model, and literature review. *Personnel Psychology* 31(4):665–99.

Bélanger, J., P. K. Edwards, and M. Wright. 2003. Commitment at work and independence from management—A study of advanced teamwork. *Work and Occupations* 30(2):234–52.

Berns, G. 2008. In hard times, fear can impair decision making. *New York Times,* December 7.

Bigos, S., M. Battie, D. Spengler, L. Fisher, W. Fordyce, T. Hansson, A. Nachemson, and J. Zeh. 1992. A longitudinal, prospective study of industrial back injury reporting. *Clinical Orthopaedics and Related Research* 279:21–34.

Black, J. R. 2009. Lean manufacturing: Former Boeing executive describes why now is the time to change. *Tooling and Production.*

Blanchard, O. J., and J. Tirole. 2003. Contours of employment protection reform. MIT Department of Economics. Working Paper No. 03–35.

———. 2008. The joint design of unemployment insurance and employment protection: A first pass. *Journal of the European Economic Association* 6(1):45–77.

———. 2009. In Serra, N., and J. Stiglitz, eds. *The Washington Consensus Reconsidered: Towards a New Global Governance.* Oxford: Oxford University Press.

Botero, J. C., S. Djankov, R. La Porta, F. Lopez-de-Silanes, and A. Shleifer. 2004. The regulation of labor. *Quarterly Journal of Economics* 119(4):1339–82.

Buchanan, J. M., and T. Gordon. 1975. Polluters' profits and political response: Direct controls versus taxes. *American Economic Review* 65(1):139.

Burke, R. J., and C. A. McKeen. 1994. Career development among managerial and professional women. In *Women in management: current research issues,* eds. M. J. Davidson and R. J. Burke. London: Paul Chapman Pub, 65–79.

BusinessDictionary.com. Manager definition. Retrieved June 16, 2009, from http://www .businessdictionary.com/definition/manager.html.

Business Week. 1996. Boeing. September 30, 119–25.

Byron, K. 2005. A meta-analytic review of work-family conflict and its antecedents. *Journal of Vocational Behavior* 67(2):169–98.

Callahan, P. 2004. So why does Harry Stonecipher think he can turn around Boeing? *Chicago Tribune,* February 29.

Cammann, C., M. Fichman, G. D. Jenkins, Jr., and J. R. Klesh. 1983. Assessing the attitudes and perceptions of organizational members. In *Assessing organizational change: A guide to methods, measures, and practices,* ed. S. E. Seashore. New York: Wiley, 71–138.

Cappelli, P. 1999. *The new deal at work: Managing the market-driven workforce.* Boston: Harvard Business School Press.

———. 2002. The path to the top: The changing model of career development. Conference paper, June 13–15. London, England.

———. 2008. *Employment relationships: New models of white collar work.* Cambridge: Cambridge University Press.

Cappelli, P., L. Bassi, H. Katz, D. Knoke, P. Osterman, and Useem, et al. 1997. *Change at work.* New York: Oxford University Press.

Carron, A. V., L. R. Brawley, M. A. Eys, S. Bray, K. Dorsch, P. Estabrooks, C. R. Hall, J. Hardy, H. Hausenblas, R. Madison, D. Paskevich, and M. M. Patterson. 2003. Do individual perceptions of group cohesion reflect shared beliefs? *Small Group Research* 34(4):468–96.

Cawley, J., C. Meyerhoefer, and D. Newhouse. 2007. The correlation of youth physical activity with state policies. *Contemporary Economic Policy* 25(4):506–17.

Chandler, A. *Scale and Scope: The Dynamics of Industrial Capitalism.* Cambridge: Harvard University Press, 1990.

Chen, C., M. Dufour, and H. Yi. 2004/2005. Alcohol consumption among young adults ages 18–24 in the United States: Results from the 2001–2002 NESARC Survey. *Alcohol Research & Health,* 28(4):269–80.

Clark, A., and F. Postel-Vinayy. 2009. Job security and job protection. *Oxford Economic Papers* 61:207–39.

Cobb, S., and S. Kasl. 1977. *Termination: The consequences of job loss.* Cincinnati: NIOSH.

Colby, A. G. 2009. Making the new career development model work. *HR Magazine* 40, July 30.

Cole, J. 1998a. Boeing's cultural revolution. *Seattle Times,* December 13.

———. 1998b. Ron Woodard: Not bitter, but incredulous at his ouster. *Seattle Times,* December 13.

Collard, B. A., J. A. Waterman, and R. H. Waterman, Jr. 2001. Toward a career-resilient workforce. In Harvard Business Review On finding and keeping the best people. Boston: Harvard Business School Press, 1–25.

Collins, J. 2001. *Good to great: Why some companies make the leap—and others don't.* New York: HarperBusiness.

Collins, J. C., and J. I. Porras. 1994. *Built to last: Successful habits of visionary companies.* New York: HarperBusiness.

Cooper, M. L., M. Russell, and W. H. George. 1988. Coping, expectancies, and alcohol abuse: A test of social learning formulations. *Journal of Abnormal Psychology* 97(2):218–30.

Cort, A. 2006. Living the Dream. *Assembly Magazine,* August 1. http://www.assemblymag .com/CDA/Articles/Cover_Story/9426d3a40438c010VgnVCM100000f932a8c0____.

Coser, L. A. 1974. *Greedy institutions: Patterns of undivided commitment.* New York: Free Press.

Courtney, K. E., and J. Polich. 2009. Binge drinking in young adults: Data, definitions, and determinants. *Psychological Bulletin* 135(1):142–56.

Dahl, R. A. 1989. *Democracy and its critics.* New Haven: Yale University Press.

Darr, W., and G. Johns. 2008. Work strain, health, and absenteeism: A meta-analysis. *Journal of Occupational Health Psychology* 13(4):293–318.

Deetz, S. 1992. *Democracy in an age of corporate colonization: Developments in communication and the politics of everyday life.* Albany: State University of New York.

Deetz, S. A., S. J. Tracy, and J. L. Simpson. 2000. *Leading organizations through transition: Communication and cultural change.* Thousand Oaks, CA: Sage Publications.

Dempsey, P. S., and L. E. Gesell. 1997. *Air transportation: Foundations for the 21st century.* Chandler, AZ: Coast Aire Publications.

Devine, D. J. 2002. A review and integration of classification systems relevant to teams in organizations. *Group dynamics: Theory, research and practice* 6(4):291–310.

Devine, K., R. Trish, L. Stainton, and R. Collins-Nakai. 2009. Downsizing outcomes: Better a victim than a survivor? *Human Resource Management* 42(2):109–24.

Dicken, P. 2007. *Global shift.* 5th ed. New York: Guilford Press.

Dion, K. L. 2000. Group cohesion: From "field of forces" to multidimensional construct. *Group Dynamics: Theory, Research, and Practice* 4:7–26.

Dooley, K. 2002. Organizational complexity. In *International encyclopedia of business and management,* ed. M. Warner. London: Thompson Learning, 5013–22.

Dunham, R. B., J. A. Grube, and M. B. Castaneda. 1994. Organizational commitment: The utility of an integrative definition. *Journal of Applied Psychology* 79(3):370–80.

Duvall, M., and D. Bartholomew. 2007. The promise and peril of PLM. *Baseline E Magazine.*

Duxbury, L., and C. Higgins. 2001. Work-life balance in the new millennium: Where are we? Where do we need to go? Canadian Policy Research Networks Discussion Paper W/12. Ottawa, ON.

Dvorak, P., and S. Thurm. Slump prods firms to seek new compact with workers. *Wall Street Journal,* October 20, 2009.

Eagly, A., M. Johannesen-Schmidt, and M. van Engen. 2003. Transformational, transactional, and laissez-faire leadership styles: A meta-analysis comparing women and men. *Psychological Bulletin* 129(4):569–91.

Eagly, A., and S. Karau. 2002. Role congruity theory of prejudice toward female leaders. *Psychological Review* 109(3):573–98.

Eby, L., W. Casper, A. Lockwood, C. Bordeaux, and A. Brinley. 2005. Work and family research in IO/OB: Content analysis and review of the literature (1980–2002). *Journal of Vocational Behavior* 66(1):124–97.

Farber, H. S. 2005. What do we know about job loss in the United States? Evidence from the Displaced Workers Survey, 1984–2004. *FRB Chicago Economic Perspectives* 29(2):13–28, http://www.chicagofed.org/publications/economicperspectives/ep_2qtr2005_part2_farber.pdf.

———. 2007. Is the company man an anachronism? Trends in long term employment in the U.S., 1973–2006. Princeton University Working Paper #518.

Fisher, K. 1993. *Leading self-directed work teams.* New York: McGraw-Hill.

Florkowski, G. W., and M. H. Schuster. 1992. Support for profit sharing and organizational commitment: A path analysis. *Human Relations* 45(5):507–23.

Freeman, R. B., and J. Rogers. 1999. *What workers want.* Ithaca, NY: ILR Press.

Gates, D. 2005. The decline of Boeing jobs. *Seattle Times,* April 17.

———. 2008. Big raises in SPEEA pact with Boeing. *Seattle Times,* November 15.

———. 2009. Boeing fix-it guy leads airliner unit. *Seattle Times,* September 1.

Gioia, D., and K. Chittipeddi. 1991. Sensemaking and sensegiving in strategic change initiation. *Strategic Management Journal* 12(6):433–48.

Glassop, L. 2002. The organizational benefits of teams. *Human Relations* 55(2):225–49.

Golden, T., J. Veiga, and R. Dino. 2008. The impact of professional isolation on teleworker job performance and turnover intentions: Does time spent teleworking, interacting face-to-face, or having access to communication-enhancing technology matter? *Journal of Applied Psychology* 93(6):1412–21.

Goldfield, M. 1989. The decline of organized labor in the United States. Chicago: University of Chicago Press.

Goodman, P., S. Davadas, and T. L. Hughson. 1988. Groups and productivity. In *Productivity in organizations,* ed. J. P. Campbell. San Francisco: Jossey-Bass and Associates.

Gosselin, P. 2008. *High wire: The precarious financial lives of American families.* New York: Basic Books.

Grant, A. M., and S. K. Parker. 2009. Redesigning work design theories: The rise of relational and proactive perspectives. *Academy of Management Annals* 3:317–75.

Greenberg, E. S. 1986. *Workplace democracy: The political effects of participation.* Ithaca, NY: Cornell University Press.

Greenberg, E., and L. Grunberg. 2003. The changing American workplace and sense of mastery: Assessing the impacts of downsizing, job redesign, and teaming. Working Paper IBS—University of Colorado Boulder.

Greenberg, E., and B. Page. 2009. *The struggle for democracy.* 9th ed. New York: Pearson Longman.

Greenhouse, S. 2008. *The big squeeze: Tough times for the American worker.* New York: Alfred Knopf.

Grunberg, L., R. Anderson-Connolly, and E. Greenberg. 2000. Surviving layoffs—The effects on organizational commitment and job performance. *Work and Occupations* 27(1):7–31.

Grunberg, L., S. Moore, and E. Greenberg. 2001. Differences in psychological and physical health among layoff survivors: The effect of layoff contact. *Journal of Occupational Health Psychology* 6(1):15–25.

———. 2006. Managers' reactions to implementing layoffs: Relationship to health problems and withdrawal behaviors. *Human Resource Management* 45(2):159–78.

———. Minimizing the impact of layoffs on front-line managers: Ensuring that layoffs are conducted fairly can help reduce negative feelings among managers who must give notice to workers. *Journal of Employee Assistance* 39(1), published online: http://search.rdsinc .com/texis/rds/suite/+fdeQWZJeAxbtqo15nG18XvXewx11qmwwwwewhanmew64Pez Rfwww/showdoc.html?thisTbl=BMP.

Hacker, J. S. 2006. *The great risk shift: The assault on American jobs, families, health care, and retirement and how you can fight back.* Oxford: Oxford University Press.

Hackman, J. R. 1987. The design of work teams. In *Handbook of organizational behavior,* ed. J. Lorsch. Englewood Cliffs, NJ: Prentice-Hall.

Hackman, J. R., and G. R. Oldham. 1980. *Work redesign.* Reading, MA: Addison-Wesley.

Hall, D. T. 2002. *Careers in and out of organizations.* Thousand Oaks, CA: Sage.

Hall, D. T., and J. E. Moss. 1998. The new Protean career contract: Helping organizations and employees adapt. *Organizational Dynamics* 26(3):22–37.

Hamilton Project: http://www.brookings.edu/projects/hamiltonproject/econsecurity_pillar .aspx.

Happenheimer, T. A. 1995. *Turbulent Skies: The history of commercial aviation.* New York: John Wiley and Sons.

Haskins, M., J. Liedtka, and J. Rosenblum. 1998. Beyond teams: Toward an ethic of collaboration. *Organizational Dynamics* 26(4):34–50.

Heckman, J., and C. Pagés-Serra. 2000. The cost of job security regulation: Evidence from Latin American labor markets. *Economia* 1(1):109–54.

Hodson, R. 2002. Worker participation and teams: New evidence from analyzing organizational ethnographies. *Economic and Industrial Democracy* 23(4):491–528.

Holmes, S. 1995. Boeing cuts: Who will be next? *Seattle Times,* October 8.

———. 2003. Boeing: What really happened. Retrieved December 15 from *Business Week,* http://www.businessweek.com/magazine/content/03_50/b3862001_mz001.htm.

———. 1995. When jobs go south—Mounting pressure to cut costs has caused Boeing to send assembly work to Mexico and overseas. In the U.S., employees lose their jobs, and in Mexico, workers are paid barely enough to subsist. *Seattle Times,* November 12.

Holmes, S., and M. France. 2004. Coverup at Boeing? *Business Week* 3889:84–90.

Jacoby, S. M. 1997. *Modern manors: Welfare capitalism since the New Deal.* Princeton, NJ: Princeton University Press.

Johnson, J., W. Stewart, E. Hall, P. Fredlund, and T. Theorell. 1996. Long-term psychosocial work environment and cardiovascular mortality among Swedish men. *American Journal of Public Health* 86(3):324–31.

Karasek, R. A. 1979. Job demands, job decision latitude, and mental strain: Implications for job redesign. *Administration Science Quarterly* 24(2):285–308.

Karasek, R. A., and T. Theorell. 1990. *Healthy work: Stress, productivity, and the reconstruction of working life.* New York: Basic Books.

Karoly, L. A., and C. W. A. Panis. 2004. *The 21st century at work: Forces shaping the future workforce and workplace in the United States.* Santa Monica, CA: RAND.

Katz, D., and R. L. Kahn. 1978. *The social psychology of organization.* 2nd ed. New York: Wiley.

Katzenbach, J. R., and D. K. Smith. 1993. *The wisdom of teams: Creating the high performance organization.* Boston: Harvard Business School Press.

Kemp, K. 2006. *Flight of the Titans: Boeing, Airbus and the battle for the future of air travel.* London: Virgin.

Kets de Vries, M., and K. Balazs. 1997. The downside of downsizing. *Human Relations* 50:11–50.

Kirkman, B., and B. Rosen. 2000. Powering up teams. *Organizational Dynamics* 28(3):48–66.

Kivimaki, M., J. Vahtera, M. Elovainio, J. Pentti, and M. Virtanen. 2003. Human costs of organizational downsizing: Comparing health trends between leavers and stayers. *American Journal of Community Psychology* 32(1–2):57–67.

Kivimaki, M., J. Vahtera, J. Pentti, and J. Ferrie. 2000. Factors underlying the effect of organisational downsizing on health of employees: Longitudinal cohort study. *British Medical Journal* 320(7240):971–75.

Klainin, P. 2009. Stress and health outcomes: The mediating role of negative affectivity in female health care workers. *International Journal of Stress Management* 16(1):45–64.

Kruse, D. 2003. *Motivating employee-owners in ESOP firms: Human resource policies and company performance.* Cambridge, MA: National Bureau of Economic Research.

Kuper, H., and M. Marmot. 2003. Job strain, job demands, decision latitude, and risk of coronary heart disease within the Whitehall II study. *Journal of Epidemiology and Community Health* 57(2):147–53.

Kusnet, D. 2008. *Love the work, hate the job: Why America's best workers are more unhappy than ever.* Hoboken, NJ: John Wiley and Sons, Inc.

Kuttner, R. 2008. The Copenhagen consensus—Reading Adam Smith in Denmark. *Foreign Affairs* 87(2):78–94.

Lave, L. B. 1981. *The strategy of social regulation: Decision frameworks for policy.* Washington, D.C.: Brookings Institution.

Lawler, E. E., and J. O'Toole. 2006. *America at work: Choices and challenges.* 1st ed. New York: Palgrave Macmillan.

Lawrence, P. K., and D. W. Thornton. 2005. *Deep stall: The turbulent story of Boeing Commercial Airplanes.* Aldershot, England: Ashgate.

Lazonick, W. 2005. Corporate restructuring. In *The Oxford Handbook of Work and Organization.* Ed. S. Ackroyd, R. Batt, P. Thompson, and P. S. Tolbert. Oxford, UK: Oxford University Press, 577–601.

Lazonick, W., and M. O'Sullivan. 2000. Maximizing shareholder value: A new ideology for corporate governance. *Economy and Society* 29(1):13–35.

Levine, D. I. 1995. *Reinventing the workplace: How business and employees can both win.* Washington D.C.: Brookings Institution.

Lindblom, C. E. (1977). *Politics and markets: The world's political-economic systems.* New York: Basic Books, 1977.

Lincoln, J. R., and A. L. Kalleberg. 1990. *Culture, control, and commitment: A study of work organization and work attitudes in the United States and Japan.* Cambridge: Cambridge University Press.

Lipset, S. M., and J. M. Lakin. 2004. *The Democratic century.* Norman, OK: University of Oklahoma Press.

Lunsford, L. 2002. Boeing and machinists union heading for contract showdown. *Wall Street Journal,* August 27.

———. 2008. Boeing strikers dig in heels even as economy turns sour. *Wall Street Journal,* October 23.

Luthans, B. C., and S. M. Sommer. 1999. The impact of downsizing on workplace attitudes. *Group & Organization Management* 24(1):46–70.

MacPherson, A., and D. Pritchard. 2007. Boeing's diffusion of commercial aircraft technology to Japan. *Journal of Labor Research* 28(3):552–66.

Madslien, J. 2009. Military spending sets new record. *BBC Online,* June 8, http://news.bbc.co.uk/2/hi/business/8086117.stm.

Martin, A. J., E. S. Jones, and V. J. Callan. 2006. Status differences in employee adjustment during organizational change. *Journal of Managerial Psychology* 21(2):145–62.

Mason, C. M., and M. A. Griffin. 2003. Identifying group task satisfaction at work. *Small Group Research* 34(4):413–42.

Mason, R. M. 1982. *Participatory and workplace democracy: A theoretical development in critique of liberalism.* Carbondale, IL: Southern Illinois University.

McGregor, D. 1960. *The human side of enterprise.* New York: McGraw-Hill.

McLagan, P., and C. Nel. 1995. *The age of participation: New governance for the workplace and the world.* San Francisco: Berrett-Koehler.

Meyer, J. P., and N. J. Allen. 1991. A three component conceptualization of organizational commitment. *Human Resource Management Review* 91(1):61.

Meyer, J. P., D. J. Stanley, L. Herscovitch, and L. Topolnytsky. 2002. Affective, continuance, and normative commitment to the organization: A meta-analysis of antecedents, correlates, and consequences. *Journal of Vocational Behavior* 61(1):20–52.

Micklethwait, J., and A. Wooldridge. 1996. *The witch doctors: Making sense of the management gurus.* New York: Times Books/Random House.

Mills, J. H. 2003. *Making sense of organizational change.* New York: Routledge.

Mirowsky, J., and C. E. Ross. 1989. *Social causes of psychological distress.* New York: de Gruyter.

Mitchell, N. J. 1997. *The conspicuous corporation: Business, public policy, and representative democracy.* Ann Arbor: University of Michigan Press.

Moore, S., L. Grunberg, and E. Greenberg. 2003. A longitudinal exploration of alcohol use and problems comparing managerial and non-managerial men and women. *Addictive Behavior* 28:687–703.

Moos, R. H., R. C. Cronkite, J. W. Finney, and A. G. Billings. 1986. *Health and daily living form manual.* Rev. ed. Palo Alto, CA: Veterans Administration and Stanford University Medical Center.

Muellerleile, C. M. 2009. Financialization takes off at Boeing. *Journal of Economic Geography* 9(5):663–77.

Newhouse, J. 2007. *Boeing versus Airbus: The inside story of the greatest international competition in business.* 1st ed. New York: A. A. Knopf.

NIAAA. 2004. Percent reporting alcohol use in the past year by age group and demographic characteristics: NSDUH (NHSDA), 1994–2002. From http://www.niaaa.nih.gov/niaaa .nih.gov/Templates/TablePage.aspx?NRMODE=Published&NRNODEGUID={5D6D8 C92–09B8–4C40–98F6-DCBECE24C967}&NRORIGINALURL=%2fResources %2fDatabaseResources%2fQuickFacts%2fAlcoholConsumption%2fdkpat3.htm& NRCACHEHINT=Guest.

Niehoff, B., R. Moorman, G. Blakely, and J. Fuller. 2001. The influence of empowerment and job enrichment on employee loyalty in a downsizing environment. *Group & Organization Management* 26(1):93–113.

Nishitani, N., and H. Sakakibara. 2006. Relationship of obesity to job stress and eating behavior in male Japanese workers. *International Journal of Obesity* 30(3):528–33.

Offermann, L., and R. Spiros. 2001. The science and practice of team development: Improving the link. *Academy of Management Journal* 44(2):376–92.

O'Kane, P., and O. Hargie. 2007. Intentional and unintentional consequences of substituting face-to-face interaction with e-mail: An employee-based perspective. *Interacting with Computers* 19(1):20–31.

Osterman, P. 2006. The changing employment circumstances of managers. In *America at work: Choices and challenges,* ed. E. E. Lawler and J. O'Toole. 1st ed. New York: Palgrave Macmillan.

———. 2009. *The truth about middle managers: Who they are, how they work, why they matter.* Boston: Harvard Business School Press.

O'Toole, J., and E. E. Lawler III. 2007. *The new American workplace.* New York: Palgrave, Macmillan.

Pateman, C. 1970. *Participation and democratic theory.* Cambridge: Cambridge University Press.

Pearlin, L. I., and C. Schooler. 1978. The structure of coping. *Journal of Health and Social Behavior* 19(1):2–21.

Peters, T., and R. Waterman. 1982. *In search of excellence: Lessons from America's best run companies.* New York: Harper & Row.

Pfeffer, J. 1998. *The human equation: Building profits by putting people first.* Boston: Harvard Business School Press.

———. 2006. Working alone: Whatever happened to the idea of organizations as communities? In *America at work: Choices and challenges,* ed. E. E. Lawler and J. O'Toole. 1st ed. New York: Palgrave Macmillan, 3–21.

Podsakoff, N. P., S. W. Whiting, P. M. Podsakoff, and B. D. Blume. 2009. Individual- and organizational-level consequences of organizational citizenship behaviors: A meta-analysis. *Journal of Applied Psychology* 94(1):122–41.

Quick, J. D., R. S. Horn, and J. C. Quick. 1986. Health consequences of stress. Special issue: Job stress: From theory to suggestion. *Journal of Organizational Behavior Management* 8(2):19–36. Fal-Win.

Quinn, R. P., and G. L. Staines. 1978. *The 1977 quality of employment survey.* Ann Arbor, MI: Institute for Social Research, University of Michigan.

Ragland, D. R., and G. M. Ames. 1996. Current developments in the study of stress and alcohol consumption. *Alcoholism: Clinical and Experimental Research* 20(8):51a–53a.

Rappaport, A. 1986. *Creating shareholder value: The new standard for business performance.* New York: Free Press.

Reich, R. B. 1992. *The work of nations: Preparing ourselves for the 21st century.* New York: Vintage.

———. 2007. *Supercapitalism: The transformation of business, democracy, and everyday life.* 1st ed. New York: Alfred A. Knopf.

Reuters. 2004. Aerospace firms battle it out at upbeat air show. Available from *AirWise News,* http://news.airwise.com/stories/2004/07/1090528504.html, September 21.

Rice, P. L. 1992. *Stress and health.* 2nd ed. Boston: Brooks/Cole Publishing Company.

Richman, J. A., K. M. Rospenda, S. J. Nawyn, J. A. Flaherty, M. Feindrich, M. L. Drum, et al. 1999. Sexual harassment and generalized workplace abuse among university employees: Prevalence and mental health correlates. *American Journal of Public Health* 89(3):358–63.

Robinson, S. L., M. S. Kraatz, and D. M. Rousseau. 1994. Changing obligations and the psychological contract: A longitudinal study. *Academy of Management Journal* 37: 137–52.

Robinson, S. L., and D. M. Rousseau. 1994. Violating the psychological contract: Not the exception but the norm. *Journal of Organizational Behavior* 15(3):245–59.

Rousseau, D. M. 1998. Why workers still identify with organizations. *Journal of Organizational Behavior* 19(3).

Sabbagh, K. 1996. *21st century jet: The making and marketing of the Boeing 777.* New York: Scribner.

Sennett, R. 1998. *The corrosion of character: The personal consequences of work in the new capitalism.* 1st ed. New York: Norton.

Serling, R. J. 1992. *Legend and legacy: The story of Boeing and its people.* New York: St. Martin's Press.

Shead, M. 2007. Definition of Management. Retrieved June 16, 2009, from http://www.leadership501.com/definition-of-management/21/

Sikora, P. B., E. D. Beaty, and J. Forward. 2004. Updating theory on organizational stress: The asynchronous multiple overlapping change (AMOC) model of workplace stress. *Human Resources Development Review* 3:3–35.

Sinha, K., and A. Van de Ven. 2005. Designing work within and between organizations. *Organization Science* 16(4):389–408.

Solinger, O. N., W. van Olffen, and R. A. Roe. 2008. Beyond the three-component model of organizational commitment. *Journal of Applied Psychology* 93(1):70–83.

Sorscher, S. 2009. Aerospace engineer strikes. In *The encyclopedia of strikes in American history,* ed. Aaron Brenner, Benjamin Day, and Immanuel Ness. New York: M. E. Sharpe.

Spreitzer, G. M. 1996. Social structural characteristics of psychological empowerment. *Academy of Management Journal* 39(2):483–504.

Stanton, J. M., W. K. Balzer, P. C. Smith, L. F. Parra, and G. Ironson. 2001. A general measure of work stress: The stress in general scale. *Educational and Psychological Measurement* 61(5):866–88.

Steele, C. M. 1997. A threat in the air: How stereotypes shape intellectual identity and performance. *American Psychologist* 52(6):613–29.

Sun, J., S. Wang, J. Zhang, and W. Li. 2007. Assessing the cumulative effects of stress: The association between job stress and allostatic load in a large sample of Chinese employees. *Work and Stress* 21(4):333–47.

Sweet, S., and P. Meiksins. 2008. *Changing Contours of Work: Jobs and Opportunities in the New Economy.* Thousand Oaks, CA: Pine Forge Press.

Tafti, A., S. Mithas, and M. S. Krishnan. 2007. Information technology and the autonomy-control duality: Toward theory. *Information Technology Management* 8:147–66.

Tian, J., and X. Wang. 2005. Short communication: An epidemiological survey of job stress and health in four occupational populations in Fuzhou city of China. *Stress and Health* 21(2):107–12.

Towers, I., L. Duxbury, C. Higgins, and J. Thomas. 2006. Time thieves and space invaders: Technology, work and the organization. *Journal of Organizational Change Management* 19(5):593–618.

Tversky, A., and D. Kahneman. 1974. Judgment under uncertainty: Heuristics and biases. *Science* 185(4157):1124–31.

Velocci, A. L., Jr. 1995. Boeing, labor talks ripple industry wide. *Aviation Week & Space Technology,* August 14, 20–21.

Vogel, D. 1989. *Fluctuating fortunes: The political power of business in America.* New York: Basic Books.

Wall, R. 2007. Questions hang over Airbus Power8 initiative. *Aviation Week,* May 5.

Wallace, J. 2009. *Airbus: A candid assessment of the 787.* Blog post, *Seattle Post-Intelligencer,* January 12. http://blog.seattlepi.nwsource.com/aerospace.

Wang, K., Q. Shu, and Q. Tu. 2008. Technostress under different organizational environments: An empirical investigation. *Computers in Human Behavior* 24(6):3002–13.

Waters, L. 2007. Experiential differences between voluntary and involuntary job redundancy on depression, job-search activity, affective employee outcomes, and re-employment quality. *Journal of Occupational & Organizational Psychology* 80:279–99.

Weick, K. E. 1995. *Sensemaking in organizations.* Thousand Oaks: Sage Publications.

Weidenbaum, M. L. 1978. Budgets and bureaucrats: The sources of government growth. Ed. Thomas E. Borcherding. *Journal of Economic Literature* 16(3):1009–11.

Wharton, A., and M. Blair-Loy. 2006. Long work hours and family life—A cross-national study of employees' concerns. *Journal of Family Issues* 27(3):415–36.

Wheeler, H. 2002. *The future of the American labor movement.* Cambridge: Cambridge University Press.

Wilthagen, T., and F. Troos. 2004. The concept of 'flexicurity': A new approach regulating employment and labour markets. *Transfer* 10(2):166–86.

Winkelmann, L., and R. Winkelmann. 1998. Why are the unemployed so unhappy? Evidence from panel data. *Economica* 65(257):1–15.

Wolfe, A. 2006. *Does American Democracy Still Work?* New Haven: Yale University Press.

Womack, J. P., D. T. Jones, and D. Roos. 1991. *The machine that changed the world: How Japan's secret weapon in the global auto wars will revolutionize western industry.* 1st Harper-Perennial ed. New York: HarperPerennial.

Wright, P. M., K. M. Kacmar, G. C. McMahan, and K. Jansen. 1997. *Impact of information technology on employee attitudes: A longitudinal field study.* CAHRS Working Paper #97–11. Ithaca, NY: Cornell University, School of Industrial and Labor Relations, Center for Advanced Human Resource Studies.

Yergin, D., and J. Stanislaw. 1999. *The commanding heights: The battle between government and the marketplace that is remaking the modern world.* 1st Touchstone ed. New York: Simon & Schuster.

Index

Page numbers in *italics* refer to illustrations and tables.

Boeing Corporation (*continued*)
with McDonnell Douglas, 13, 25, 34–
35, 40, 48–51, 53, 56, 91, 153, 174; passenger airplane division, *see* Boeing
Commercial Airplanes; profitability of,
20, 21–22, 23, 192; reputation of, 9–10,
53; stock purchase of, 218n5
Booz Allen, 32

careers, redefinition of, 188
Caterpillar, 179
change: cost-cutting, 34–37, 53; decisions
about, 20–21; during research period,
12–14; effects on employees, 13, 37–38,
40; necessity for, 3, 19–25, 174–77;
new work initiatives, 186; origins of,
128, 208n10; positive responses to, 57–
60, *59;* resistance to, 46, 104; transformative, 25–34; unrelenting pace of,
104, 186–87
Cisco Systems, 179
Civil Aeronautics Board (CAB), 21–23
Collins, Jim, 9
competition, 20, 178–80; from Airbus,
23–25, 35, 36–37, 43, 49, 58, 63, 176–
77; global, 22–24; and job security,
178–79; and mergers, 25, 34; and productivity, 183–84; World Class Competitiveness (WCC), 47, 82
Condit, Phil, 20, 25, 182; Chairman's Initiative of, 219n21; departure of, 49, 54;
and merger, 34, 35, 49; and risk aversion, 56; and 777 program, 46; and
shareholder value, 39, 40, 49; and
unions, 66
continuing education, 5, 13, 58, 71, 189
continuous improvement, 13, 89
corporate culture, 39–60; bureaucratic,
42–43, 44, 47–48, 86, 107–8; conservative, 57–58; deep structure identification with, 211n18; of efficiency, 43–
48; engineering, 22, 41; every man for
himself, 91–92; as family, 41–42, 49–

50, 51, 60, 75; gender in, 130–38;
legacy of, 41–43; macho, 128, 130–32,
138–39, 143–46, 149; and merger, 35,
40, 48–51; and outsourcing, 55–57; paternalistic, 42, 43, 128; risk management, 55–56; short-term shareholder
value, 3, 9, 13, 21, 39–40, 48–53, 105;
standardization in, 6, 29–31; teams,
82–84, 91, 105, 169; win at any cost,
53–55

DCAC/MRM, 6, 29–31, 44, 92, 93, 95, 96
Denmark, "flexicurity" system in, 193
design: globalization of, 27; moderniza-
tion of, 175; outsourcing, 31, 55, 112;
standards of, 22; virtual, 26–27, 34, 93
Douglas aircraft: competition for, 24; as
McDonnell-Douglas, 13, 25; profitability of, 21
downsizing, *see* layoffs
DuPont, 179

eating habits, 158–60, *159*
employees, *see* workers
engineers: corporate culture of, 22, 41;
and cost-cutting, 53; morale of, 8, 9;
and outsourcing, 33, 34, 55, 57, 63–64,
112; respect for, 66; shrinking numbers
of, 27, 33, 66; strikes by, 52–53, 66
Ethical Leadership Group, 42
ethics, 53–55
executive compensation, 182

Farber, Henry, 178
Ford Motor Co., 179, 185
Frontier Airlines, 23

General Electric, 31, 35, 179, 184
General Motors, 178–79, 185
Genpact, 179
glass ceiling, 129
Goforth, Ray, 67
Google, 183, 185